George Lamming was born in Barbados. He wrote his first novel, *In the Castle of My Skin*, shortly after arriving in England in 1950, when he was twenty-three. It was awarded the Somerset Maugham Award for Literature in 1958, and was followed by *The Emigrants*, *Of Age and Innocence*, *Season of Adventure*, *The Pleasures of Exile* (a collection of essays), *Water with Berries* and *Natives of My Person* – published in Picador at the same time as *Cannon Shot and Glass Beads*. George Lamming received a Guggenheim Fellowship to the USA from 1955–6, a Canada Council Fellowship in 1962, and was writer in residence at the University of the West Indies from 1967–8. From 1971–3 he held lectureships at several American universities.

Cannon Shot and Glass Beads

Modern Black Writing edited by
GEORGE LAMMING

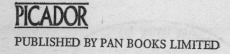

PICADOR

PUBLISHED BY PAN BOOKS LIMITED

First published in Picador by
Pan Books Ltd, Cavaye Place, London SW10 9PG
© Pan Books Ltd 1974
Introduction © George Lamming 1974
Printed in Great Britain by
Richard Clay (The Chaucer Press), Ltd, Bungay, Suffolk

ISBN 0 330 23937 6

for
ANDAIYE
(sandra williams)

CONTENTS

ACKNOWLEDGEMENTS AND COPYRIGHT NOTICES

Peter Blackman, from 'My Song is for All Men', and 'In Memory of Claudia Jones'. Reprinted by permission of the author.

Edward Brathwaite, 'Jah' from *Islands* by Edward Brathwaite. Copyright © Oxford University Press 1969. Reprinted by permission of the publisher.

Aimé Césaire, from *Return to My Native Land* by Aimé Césaire. Reprinted by permission of the translator, John Berger.

Neville Dawes, from *The Last Enchantment* by Neville Dawes. Reprinted by permission of the author.

Ralph Ellison, from *Invisible Man* by Ralph Ellison. Proprietors: Random House Inc. Reprinted by permission of Laurence Pollinger Ltd.

Evan Jones, 'The Song of the Banana Man' and 'The Lament of the Banana Man'. Copyright © Southbend Investments Ltd, Nassau, Bahamas. Reprinted by permission of the author.

C. H. Kane, from *Ambiguous Adventure* by C. H. Kane. Reprinted by permission of Walker and Company Inc, New York, NY.

George Lamming, from *The Emigrants* by George Lamming. Reprinted by permission of the author. Introduction copyright © 1974 George Lamming.

Paule Marshall, 'Brazil' from *Soul Clap Hands and Sing* by Paule Marshall. Reprinted by permission of the author.

Louise M. Meriwether, 'A Happening in Barbados'. Reprinted by permission of the author.

Ezekiel Mphahlele, 'Mrs Plum'. Reprinted by permission of the author.

Ngugi Wa Thiong'o (James Ngugi), from *A Grain of Wheat* by James Ngugi. Reprinted by permission of the publisher, Heinemann Educational Books Ltd.

Sembene Ousmane, from *God's Bits of Wood* by Sembene Ousmane. Reprinted by permission of Mary Yost Associates, New York, NY.

Ferdinand Oyono, from *The Old Man and the Medal* by Ferdinand Oyono. Reprinted by permission of the publisher, Heinemann Educational Books Ltd.

Okot p'Bitek, from *Song of Lawino* by Okot p'Bitek. Reprinted by permission of East African Publishing House, Nairobi, Kenya.

Samuel Selvon, from *The Lonely Londoners* by Samuel Selvon. Reprinted by permission of the author.

Wole Soyinka, from *The Interpreters* by Wole Soyinka. Reprinted by permission of the publisher, Andre Deutsch Ltd.

Derek Walcott, 'Ruins of a Great House' from *In a Green Night* by Derek Walcott. Reprinted by permission of the publisher, Jonathan Cape Ltd.

Every effort has been made to trace the owners of the remaining copyright material, but without success. On hearing from the writers concerned, the publisher will be pleased to rectify the matter immediately.

Introduction

It is fairly safe to assume that so long as this country lasts there will be a substantial Black population in it, and that the overwhelming majority will, with time, be native to this land. Reading will therefore cease to be a participation in exclusively White experience. There will be an increasing demand by Black literacy for the imaginative rendering of a social history with which Black people can easily identify. Such a population will, of course, create its own literature. This is inevitable. But there must remain the need to experience some spiritual intimacy with its immediate as well as its ancestral past. This is one aspect of what this anthology is about.

The central theme concerns the historic encounter between Europe and Africa and the nature of the experience, which is sometimes much too loosely called colonial. There was a quality of upheaval in the association of these peoples which will remain a pervasive influence in their relations long after the last structure of empire has been dismantled. The geography of the fiction extends therefore from Africa to Europe to the Americas and the Caribbean. It is the second aim of our selection to offer a comparative survey of Black response to the politics and culture of White racism.

This is the honest and most obvious way to define Black/White relations; but the importance of an imaginative literature is that it takes us on the inside, charts a way into the human interior where definition often fails to illuminate the essence of what it defines. If there is a central theme which the writers share, what emerges from the cumulative impact of the selection is the great variety of tone and vision which distinguishes these writers.

In the extract from Ngugi Wa Thiong'o's novel *A Grain of Wheat* we are treated to a brutal reversal of fortune in the career of a man whom history has suddenly robbed not only of privilege but of his original conception of his role as a District Officer in colonial Kenya. With a deep sense of betrayal he now reads of the preparations for the Independence celebrations. The Queen's husband will, in her absence, bear witness to the final lowering of the British flag. Such knowledge makes him sad, and his mind hurries him back to a more consoling period when the Queen, then a princess, had visited Kenya:

> '... Thompson forgot the newspaper and relived that moment when the young woman shook hands with him ... He felt a thrill: his heart-beat had quickened almost as if a covenant had been made between him and her. Then, there, he would have done anything for her, would have stabbed himself to prove his readiness to carry out that mission which though unspoken seemed embodied in her person and smile. Recalling that rapture, Thompson involuntarily pushed away the paper and rose to his feet. There was a flicker in his eyes, a watery glint. He walked towards the window muttering under his breath: "What the hell was it all about!" '

There is a tragic irony in the fate of such a man who must now breathe murder whenever a Black youth crosses his path in a London street.

The episode invites comparison with a similar misconception of roles in the extract from Ellison's *Invisible Man*. The terrain is no longer colonial Africa but the Black South of the United States. The millionaire philanthropist Mr Norton is taken ill during a tour of the Black college which he supports. The Black narrator student panics and seeks help in the Golden Inn, a brothel and gambling house which some ex-soldiers, now mental patients in the nearby asylum, are allowed to visit under supervision. The young student guide is familiar with the scene, but it is a knowledge which increases his confusion:

> 'Many of the men had been doctors, lawyers, teachers, Civil Service workers; there were several cooks, a preacher, a politician, and an artist ... Whenever I saw them I felt uncomfortable. They were supposed to be members of the professions towards which at various times I vaguely aspired myself, and even though they never seemed to see me I could never believe that they were really patients. Sometimes it appeared as though they had played some vast and complicated game with me and the rest of the school folk, a game whose goal was laughter and whose rules and subtleties I could never grasp.'

But the young Black student is an innocent whose ambitions serve to reinforce the fantasies of Mr Norton's private world which is also a fact of immense public power. Vaguely aware of his surroundings, Mr Norton is soon engaged in very purposeful dialogue with one of the men:

' "Tell me," the vet said, suddenly calm. "Why have you been interested in the school, Mr Norton?"

"Out of a sense of my destined role," Mr Norton said shakily. "I felt, and I still feel, that your people are in some important manner tied to my destiny."

"What do you mean, destiny?" the vet asked.

"Why, the success of my work, of course."

"And would you recognize it if you saw it?"

"Why, of course I would," Mr Norton said indignantly. "I've watched it grow each year I've returned to the campus."

"Campus? Why the campus?"

"It is there that my destiny is being made." '

The School as a symbol of political tutelage and cultural conflict will appear time and again in the work of almost all Black writers whose education was a product of colonial experience and who came to maturity before the formal independence of their respective countries. It is a most impressive continuity of circumstance which provides every African, West Indian and Black American with a universal ground of sympathy. And it is an essential part of the intention that the present anthology should communicate this fact and quicken the urgency for a common struggle against four centuries of cultural imperialism.

George Lamming

C. H. Kane

from Ambiguous Adventure

The country of the Diallobé was not the only one which had been awakened by a great clamour early one day. The entire black continent had had its moment of clamour.

Strange dawn! The morning of the Occident in black Africa was spangled over with smiles, with cannon shots, with shining glass beads. Those who had no history were encountering those who carried the world on their shoulders. It was a morning of accouchement: the known world was enriching itself by a birth that took place in mire and blood.

From shock, the one side made no resistance. They were a people without a past, therefore without memory. The men who were landing on their shores were white, and mad. Nothing like them had ever been known. The deed was accomplished before the people were even conscious of what had happened.

Some among the Africans, such as the Diallobé, brandished their shields, pointed their lances, and aimed their guns. They were allowed to come close, then the cannon were fired. The vanquished did not understand...

Others wanted to parley. They were given a choice: friendship or war. Very sensibly, they chose friendship. They had no experience at all.

The result was the same, nevertheless, everywhere.

Those who had shown fight and those who had surrendered, those who had come to terms and those who had been obstinate – they all found themselves, when the day came, checked by census, divided up, classified, labelled, conscripted, administrated.

For the newcomers did not know only how to fight. They were strange people. If they knew how to kill with effectiveness, they also knew how to cure, with the same art. Where they had brought disorder, they established a new order. They destroyed and they constructed. On the black continent it began to be understood that their true power lay not in the cannons of the first morning, but rather in what followed the cannons.

Thus, behind the gunboats, the clear gaze of the Most Royal Lady of the Diallobé had seen the new school.

The new school shares at the same time the characteristics of cannon and of magnet. From the cannon it draws its efficacy as an arm of combat. Better than the cannon, it makes conquest permanent. The cannon compels the body, the school bewitches the soul. Where the cannon has made a pit of ashes and of death, in the sticky mould of which men would not have rebounded from the ruins, the new school establishes peace. The morning of rebirth will be a morning of benediction through the appeasing virtue of the new school.

From the magnet, the school takes its radiating force. It is bound up with a new order, as a magnetic stone is bound up with a field. The upheaval of the life of man within this new order is similar to the overturn of certain physical laws in a magnetic field. Men are seen to be composing themselves, conquered, along the lines of invisible and imperious forces. Disorder is organized, rebellion is appeased, the mornings of resentment resound with songs of a universal thanksgiving.

Only such an upheaval in the natural order can explain how, without either of them wanting it, the new man and the new school come together just the same. For neither of them wants the other. The man does not want the school because in order that he may live – that is, be free, feed and clothe himself – it imposes upon him the necessity of sitting henceforth, for the required period, upon its benches. No more does the school want the man because in order to survive – that is, extend itself and take roots where its necessity has landed it – it is obliged to take account of him.

When the Lacroix family arrived in the little Negro town of L, they found a school there. It was on the classroom benches of this school, filled with little black children, that Jean Lacroix made the acquaintance of Samba Diallo.

On the morning of their fifteenth day at L, M Lacroix had taken his two children, Jean and Georgette, to the school of the little town. At Pau, the little boy and girl had not gone above the lower grades. Here, the class of M N'Diaye corresponded broadly to what they needed.

The story of Samba Diallo is a serious story. If it had been a gay recital, we should have told you of the bewilderment of the two white children, on the first morning of their sojourn among little Negroes, in finding themselves in the presence of so many black faces. Such were the peripheries of this vast movement of approach that Jean and his sister felt it was closing in about them, little by little, like some fantastic and patient ballet. What was their childish surprise, one might have said, to realize after some time, how much, under their kinky heads and their dark skins, their new school-mates resembled those they had left behind in Pau ...

But nothing more will be said of all that, because these memories would revive others, all of them also happy, and would bring gaiety to this recital of which the profound truth is wholly sad.

Long afterwards, thinking of this, Jean Lacroix believed that he remembered perceiving this sadness – though in a diffuse and imprecise way – from his first moments of contact with Samba Diallo.

It was in M N'Diaye's class that he first felt this. In this class he had had, as it were, the impression of a point where all noises were absorbed, where all rustling sounds were lost. One might have said that somewhere in the ambient air there was a break in continuity. So, when it happened that the whole class would be laughing or shrieking, his attentive ear would perceive something like a pit of silence not far from where he sat. As the hour of dismissal approached, and a quiver would run through all the benches, slates would be shaken and then surreptitiously put away, and there would be a dropping of things that had been gathered together, Jean's whole person would feel at the heart of this agitation something like a break of peace.

As a matter of fact, although he might have noticed it from the outset, it was only after some ten days in M N'Diaye's classroom that Jean became clearly conscious of this universal false note. From that moment, all his senses were on the alert.

One morning M N'Diaye was questioning the class and had – fairly enough – taken the presence of Jean and Georgette as pretext for an interrogation on the geography and history of France. The interchange between master and pupils was sustained and swift. Then suddenly a silence, an embarrassed silence, fell upon the class.

'Let us see, my children,' M N'Diaye insisted, 'Pau is in a department of which it is the capital. What is this department? You remember Pau?'

Jean, to whom the question was not addressed, perceived very clearly, then, that someone not far from him was not embarrassed by this silence, someone was enjoying this silence and prolonging it at his pleasure, someone who could break it, who was about to break it. He slowly turned his head and, for the first time, observed his neighbour on the right, the pupil who with Georgette and himself shared the first table of the central row. It was like a revelation. The pit of silence, the break of peace – it was this boy! He who at this moment was attracting all glances by a sort of restrained radiation, he whom Jean had not noticed but whose presence in this class had troubled him from the first days . . .

Jean observed him in profile. He could do so at ease, for the other had raised his head and was fixing all his attention on M N'Diaye. The class was looking at him, and he was looking at the teacher. He seemed tense. His countenance, the regularity of which Jean noted, was beaming. Jean had the impression that if he leaned over and looked straight at his companion, he could read on his face – so great was its effulgence – the answer that M N'Diaye was expecting. But, one might say in spite of this tension and this radiation, nothing about the boy stirred. Jean was later to think back and realize that he never raised his hand, though when a pupil wished to answer a question, it was the custom for him to raise his hand and snap his fingers. Jean's neighbour remained motionless and tense, as if he had his heart in his mouth. M N'Diaye turned towards him, and Jean noted something like a muscular relaxation on the other's part. He smiled, and had the air of being confused. Then he got up.

'The department of which Pau is the capital is the Basses-Pyrénées. Pau is the city in which Henri IV was born.'

His voice was clear-cut and his language correct. He was speaking to M N'Diaye, but Jean had the impression that he was speaking to the class, that it was to them that he was giving account.

When he had finished speaking he sat down again, on a sign from M N'Diaye. Jean was still staring at him. He noticed that this embarrassed the other boy, and gave himself over to the contemplation of his slate.

Having paused for a moment, the class went back to its routine. Then only did Jean remember that it was not by chance that he was sitting near Samba Diallo. He recalled that when he arrived he had wished to lead his sister to a table where there were two vacant places, as he had noticed. M N'Diaye had intervened, and had had them sit at the first table, next to Samba Diallo.

When the noon bell had rung, when M N'Diaye had dismissed his pupils and Georgette and Jean had gone out, it was impossible for the latter to find Samba Diallo again. Jean was standing on his tiptoes, looking about him on all sides, when someone touched his shoulder. He turned around. It was Ammar Lô, the first boy in the class that he had made friends with.

'Who are you looking for, the Diallobé?'

'Who is that?'

'But that is your neighbour, Samba Diallo.'

Jean was surprised and a little put out that Ammar Lô should have guessed his thought. He did not reply.

'Don't wait any longer for Samba Diallo. He has gone,' Ammar Lô volunteered. Then he turned his back and went away.

M Lacroix had come in a car to get his children. When Jean went back to school in the afternoon Samba Diallo was not there, and he was conscious of some chagrin.

The next day was Thursday.* Jean did not go out in the morning, but in the afternoon he betook himself to his father's office in the Résidence du Cercle. He knocked at the door and went in. There were two people in the room he entered, occupying two separate desks. One of them was his father. He made his way towards him, but he was looking at the other man, who was a Negro.

He was a tall man, something which one noticed at once, even though he was seated. The boubous he wore were white, and full-cut. Under his clothing one sensed a stature which was powerful without being fleshy. His hands were at once large and finely moulded. His bearing helped to give a hieratic posture to his head, which one would have said was cut out of gleaming black sandstone. Why, on looking at him, did Jean think of a certain engraving in his history textbook, which showed a knight of the Middle Ages clad in his dalmatic vestments? The man, on whose face there was a lightly sketched smile, slowly turned his head so that his glance followed the boy. Jean, for his part, was watching him so attentively that he almost bumped into a chair.

'Well, Jean, say good afternoon to this gentleman,' his father said.

Jean took a few steps towards the man, who smiled once more and held out his hand – a gesture which spread his wide boubou more amply about him.

'Well, young man, how are you?'

His hand enveloped Jean's in a pressure which was vigorous but not rough. The man was looking at the child, and his face, his beautiful face of shadow set in light, was all smiles for him. Jean had the impression that this man had known him for ever, and that while he was smiling at him nothing else existed, nothing else had any importance.

'This is my son, Jean. He is not stupid, but he is very often on a trip to the moon.'

That deplorable habit his father had of always divulging the family secrets! Jean would still have endured it, under all circumstances, but before this man!

'Sh ... Don't make this big young man blush. I am sure that his

* Thursday is the holiday in French schools. Tr.

journeys to the moon are thrilling – aren't they?'

Jean's confusion would have known no bounds if at this moment his attention had not been distracted by two light but firm raps on the door. Samba Diallo appeared. Jean's confusion gave way to surprise. Wearing a long white caftan and white sandals, Samba Diallo entered the room with a graceful and silent step, and made his way first towards M Lacroix, who smilingly held out his hand. Then, with his own hand open, he stepped up to Jean:

'How do you do, Jean?'

'How do you do, Samba Diallo?'

Their hands met. Then Samba Diallo turned away and greeted the knight in the dalmatic. Neither of them was smiling any longer; they merely looked each other in the eyes for the space of several seconds, then, with the same movement, moved aside, their faces lighted up anew.

'I see that these young people are already acquainted,' M Lacroix said.

'Samba Diallo is my son,' added the knight. 'Where have you met, then – if that is not an indiscreet question?'

His tone was ironic as he spoke the last words.

'We sit at the same table in M N'Diaye's class,' Samba Diallo replied, without taking his eyes off Jean. 'Only we have hardly had any opportunity to talk together, have we?'

Samba Diallo's ease of manner, since he came into the room, left no doubt in Jean's mind: the knight's son had already met M Lacroix. But none of this had been allowed to be seen at the school.

Blushing, Jean confirmed the fact that they had never spoken with each other.

Samba Diallo began to talk to his father in a low voice. Jean took advantage of this to go over to M Lacroix.

The two boys left the office at the same time. Without speaking, they made their way into the white marl roadway, bordered with red flowers, which led to the portal of the Résidence. Samba Diallo snipped off a flower and began to look closely at it. After a short time he held it out to Jean.

'See, Jean, how beautiful this flower is,' he said. 'It smells good.'

He was silent for an instant, then he added, unexpectedly,

'But it is going to die.'

His eyes had been sparkling, and his nostrils had quivered a little, when he said that the flower was beautiful. A moment later he was obviously sad.

'It is going to die because you plucked it,' Jean ventured to say.

'Yes – and if I had not done that, look what would have happened to it.'

He picked a dry and spiny pod and showed it to Jean. Then, with a springlike motion, he turned clear around, threw the pod away, and turned back to Jean, smiling:

'You wouldn't like to come and take a walk with me?'

'I should like it very much,' Jean answered.

They went away from the Résidence and took one of those long streets of white marl that furrow the red sand of the little town of L. They walked along for some time without speaking, and soon abandoned the white marl for the red sand, a broad stretch of which, surrounded by milky euphorbia, lay straight ahead of them. In the middle of it Samba Diallo stopped, sat down, then lay out flat on his back, his hands at the nape of his neck and his face to the sky. Jean seated himself.

The sun was setting in an immense sweep of sky. Its rays, which are golden at this time of the day, had been dyed purple in their passage through the clouds that were setting the west afire. Struck diagonally by the light, the red sand was like seething gold.

Samba Diallo's basalt countenance had purple reflections. Basalt? It was a face of basalt because, also, it was as if turned to stone. No muscle in it, now, was moving. In his eyes the sky showed red. Since he lay down on the ground had Samba Diallo become riveted to it? Had he ceased to live? Jean was frightened.

'Tell me, Samba Diallo,' he ventured, 'what is a Diallobé?'

He had spoken for the sake of saying something. The enchantment was shattered. Samba Diallo burst out laughing.

'Ah, they have been talking to you about me ... A Diallobé ... Well, my family, the Dialloubé, belong to the Diallobé people. We come from the banks of a great river. Our country is also called the Diallobé. I am the only one from this country in M N'Diaye's class. They take advantage of that to joke about me.'

'If you are a Diallobé, why didn't you stay in the Diallobé country?'

'And you, why did you leave Pau?'

Jean was embarrassed. But Samba Diallo went on at once:

'This is where I live, it is where I live all the time. It is true that I should have preferred to stay in the country, but my father lives here.'

'He is a big man, your father. He is a bigger man than mine.'

'Yes, he is a very big man.'

While they were talking twilight had fallen. The golden rays had thinned out a little, and the purple had turned to pink. Along their lower edges the clouds had become a frozen blue. The sun had disappeared, but already in the east the moon had risen, and it, too, shed a light. One could see that the ambient light was made up of the paling rose from the sun, the milky whiteness from the moon, and also the peaceful penumbra of a night which was felt to be imminent.

'Excuse me, Jean,' said Samba Diallo. 'It is twilight, and I must pray.'

He rose, turned towards the east, lifted his arms, with his hands open, and slowly let them fall. His voice echoed in the quiet air. Jean did not dare to walk around his companion in order to see his face, but it seemed to him that this voice was no longer his. Samba Diallo remained motionless. Nothing in him was alive except this voice, speaking in the twilight a language which Jean did not understand. Then his long white caftan – turned violet now by the evening light – was swept through by a kind of shiver, which grew more pronounced in measure as the voice was rising. The shiver became a tremor which shook his entire body, and the voice turned to a sob. To the east the sky was like an immense lilac-coloured crystal.

Jean did not know how long he remained there, held fascinated by Samba Diallo weeping under the sky. He never knew how much time was consumed by this pathetic and beautiful death of the day. He only regained consciousness of his surroundings when he heard the sound of footsteps not far away. He raised his head and saw the knight of the dalmatic, who came towards him, smiling, and held out his hand to help him get up. Samba Diallo was crouched on the ground, his head lowered, his body still trembling. The knight knelt down, took his son by the shoulders, set him on his feet, and smiled at him. Through his tears Samba Diallo smiled back, a bright smile. With a fold of his boubou the knight wiped the boy's face, very tenderly.

They conducted Jean, in silence, back to the marl street, then they retraced their steps to go to their own home. In the moonlight the street had the white sheen of lilies. Jean had watched the two figures disappearing in the distance, holding each other by the hand, then, slowly, he had gone back to his own house.

That night, thinking of Samba Diallo, he was overcome by fear. But that happened very late, when everyone had retired and Jean was alone, in his bed. That twilight's violence and splendour were not the cause of Samba Diallo's tears. Why had he wept?

For a long time the little boy was haunted by the two faces, of the father and the son. They continued to obsess him, until the moment when he sank into sleep.

Derek Walcott

Ruins of a Great House

*though our longest sun sets at right
declensions and makes but winter
arches, it cannot be long before we
lie down in darkness, and have our
light in ashes ...*
> Browne: *Urn Burial*

Stones only, the *disjecta membra* of this Great House,
Whose moth-like girls are mixed with candledust,
Remain to file the lizard's dragonish claws;
The mouths of those gate cherubs streaked with stain.
Axle and coachwheel silted under the muck
Of cattle droppings.

Three crows flap for the trees,
And settle, creaking the eucalyptus boughs.
A smell of dead limes quickens in the nose
The leprosy of Empire.

'Farewell, green fields'
'Farewell, ye happy groves!'

Marble as Greece, like Faulkner's south in stone,
Deciduous beauty prospered and is gone;
But where the lawn breaks in a rash of trees
A spade below dead leaves will ring the bone
Of some dead animal or human thing
Fallen from evil days, from evil times.
It seems that the original crops were limes
Grown in the silt that clogs the river's skirt;
The imperious rakes are gone, their bright girls gone,
The river flows, obliterating hurt.

I climbed a wall with the grill ironwork
Of exiled craftsmen, protecting that great house
From guilt, perhaps, but not from the worm's rent,
Nor from the padded cavalry of the mouse.
And when a wind shook in the limes I heard
What Kipling heard; the death of a great empire, the abuse
Of ignorance by Bible and by sword.

A green lawn, broken by low walls of stone
Dipped to the rivulet, and pacing, I thought next
Of men like Hawkins, Walter Raleigh, Drake,
Ancestral murderers and poets, more perplexed
In memory now by every ulcerous crime.
The world's green age then was a rotting lime
Whose stench became the charnel galleon's text.
The rot remains with us, the men are gone.
But, as dead ash is lifted in a wind,
That fans the blackening ember of the mind,
My eyes burned from the ashen prose of Donne.

Ablaze with rage, I thought
Some slave is rotting in this manorial lake,
And still the coal of my compassion fought:
That Albion too, was once
A colony like ours, 'Part of the continent, piece of the main'
Nook-shotten, rook o'er blown, deranged
By foaming channels, and the vain expense
Of bitter faction.
                    All in compassion ends
So differently from what the heart arranged:
'as well as if a manor of thy friend's . . .'

Ralph Ellison

from Invisible Man

I saw them as we approached the short stretch that lay between the
railroad tracks and the Golden Day. At first I failed to recognize them.
They straggled down the highway in a loose body, blocking the way
from the white line to the frazzled weeds that bordered the sun-heated
concrete slab. I cursed them silently. They were blocking the road and
Mr Norton was gasping for breath. Ahead of the radiator's gleaming
curve they looked like a chain gang on its way to make a road. But a
chain gang marches single file and I saw no guards on horseback. As I
drew nearer I recognized the loose grey shirts and pants worn by the
veterans. Damn! They were heading for the Golden Day.

'A little stimulant,' I heard behind me.

'In a few minutes, sir.'

Up ahead I saw the one who thought he was a drum major strutting in
front, giving orders as he moved energetically in long, hip-swinging
strides, a cane held above his head, rising and falling as though in time
to music. I slowed the car as I saw him turn to face the men, his cane
held at chest level as he shortened the pace. The men continued to
ignore him, walking along in a mass, some talking in groups and others
talking and gesticulating to themselves.

Suddenly, the drum major saw the car and shook his cane-baton at
me. I blew the horn, seeing the men move over to the side as I nosed
the car slowly forward. He held his ground, his legs braced, hands on
hips, and to keep from hitting him I slammed on the brakes.

The drum major rushed past the men towards the car, and I heard
the cane bang down upon the hood as he rushed towards me.

'Who the hell you think you are, running down the army? Give the
countersign. Who's in command of this outfit? You trucking bastards
was always too big for your britches. Countersign me!'

'This is General Pershing's car, sir,' I said, remembering hearing that
he responded to the name of his wartime Commander-in-Chief. Sud
denly the wild look changed in his eyes and he stepped back and sal-
uted with stiff precision. Then looking suspiciously into the back seat,
he barked,

'Where's the General?'

'There,' I said, turning and seeing Mr Norton raising himself, weak and white-faced, from the seat.

'What is it? Why have we stopped?'

'The sergeant stopped us, sir ...'

'Sergeant? What sergeant?' He sat up.

'Is that you, General?' the vet said, saluting. 'I didn't know you were inspecting the front lines today. I'm very sorry, sir.'

'What ... ?' Mr Norton said.

'The General's in a hurry,' I said quickly.

'Sure is,' the vet said. 'He's got a lot to see. Discipline is bad. Artillery's shot to hell.' Then he called to the men walking up the road, 'Get the hell out of the General's road. General Pershing's coming through. Make way for General Pershing!'

He stepped aside and I shot the car across the line to avoid the men and stayed there on the wrong side as I headed for the Golden Day.

'Who was that man?' Mr Norton gasped from the back seat.

'A former soldier, sir. A vet. They're all vets, a little shell-shocked.'

'But where is the attendant?'

'I don't see one, sir. They're harmless though.'

'Nevertheless, they should have an attendant.'

I had to get him there and away before they arrived. This was their day to visit the girls, and the Golden Day would be pretty rowdy. I wondered where the rest of them were. There should have been about fifty. Well, I would rush in and get the whisky and leave. What was wrong with Mr Norton anyway, why should he get *that* upset over Trueblood? I had felt ashamed and several times I had wanted to laugh, but it had made him sick. Maybe he needed a doctor. Hell, he didn't ask for any doctor. Damn that bastard Trueblood.

I would run in, get a pint, and run out again, I thought. Then he wouldn't see the Golden Day. I seldom went there myself except with some of the fellows when word got out that a new bunch of girls had arrived from New Orleans. The school had tried to make the Golden Day respectable, but the local white folks had a hand in it somehow and they got nowhere. The best the school could do was to make it hot for any student caught going there.

He lay like a man asleep as I left the car and ran into the Golden Day. I wanted to ask him for money but decided to use my own. At the door I paused; the place was already full, jammed with vets in loose grey shirts and trousers and women in short, tight-fitting, stiffly starched gingham aprons. The stale beer smell struck like a club through the noise of voices and the juke box. Just as I got inside the door a stolid-faced man gripped me by the arm and looked stonily into my eyes.

'It will occur at 5.30,' he said, looking straight through me.

'What?'

'The great all-embracing, absolute Armistice, the end of the world!' he said.

Before I could answer, a small plump woman smiled into my face and pulled him away.

'It's your turn, Doc,' she said. 'Don't let it happen till after me and you done been upstairs. How come I always have to come get you?'

'No, it is true,' he said. 'They wirelessed me from Paris this morning.'

'Then, baby, me an' you better hurry. There's lots of money I got to make in here before that thing happens. You hold it back a while, will you?'

She winked at me as she pulled him through the crowd towards the stairs. I elbowed my way nervously towards the bar.

Many of the men had been doctors, lawyers, teachers, Civil Service workers; there were several cooks, a preacher, a politician and an artist. One very nutty one had been a psychiatrist. Whenever I saw them I felt uncomfortable. They were supposed to be members of the professions towards which at various times I vaguely aspired myself, and even though they never seemed to see me I could never believe that they were really patients. Sometimes it appeared as though they played some vast and complicated game with me and the rest of the school folk, a game whose goal was laughter and whose rules and subtleties I could never grasp.

Two men stood directly in front of me, one speaking with intense earnestness. '... and Johnson hit Jeffries at an angle of forty-five degrees from his lower left lateral incisor, producing an instantaneous blocking of his entire thalamic rine, frosting it over like the freezing unit of a refrigerator, thus shattering his autonomous nervous system and rocking the big brick-laying creampuff with extreme hyperspasmic muscular tremors which dropped him dead on the extreme tip of his coccyx, which, in turn, produced a sharp traumatic reaction in his sphincter nerve and muscle, and then, my dear colleague, they swept him up, sprinkled him with quicklime and rolled him away in a barrow. Naturally, there was no other therapy possible '

'Excuse me,' I said, pushing past.

Big Halley was behind the bar, his dark skin showing through his sweat-wet shirt.

'Whatcha saying, schoolboy?'

'I want a double whisky, Halley. Put it in something deep so I can get it out of here without spilling it. It's for somebody outside.'

His mouth shot out, 'Hell, naw!'

'Why?' I asked, surprised at the anger in his thyroid eyes.

'You still up at the school, ain't you?'

'Sure.'

'Well, those bastards is trying to close me up agin, that's why. You can drink till you blue in the face in here, but I wouldn't sell you enough to spit through your teeth to take outside.'

'But I've got a sick man out in the car.'

'What car? You never had no car.'

'The white man's car. I'm driving for him.'

'Ain't you in school?'

'He's *from* the school.'

'Well, who's sick?'

'He is.'

'He too good to come in? Tell him we don't Jimcrow nobody.'

'But he's sick.'

'He can die!'

'He's important, Halley, a trustee. He's rich and sick and if anything happens to him, they'll have me packed and on my way home.'

'Can't help it, schoolboy. Bring him inside and he can buy enough to swim in. He can drink outta my own private bottle.'

He sliced the white heads off a couple of beers with an ivory paddle and passed them up the bar. I felt sick inside. Mr Norton wouldn't want to come in here. He was too sick. And besides I didn't want him to see the patients and the girls. Things were getting wilder as I made my way out. Supercargo, the white-uniformed attendant who usually kept the men quiet, was nowhere to be seen. I didn't like it, for when he was upstairs they had absolutely no inhibitions. I made my way out to the car. What could I tell Mr Norton? He was lying very still when I opened the door.

'Mr Norton, sir. They refuse to sell me whisky to bring out.'

He lay very still.

'Mr Norton.'

He lay like a figure of chalk. I shook him gently, feeling dread within me. He barely breathed. I shook him violently, seeing his head wobble grotesquely. His lips parted, bluish, revealing a row of long, slender, amazingly animal-like teeth.

'sir!'

In a panic I ran back into the Golden Day, bursting through the noise as through an invisible wall.

'Halley! Help me, he's dying!'

I tried to get through but no one seemed to have heard me. I was blocked on both sides. They were jammed together.

'Halley!'

Two patients turned and looked me in the face, their eyes two inches from my nose.

'What is wrong with this gentleman, Sylvester?' the tall one said.

'A man's dying outside!' I said.

'Someone is always dying,' the other one said.

'Yes, and it's good to die beneath God's great tent of sky.'

'He's got to have some whisky!'

'Oh, that's different,' one of them said and they began pushing a path to the bar. 'A last bright drink to keep the anguish down. Step aside, please!'

'Schoolboy, you back already?' Halley said.

'Give me some whisky. He's dying!'

'I done told you, schoolboy, you better bring him in here. He can die, but I still got to pay my bills.'

'Please, they'll put me in jail.'

'You going to college, figure it out,' he said.

'You'd better bring the gentleman inside,' the one called Sylvester said. 'Come, let us assist you.'

We fought our way out of the crowd. He was just as I left him.

'Look, Sylvester, it's Thomas Jefferson!'

'I was just about to say, I've long wanted to discourse with him.'

I looked at them speechlessly; they were both crazy. Or were they joking?

'Give me a hand,' I said.

'Gladly.'

I shook him. 'Mr Norton!'

'We'd better hurry if he's to enjoy his drink,' one of them said thoughtfully.

We picked him up. He swung between us like a sack of old clothes.

'Hurry!'

As we carried him towards the Golden Day one of the men stopped suddenly and Mr Norton's head hung down, his white hair dragging in the dust.

'Gentlemen, this man is my grandfather!'

'But he's *white*, his name's Norton.'

'I should know my own grandfather! He's Thomas Jefferson and I'm his grandson – on the "field-nigger" side,' the tall man said.

'Sylvester, I do believe that you're right. I certainly do,' he said, staring at Mr Norton. 'Look at those features. Exactly like yours – from the identical mould. Are you sure he didn't spit you upon the earth, fully clothed?'

'No, no, that was my father,' the man said earnestly.

And he began to curse his father violently as we moved for the door. Halley was there waiting. Somehow he'd gotten the crowd to quiet down and a space was cleared in the centre of the room. The men came close to look at Mr Norton.

'Somebody bring a chair.'

'Yeah, let Mister Eddy sit down.'

'That ain't no Mister Eddy, man, that's John D. Rockefeller,' someone said.

'Here's a chair for the Messiah.'

'Stand back y'all,' Halley ordered. 'Give him some room.'

Burnside, who had been a doctor, rushed forward and felt for Mr Norton's pulse.

'It's solid! This man has a *solid* pulse! Instead of beating, it *vibrates*. That's very unusual. Very.'

Someone pulled him away. Halley reappeared with a bottle and a glass. 'Here, some of y'all tilt his head back.'

And before I could move, a short, pock-marked man appeared and took Mr Norton's head between his hands, tilting it at arm's length and then, pinching the chin gently like a barber about to apply a razor, gave a sharp, swift movement.

'Pow!'

Mr Norton's head jerked like a jabbed punching bag. Five pale red lines bloomed on the white cheek, glowing like fire beneath translucent stone. I could not believe my eyes. I wanted to run. A woman tittered. I saw several men rush for the door.

'Cut it out, you damn fool!'

'A case of hysteria,' the pock-marked man said quietly.

'Git the hell out of the way,' Halley said. 'Somebody git that stool-pigeon attendant from upstairs. Git him down here, quick!'

'A mere mild case of hysteria,' the pock-marked man said as they pushed him away.

'Hurry with the drink, Halley!'

'Heah, schoolboy, you hold the glass. This here's brandy I been saving for myself.'

Someone whispered tonelessly into my ear, 'You see, I told you that it would occur at 5.30. Already the Creator has come.' It was the stolid-faced man.

I saw Halley tilt the bottle and the oily amber of brandy sloshing into the glass. Then tilting Mr Norton's head back, I put the glass to his lips and poured. A fine brown stream ran from the corner of his mouth, down his delicate chin. The room was suddenly quiet. I felt a slight movement against my hand, like a child's breast when it whimpers at the end of a spell of crying. The fine-veined eyelids flickered. He coughed. I saw a slow red flush creep, then spurt, up his neck, spreading over his face.

'Hold it under his nose, schoolboy. Let 'im smell it.'

I waved the glass beneath Mr Norton's nose. He opened his pale blue eyes. They seemed watery now in the red flush that bathed his face. He tried to sit up, his right hand fluttering to his chin. His eyes widened, moved quickly from face to face. Then coming to mine, the moist eyes focused with recognition.

'You were unconscious, sir,' I said.

'Where am I, young man?' he asked wearily.

'This is the Golden Day, sir.'

'What?'

'The Golden Day. It's a kind of sporting-and-gambling house,' I added reluctantly.

'Now give him another drinka brandy,' Halley said. I poured a drink and handed it to him. He sniffed it, closed his eyes as in puzzlement, then drank; his cheeks filled out like small bellows; he was rinsing his mouth.

'Thank you,' he said, a little stronger now. 'What is this place?'

'The Golden Day,' said several patients in unison.

He looked slowly around him, up to the balcony, with its scrolled and carved wood. A large flag hung lank above the floor. He frowned.

'What was this building used for in the past?' he said.

'It was a church, then a bank, then it was a restaurant and a fancy gambling house, and now *we* got it,' Halley explained. 'I think some-body said it used to be a jail-house too.'

'They let us come here once a week to raise a little hell,' someone said.

'I couldn't buy a drink to take out, sir, so I had to bring you inside,' I explained in dread.

He looked about him. I followed his eyes and was amazed to see the varied expressions on the patients' faces as they silently returned his gaze. Some were hostile, some cringing, some horrified; some, who when among themselves were most violent, now appeared as submissive as children. And some seemed strangely amused.

'Are all of you patients?' Mr Norton asked.

'Me, I just runs the joint,' Halley said. 'These here other fellows ...'

'We're patients sent here as therapy,' a short, fat, very intelligent-looking man said. 'But,' he smiled, 'they send along an attendant, a kind of censor, to see that the therapy fails.'

'You're nuts. I'm a dynamo of energy. I come to charge my batteries,' one of the vets insisted.

'I'm a student of history, sir,' another interrupted with dramatic gestures. 'The world moves in a circle like a roulette wheel. In the beginning, black is on top, in the middle epochs, white holds the odds, but soon Ethiopia shall stretch forth her noble wings! Then place your money on the black!' His voice throbbed with emotion. 'Until then, the sun holds no heat, there's ice in the heart of the earth. Two years from now and I'll be old enough to give my mulatto mother a bath, the half-white bitch!' he added, beginning to leap up and down in an explosion of glassy-eyed fury.

Mr Norton blinked his eyes and straightened up.

'I'm a physician, may I take your pulse?' Burnside said, seizing Mr Norton's wrist.

'Don't pay him no mind, mister. He ain't been no doctor in ten years. They caught him trying to change some blood into money.'

'I did too!' the man screamed. 'I discovered it and John D. Rockefeller stole the formula from me.'

'Mr Rockefeller did you say?' Mr Norton said. 'I'm sure you must be mistaken.'

'WHAT'S GOING ON DOWN THERE?' a voice shouted from the balcony. Everyone turned. I saw a huge black giant of a man, dressed only in white shorts, swaying on the stairs. It was Supercargo, the attendant. I hardly recognized him without his hard-starched white uniform. Usually he walked around threatening the men with a strait jacket which he always carried over his arm, and usually they were quiet and submissive in his presence. But now they seemed not to recognize him and began shouting curses.

'How you gon keep order in the place if you gon git drunk?' Halley shouted. 'Charlene! Charlene!'

'Yeah?' a woman's voice, startling in its carrying power, answered sulkily from a room off the balcony.

'I want you to git that stool-pigeoning, joy-killing, nut-crushing bum back in there with you and sober him up. Then git him in his white suit and down here to keep order. We got white folks in the house.'

A woman appeared on the balcony, drawing a woolly pink robe about her. 'Now you lissen here, Halley,' she drawled, 'I'm a woman. If you want him dressed, you can do it yourself. I don't put on but one man's clothes and he's in N'Orleans.'

'Never mind all that. Git that stool pigeon sober!'

'I want order down there,' Supercargo boomed, 'and if there's white folks down there, I wan's *double* order.'

Suddenly there was an angry roar from the men back near the bar and I saw them rush the stairs.

'Get him!'

'Let's give him some order!'

'Out of my way.'

Five men charged the stairs. I saw the giant bend and clutch the posts at the top of the stairs with both hands, bracing himself, his body gleaming bare in his white shorts. The little man who had slapped Mr Norton was in front, and, as he sprang up the long flight, I saw the attendant set himself and kick, catching the little man just as he reached the top, hard in the chest, sending him backwards in a curving dive into the midst of the men behind him. Supercargo got set to swing his leg again. It was a narrow stair and only one man could get up at a time. As fast as they rushed up, the giant kicked them back. He swung his leg, kicking them down like a fungo-hitter batting out flies. Watching him, I forgot Mr Norton. The Golden Day was in an uproar. Half-dressed women appeared from the rooms off the balcony. Men hooted and yelled as at a football game.

'I WANT ORDER!' the giant shouted as he sent a man flying down the flight of stairs.

Mr Norton was gone from where I had left him. I rushed here and there through the noisy men, calling his name.

When I found him he was under the stairs. Somehow he had been pushed there by the scuffling, reeling men and he lay sprawled in the chair like an aged doll. In the dim light his features were sharp and white and his closed eyes well-defined lines in a well-tooled face. I shouted his name above the roar of the men, and got no answer. He was out again. I shook him, gently, then roughly, but still no flicker of his wrinkled lids. Then some of the milling men pushed me up against him and suddenly a mass of whiteness was looming two inches from my eyes; it was only his face but I felt a shudder of nameless horror. I had never been so close to a white person before. In a panic I struggled to get away. With his eyes closed he seemed more threatening than with them open. He was like a formless white death, suddenly appeared before me, a death which had been there all the time and which had now revealed itself in the madness of the Golden Day.

'Stop screaming!' a voice commanded, and I felt myself pulled away. It was the short fat man.

I clamped my mouth shut, aware for the first time that the shrill sound was coming from my own throat. I saw the man's face relax as he gave me a wry smile.

'That's better,' he shouted into my ear. 'He's only a man. Remember that. He's only a man!'

I wanted to tell him that Mr Norton was much more than that, that he was a rich white man and in my charge; but the very idea that I was responsible for him was too much for me to put into words.

'Let us take him to the balcony,' the man said, pushing me towards Mr Norton's feet. I moved automatically, grasping the thin ankles as he raised the white man by the armpits and backed from beneath the stairs. Mr Norton's head lolled upon his chest as though he were drunk or dead.

The vet started up the steps still smiling, climbing backwards a step at a time. I had begun to worry about him, whether he was drunk like the rest, when I saw three of the girls who had been leaning over the balustrade watching the brawl come down to help us carry Mr Norton up.

'Looks like pops couldn't take it,' one of them shouted.

'He's high as a Georgia pine.'

'Yeah, I tell you this stuff Halley got out here is too strong for white folks to drink.'

'Not drunk, ill!' the fat man said. 'Go find a bed that's not being used so he can stretch out awhile.'

'Sho, daddy. Is there any other little favours I can do for you?'

'That'll be enough,' he said.

One of the girls ran up ahead. 'Mine's just been changed. Bring him down here,' she said.

In a few minutes Mr Norton was lying upon a three-quarter bed, faintly breathing. I watched the fat man bend over him very professionally and feel for his pulse.

'You a doctor?' a girl asked.

'Not now, I'm a patient. But I have a certain knowledge.'

Another one, I thought, pushing him quickly aside. 'He'll be all right. Let him come to so I can get him out of here.'

'You needn't worry, I'm not like those down there, young fellow,' he said. 'I really was a doctor. I won't hurt him. He's had a mild shock of some kind.'

We watched him bend over Mr Norton again, feeling his pulse, pulling back his eyelid.

'It's a mild shock,' he repeated.

'This here Golden Day is enough to shock anybody,' a girl said, smoothing her apron over the smooth sensuous roll of her stomach.

Another brushed Mr Norton's white hair away from his forehead and stroked it, smiling vacantly. 'He's kinda cute,' she said. 'Just like a little white baby.'

'What kinda ole baby?' the small skinny girl asked.

'That's the kind, an *ole* baby.'

'You just like white men, Edna. That's all,' the skinny one said.

Edna shook her head and smiled as though amused at herself. 'I sho do. I just love 'em. Now this one, old as he is, he could put his shoes under my bed any night.'

'Shucks, me I'd kill an old man like that.'

'Kill him nothing,' Edna said. 'Girl, don't you know that all these rich ole white men got monkey glands and billy goat balls? These ole bastards don't never git enough. They want to have the whole world.'

The doctor looked at me and smiled. 'See, now you're learning all about endocrinology,' he said. 'I was wrong when I told you that he was only a man; it seems now that he's either part goat or part ape. Maybe he's both.'

'It's the truth,' Edna said. 'I used to have me one in Chicago —'

'Now you ain't never been to no Chicago, gal,' the other one interrupted.

'How you know I ain't? Two years ago ... Shucks, you don't know nothing. That ole white man right there might have him a coupla jackass balls!'

The fat man raised up with a quick grin. 'As a scientist and a physician I'm forced to discount that,' he said. 'That is one operation that has yet to be performed.' Then he managed to get the girls out of the room.

'If he should come around and hear that conversation,' the vet said, 'it would be enough to send him off again. Besides, their scientific curiosity might lead them to investigate whether he really does have a monkey gland. And that, I'm afraid, would be a bit obscene.'

'I've got to get him back to the school,' I said.

'All right,' he said, 'I'll do what I can to help you. Go see if you can find some ice. And don't worry.'

I went out on the balcony, seeing the tops of their heads. They were still milling around, the juke box baying, the piano thumping, and over at the end of the room, drenched with beer, Supercargo lay like a spent horse upon the bar.

Starting down, I noticed a large piece of ice glinting in the remains of an abandoned drink and seized its coldness in my hot hand and hurried back to the room.

The vet sat staring at Mr Norton, who now breathed with a slightly irregular sound.

'You were quick,' the man said, as he stood and reached for the ice. 'Swift with the speed of anxiety,' he added, as if to himself. 'Hand me that clean towel – there, from beside the basin.'

I handed him one, seeing him fold the ice inside it and apply it to Mr Norton's face.

'Is he all right?' I said.

'He will be in a few minutes. What happened to him?'

'I took him for a drive,' I said.

'Did you have an accident or something?'

'No,' I said. 'He just talked to a farmer and the heat knocked him out ... Then we got caught in the mob downstairs.'

'How old is he?'

'I don't know, but he's one of the trustees ...'

'One of the very first, no doubt,' he said, dabbing at the blue-veined eyes. 'A trustee of consciousness.'

'What was that?' I asked.

'Nothing ... There now, he's coming out of it.'

I had an impulse to run out of the room. I feared what Mr Norton would say to me, the expression that might come into his eyes. And yet, I was afraid to leave. My eyes could not leave the face with its flickering lids. The head moved from side to side in the pale glow of the light bulb, as though denying some insistent voice which I could not hear. Then the lids opened, revealing pale pools of blue vagueness that finally solidified into points that froze upon the vet, who looked down unsmilingly.

Men like us did not look at a man like Mr Norton in that manner, and I stepped hurriedly forward.

'He's a real doctor, sir,' I said.

'I'll explain,' the vet said. 'Get a glass of water.'

I hesitated. He looked at me firmly. 'Get the water,' he said, turning to help Mr Norton to sit up.

Outside I asked Edna for a glass of water and she led me down the hall to a small kitchen; drawing it for me from a green old-fashioned cooler.

'I got some good liquor, baby, if you want to give him a drink,' she said.

'This will do,' I said. My hands trembled so that the water spilled. When I returned, Mr Norton was sitting up unaided, carrying on a conversation with the vet.

'Here's some water, sir,' I said, extending the glass.

He took it. 'Thank you,' he said.

'Not too much,' the vet cautioned.

'Your diagnosis is exactly that of my specialist,' Mr Norton said, 'and I went to several fine physicians before one could diagnose it. How did you know?'

'I too was a specialist,' the vet said.

'But how? Only a few men in the whole country possess the knowledge —'

'Then one of them is an inmate of a semi-madhouse,' the vet said. 'But there's nothing mysterious about it. I escaped for a while – I went to France with the Army Medical Corps and remained there after the Armistice to study and practise.'

'Oh yes, and how long were you in France?' Mr Norton asked.

'Long enough,' he said. 'Long enough to forget some fundamentals which I should never have forgotten.'

'What fundamentals?' Mr Norton said. 'What do you mean?'

The vet smiled and cocked his head. 'Things about life. Such things as most peasants and folk peoples almost always know through experience, though seldom through conscious thought . . .'

'Pardon me, sir,' I said to Mr Norton, 'but now that you feel better, shouldn't we go?'

'Not just yet,' he said. Then to the doctor, 'I'm very interested. What happened to you?' A drop of water caught in one of his eyebrows glittered like a chip of active diamond. I went over and sat on a chair. Damn this vet to hell!

'Are you sure you would like to hear?' the vet asked.

'Why, of course.'

'Then perhaps the young fellow should go downstairs and wait . . .'

The sound of shouting and destruction welled up from below as I opened the door.

'No, perhaps you should stay,' the fat man said. 'Perhaps had I overheard some of what I'm about to tell you when I was a student up there on the hill, I wouldn't be the casualty that I am.'

'Sit down, young man,' Mr Norton ordered. 'So you were a student at the college,' he said to the vet.

I sat down again, worrying about Dr Bledsoe as the fat man told Mr Norton of his attending college, then becoming a physician and going to France during the World War.

'Were you a successful physician?' Mr Norton said.

'Fairly so. I performed a few brain surgeries that won me some small attention.'

'Then why did you return?'

'Nostalgia,' the vet said.

'Then what on earth are you doing here in this ...?' Mr Norton said. 'With your ability ...'

'Ulcers,' the fat man said.

'That's terribly unfortunate, but why should ulcers stop your career?'

'Not really, but I learned along with the ulcers that my work could bring me no dignity,' the vet said.

'Now you sound bitter,' Mr Norton said, just as the door flew open.

A brown-skinned woman with red hair looked in. 'How's white-folks making out?' she said, staggering inside. 'White-folks, baby, you done come to. You want a drink?'

'Not now, Hester,' the vet said. 'He's still a little weak.'

'He sho looks it. That's how come he needs a drink. Put some iron in his blood.'

'Now, now, Hester.'

'Okay, okay ... But what y'all doing looking like you at a funeral? Don't you know this is the Golden Day?' She staggered towards me, belching elegantly and reeling. 'Just look at y'all. Here schoolboy looks like he's scared to death. And white-folks here is acting like y'all two strange poodles. Be happy y'all! I'm going down and get Halley to send you up some drinks.' She patted Mr Norton's cheek as she went past and I saw him turn a glowing red. 'Be happy, white-folks.'

'Ah hah!' the vet laughed, 'you're blushing, which means that you're better. Don't be embarrassed. Hester is a great humanitarian, a thera-pist of generous nature and great skill, and the possessor of a healing touch. Her catharsis is absolutely tremendous — ha, ha!'

'You do look better, sir,' I said, anxious to get out of the place. I could understand the vet's words but not what they conveyed, and Mr Norton looked as uncomfortable as I felt. The one thing which I did know was that the vet was acting towards the white man with a freedom which could only bring on trouble. I wanted to tell Mr Norton that the man was crazy and yet I received a fearful satisfaction from hearing him talk as he had to a white man. With the girl it was different. A woman usually got away with things a man never could.

I was wet with anxiety, but the vet talked on, ignoring the interruption.

'Rest, rest,' he said, fixing Mr Norton with his eyes. 'The clocks are all set back and the forces of destruction are rampant down below. They might suddenly realize that you are what you are, and then your life wouldn't be worth a piece of bankrupt stock. You would be cancelled, perforated, voided, become the recognized magnet attracting loose screws. Then what would you do? Such men are beyond money, and with Supercargo down, out like a felled ox, they know nothing of value. To some, you are the great white father, to others the lyncher of souls, but for all, you are confusion come even into the Golden Day.'

'What are you talking about?' I said, thinking: *Lyncher?* He was getting wilder than the men downstairs. I didn't dare look at Mr Norton, who made a sound of protest.

The vet frowned. 'It is an issue which I can confront only by evading it. An utterly stupid proposition, and these hands so lovingly trained to master a scalpel yearn to caress a trigger. I returned to save life and I was refused,' he said. 'Ten men in masks drove me out from the city at midnight and beat me with whips for saving a human life. And I was forced to the utmost degradation because I possessed skilled hands and the belief that my knowledge could bring me dignity — not wealth, only dignity — and other men health!'

Then suddenly he fixed me with his eyes. 'And now, do you understand?'

'What?' I said.

'What you've heard!'

'I don't know.'

'Why?'

I said, 'I really think it's time we left.'

'You see,' he said turning to Mr Norton, 'he has eyes and ears and a good distended African nose, but he fails to understand the simple facts of life. *Understand*. Understand? It's worse than that. He registers with his senses but short-circuits his brain. Nothing has meaning. He takes it in but he doesn't digest it. Already he is — well, bless my soul! Behold! a walking zombie! Already he's learned to repress not only his emotions but his humanity. He's invisible, a walking personification of the Negative, the most perfect achievement of your dreams, sir! The mechanical man!'

Mr Norton looked amazed.

'Tell me,' the vet said, suddenly calm. 'Why have you been interested in the school, Mr Norton?'

'Out of a sense of my destined role,' Mr Norton said shakily. 'I felt, and I still feel, that your people are in some important manner tied to my destiny.'

'What do you mean, destiny?' the vet said.

'Why, the success of my work, of course.'

'I see. And would you recognize it if you saw it?'

'Why, of course I would,' Mr Norton said indignantly. 'I've watched it grow each year I've returned to the campus.'

'Campus? Why the campus?'

'It is there that my destiny is being made.'

The vet exploded with laughter. 'The campus, what a destiny!' He stood and walked around the narrow room, laughing. Then he stopped as suddenly as he had begun.

'You will hardly recognize it, but it is very fitting that you came to the Golden Day with the young fellow,' he said.

'I came out of illness – or rather, he brought me,' Mr Norton said.

'Of course, but you came, and it was fitting.'

'What do you mean?' Mr Norton said with irritation.

'A little child shall lead them,' the vet said with a smile. 'But seriously, because you both fail to understand what is happening to you. You cannot see or hear or smell the truth of what you see – and you, looking for destiny! It's classic! And the boy, this automaton, he was made of the very mud of the region and he sees far less than you. Poor stumblers, neither of you can see the other. To you he is a mark on the score-card of your achievement, a thing and not a man; a child, or even less – a black amorphous thing. And you, for all your power, are not a man to him, but a God, a force —'

Mr Norton stood abruptly. 'Let us go, young man,' he said angrily.

'No, listen. He believes in you as he believes in the beat of his heart. He believes in that great false wisdom taught slaves and pragmatists alike, that white is right. I can tell you *his* destiny. He'll do your bidding, and for that his blindness is his chief asset. He's your man, friend. Your man and your destiny. Now the two of you descend the stairs into chaos and get the hell out of here. I'm sick of both of you pitiful obscenities! Get out before I do you both the favour of bashing in your heads!'

I saw his motion towards the big white pitcher on the washstand and stepped between him and Mr Norton, guiding Mr Norton swiftly through the doorway. Looking back, I saw him leaning against the wall making a sound that was a blending of laughter and tears.

'Hurry, the man is as insane as the rest,' Mr Norton said.

'Yes, sir,' I said, noticing a new note in his voice.

The balcony was now as noisy as the floor below. The girls and drunken vets were stumbling about with drinks in their hands. Just as we went past an open door Edna saw us and grabbed my arm.

'Where you taking white-folks?' she demanded.

'Back to school,' I said, shaking her off.

'You don't want to go up there, white-folks, baby,' she said. I tried to push past her. 'I ain't lying,' she said. 'I'm the best little home-maker in the business.'

'Okay, but please let us alone,' I pleaded. 'You'll get me into trouble.'

We were going down the stairs into the milling men now and she started to scream, 'Pay me then! If he's too good for me, let him pay!'

And before I could stop her she had pushed Mr Norton, and both of us were stumbling swiftly down the stairs. I landed against a man who looked up with the anonymous familiarity of a drunk and shoved me hard away. I saw Mr Norton spin past as I sank farther into the crowd. Somewhere I could hear the girl screaming and Halley's voice yelling, 'Hey! Hey! Hey, now!' Then I was aware of fresh air and saw that I was near the door and pushed my way free and stood panting and preparing to plunge back for Mr Norton – when I heard Halley calling, 'Make way y'all!' and saw him piloting Mr Norton to the door.

'Whew!' he said, releasing the white man and shaking his huge head.

'Thanks, Halley —' I said and got no further.

I saw Mr Norton, his face pale again, his white suit rumpled, topple and fall, his head scraping against the screen of the door.

'Hey!'

I opened the door and raised him up.

'Goddamit, out agin,' Halley said. 'How come you bring this white man here, schoolboy?'

'Is he dead?'

'DEAD!' he said, stepping back indignantly. 'He *caint* die!'

'What'll I do, Halley?'

'Not in my place, he cain't die,' he said, kneeling.

Mr Norton looked up. 'No one is dead or dying,' he said acidly. 'Remove your hands!'

Halley fell away, surprised. 'I sho am glad. You sho you all right? I thought sho you was dead this time.'

'For God's sake, be quiet!' I exploded nervously. 'You should be glad that he's all right.'

Mr Norton was visibly angry now, a raw place showing on his fore-head, and I hurried ahead of him to the car. He climbed in unaided, and I got under the wheel, smelling the heated odour of mints and cigar smoke. He was silent as I drove away.

Edward Brathwaite

Jah

1

Nairobi's male elephants uncurl
their trumpets to heaven
Toot-Toot takes it up
in Havana
in Harlem

bridges of sound curve
through the pale rigging
of saxophone stops
the ship sails, slips on banana
peel water, eating the dark men.

Has the quick drummer nerves
after the stink Sabbath's unleavened
cries in the hot hull? From the top
of the music, slack Bwana
Columbus rides out of the jungle's den.

With my blue note, my cracked note, full flatten-
ed fifth, my ten bebop fingers, my black bottom'd strut, Panama
worksong, my cabin, my hut,
my new frigged-up soul and God's heaven,
heaven, gonna walk all over God's heaven . . .

I furl
away from the trumpet
my bridge stops in the New York air
elevator speeds me to angels
heaven sways in the reinforced girders;

God is glass with his type-
writer teeth, gospel
jumps and pings off the white
paper, higher and higher;

the eagle's crook neck,
the vulture's talons clutching tight
as a blind baby's fist, still knows
the beat of the root blood
up through the rocks, up through the torn

hummingbird trees, guitar strings, eyrie;
the buffaloes' boom through the dust plains,
the antelope's sniff at the water, eland's sudden hurl
through the hurdle of fire, runnels upwards to them
through the hoof of the world.

But here God looks out over the river
yellow mix of the neon lights
high up over the crouching cotton-wool green
and we float, high up over the sighs of the city,
like fish in a gold water world

we float round and round
in the bright bubbled bowl
without hope of the hook,
of the fisherman's tugging-in root;

eyes without bait, snout
without words, teeth with nothing to kill,
skill of fin for a child's wonder,
pale scales for collectors to sell;

and God, big eyes bulging
his glass house aglobe
floating floating in heaven
without feet without wind

without wing without thunder
no stone under him
no sound to carry earth up to his fathoms
no ground to keep him down near the gods.

For the land has lost the memory of the most secret places.

We see the moon but cannot remember its meaning.
A dark skin is a chain but it cannot recall the name

of its tribe. There are no chiefs in the village.

The gods have been forgotten or hidden.
A prayer poured on the ground with water,

with rum, will not bid them come

back. Creation has burned to a spider.
It peeps over the hills with the sunrise

but prefers to spin webs in the trees.

The sea is a divider. It is not a life-giver,
Time's river. The islands are the humped

backs of mountains, green turtles

that cannot find their way. Volcanoes
are voiceless. They have shut their red eyes

to the weather. The sun that was once a doom of gold to the
    Arawaks
is now a flat boom in the sky.

Ferdinand Oyono

from The Old Man and the Medal

Meka stood bare-headed and quite still, his arms to his sides, inside
the circle painted with whitewash where he had been placed to wait for
the arrival of the White Chief. The guards were having difficulty keeping back the crowd of his fellow Africans massed behind him. In front,
under the shade of M Fouconi's veranda were the white men but Father
Vandermayer with his black cassock and his black beard was the only
one Meka could recognize. For him, white men were like antelopes,
their faces all looked the same.

Meka peered around him cautiously like an animal that feels
watched. He had to control an urge to pass his hand over his face and
wipe off the sweat which had gathered in a bead at the end of his nose.
He realized what a strange situation he was in. Neither his grandfather
nor his father nor any member of his huge family had ever been placed
as he was inside a whitewash circle, between two worlds, his own world
and the world of those others who had been called ghosts when they
first came into the land. He was not with his own people, and he was not
with the others. He wondered what he was doing out there. He could
just as well have waited with Kelara who was somewhere, he knew, in
the crowd screaming behind him and been called out for the medal when
the great Chief of the white men had arrived. What was this absurd idea
of the Chief of the Doum white men to have him inside a whitewash
circle? He had been there an hour already, perhaps longer. Still the
great Chief of the whites had not come.

It was hot. Meka began to wonder if his heart was beating in his feet.
He had put his shoes on at the top of the hill where M Fouconi's office
first comes into sight. He could hardly feel he had them on as he went
to report to the Commandant. Meka had marched to his position
underneath the flag as if he had been the King of Doum. He had not

even given a glance aside at the tribal chiefs whom he recognized by their red shoulder bands.

'More of them bursting with envy!' he said to himself. 'I despise them! I despise them!'

Then he had brought his heels together in the way he had seen soldiers do when a white man went by. A white man went by him, gave him a smile, then went over and joined the other white men, pointing back at Meka with his finger. Then Meka heard confused voices raised among the Europeans. But he stood rigidly to attention. He felt as hard as a plank of wood.

His tiredness had started first in his stiff neck. Meka again began to look around him. Now that he could feel his heart was beating in his feet, he started to worry about whether he would be able to stay in his circle until the great Chief of the white men arrived. He looked down at his shoes. They looked as if they had swollen since the morning when he had emptied out the sand he had filled them up with for the night. He tried to move one of his feet; he clasped his fists and stopped breathing. For a few seconds he felt a great sense of peace. Then he tried to put all his weight on his right foot which was hurting less than the other. His left foot grew easier but now he could not tell what was going on in his right foot. It felt as if the needle Ela had given him was going through his little toe, then up through his ankle, right up to his thigh and sticking into his backbone. The needle multiplied into a million needles swarming and pricking in every part of his body. Meka was bathed in sweat.

'It's a good job I didn't put socks on,' he said to himself.

He tried to call up in his imagination a more excruciating pain than the one he was feeling.

'But what about it?' he said to himself. 'I am a man, just as my ancestors made me and left me. They are watching me now, in this situation . . . I must not let them be ashamed of me. I was circumcized with the knife and the doctor spat out pimento on to the wound. I did not cry out . . .'

He clenched his teeth a little harder.

'I did not cry,' he thought. 'In all my life I have never cried. A man, a real man, never cries . . .'

That is what Meka was, a man and a real man. Was he not the son of the great Meka who held out for so long against the first white men? Well then, was he going to cry now in front of them and in front of his own people who knew his father or had heard the stories of him?

Transfigured, Meka looked over to the whites. He stretched out one foot and moved the other to the side. Then he did it the other way round, and brought his heels together again. He turned around and smiled at the Africans, as if he wanted to reassure them. He could not feel his shoes any more. He looked up at the flag waving above his head, he looked at the whites and at the soldiers. Then he braced his neck.

'Even if he doesn't come till the night, I will wait,' he said. 'Even if he doesn't come until tomorrow, or for a year or till the end of the world . . .'

Suddenly his forehead wrinkled and an ominous expression crossed his face. There seemed to be a heavy weight at the bottom of his belly. From far far away he could feel approaching the urge to satisfy a need.

M Fouconi was in the first row of the Doum Europeans, sitting between Gullet and his assistant, a young man with a plump figure. He had a profusion of dark hair and a wide pelvis. The Africans called him 'Man-woman-who-stands-by'.

M Fouconi came forward, down the steps and into the courtyard. His assistant joined him. They chatted for a moment a few feet away from Meka. M Fouconi looked over to him and smiled. Meka returned the widest smile he could manage. Then the two white men went over to discuss with the Chief of the soldiers. M Fouconi with his assistant still following went back to the group of white men.

'What if I just went away,' thought Meka. His feet were broiling. 'What if I just went away?'

He put the question to himself several times and shrugged his shoulders. Then taking his courage in both hands, he wiped his hand across his sweating face. He looked around as if to see if there was anyone who had noticed.

He swayed and made a vague movement. He wanted to whistle. He took a hold on himself and wiped his hand across his lips. He wondered what he ought to think about to help him forget the urge he could feel becoming more and more pressing and the heat of the fire that was consuming his feet. He would have given the whole world to be behind his hut under the magnolia tree where he crouched down every morning after his prayers. He closed his eyes.

'Almighty God,' he prayed to himself. 'Thou alone seest all that passeth in the hearts of men, Thou seest that my dearest wish at this moment as I wait for the medal and for the white Chief, alone in this circle, between two worlds' – he opened his eyes, looked in front of him and behind, then shut them again – 'between two worlds, O God, which Thou hast made utterly different from each other, that my dear wish and great longing is to take off these shoes and to have a piss ... Yes, a piss ... I am only a poor sinner and not worthy that Thou shouldest hear me ... but I beseech Thee to aid me in this position which I have never been in before in all my life. In the name of Jesus Christ our Lord. So be it. I make the sign of the cross inwardly.'

He opened his eyes and passed his tongue over his lips. He felt easier.

It was half past ten. M Fouconi was beginning to grow restless for the High Commissioner was now an hour late. They were waiting for him to take the salute. M Fouconi went over to the group of African officials, then to the group of chiefs. He crossed over in front of Meka.

'Hot, isn't it?' he said to him.

'Yes, yes,' said Meka.

That was the limit of what he could say in French. M Fouconi was joined by Gullet and his assistant. The white men began to cross back and forth in front of Meka.

'They are lucky not to suffer with their shoes,' thought Meka bitterly. 'They are wearing pith helmets and they are young ... I am a poor old man but I have to leave my head baking in the sun like a lizard.'

The Europeans passed across in front of him again. Their clothes were so white they hurt his eyes. He closed them, and his ears were tortured by the grating of the pebbles crushed by the white men's heavy feet.

Meka could not tell what hurt the most, his feet, his belly, the heat or his teeth. If he had been asked at that moment what was wrong he would not have been lying, as he usually was, when he gave his reply that the pain was everywhere at once. He was sorry he had not called at Mammy Titi's.

'At least there I could have taken something to stop me feeling the pain,' he told himself.

He looked over towards the Commercial Centre. At the same moment the bugle sounded, and excitement stirred everywhere. Meka saw a huge black car flying a small tricolour approaching smartly towards the courtyard where he was standing. The car came to a stop in front of M Fouconi and his assistant. The Commandant of Doum opened one of the doors. Two enormous white men climbed out. Meka wondered which of them could be the great Chief they were all waiting for.

The two whites followed by M Fouconi and his assistant moved up and down in front of the soldiers. Then M Fouconi led them to the veranda of his office where the Europeans of Doum were awaiting them.

A few moments later M Fouconi presented the party of African officials to them. Then the party of tribal chiefs. Here they shook a few hands. When Meka saw them coming towards him, he felt a knife blade going through his bowels. He clenched his teeth and braced his muscles as he did when he had to face danger. M Fouconi indicated Meka with the point of his chin and then turned round to his chiefs, talking all the time. Meka wondered if they hadn't guessed about his urgent need. He blinked and clenched his fists. When M Fouconi had finished what he had to say, the two white men, one after the other, each offered him a soft hand. He squeezed them like a damp rag. Then they went back to their own people.

Meka was at the end of his strength. It was so hot that he looked up into the sky to make sure the sun was still up there and not resting on his back.

'Why didn't they give him the medal? How could they leave a man of his age standing there for an hour? Had they lost the medal he was to have or forgotten to bring it?' The thought of this terrified him. What would he tell his friends, especially those who had watched him assume a kind of importance over the presentation. Ah, these whites. Nothing was straightforward with them. They ran when they walked and they were tortoises when they had made you a promise. They were taking their time over there, on the other side of the courtyard, dragging out their presentations and their salutations. He shook his head and looked down at his feet. He managed to hold himself from jumping in the air. 'I've got the feet of Nti! I've got the feet of Paul Nti,' he said in panic. He crossed his hands over the lower part of his belly. It made him feel much better.

He quickly put his heels together when he saw the two white strangers, with M Fouconi, his assistant and M Pipiniakis coming towards him. He thrust his arms as far as he could down the sides of his thighs, held his head high and stood absolutely still. He saw M Pipiniakis stand by his side. M Fouconi and the others remained a few steps in front of them.

The bugle sounded and there was a roll of drums. One of the enormous white men came towards M Pipiniakis.

'It is him, the great white Chief!' thought Meka. He had never seen anything or anybody like him. All that he noticed were the voluminous folds of skin under his chin that almost concealed the knot of his tie.

The great Chief was speaking to M Pipiniakis, as if he were speaking to someone who was deaf. M Pipiniakis stood as still as a statue. When he had finished the Chief took a medal from a small case which M

Fouconi's assistant held out for him and pinned it on to M Pipiniakis's breast. Then Meka saw the great Chief grasp his shoulders and put his cheeks one after the other against the cheeks of the Greek. At each movement the folds of skin under his chin trembled like a withered dun-coloured breast.

Then it was Meka's turn. The white Chief stood in front of him and began to shout. As he opened and shut his mouth his lower jaw went down and came up, puffing up and then deflating the skin under his chin. He took another medal from the case and came towards Meka, still talking. Meka had time to notice that it was not the same as the Greek's medal.

The white Chief was now at his shoulder. Meka looked down at him just at the moment when he was pinning the medal on to his breast. He could feel the hot breath through his khaki jacket. The Chief was sweating like a wrestler. It looked as if it had been raining over his back. A large damp patch stretched from his shoulders down to his buttocks.

Meka wondered anxiously if he was going to push his damp turkey-crop against each shoulder as he had done with M Pipiniakis. He breathed again when the white Chief, after he had pinned on the medal, took a few steps backward and shook his hand. Meka's hand swallowed up the hand of the Chief like a scrap of damp cotton rag.

Meka squinted down at his chest. The medal was certainly there, pinned on to his khaki jacket. He smiled and lifted up his head. Then he noticed that he was singing under his breath and that the whole of his face was beating time. His body was swaying in spite of himself and his knees bending and stretching like a spring. He no longer felt any pain. He could not even hear his bones cracking. The heat, his need, the pain in his feet, as if by magic they had all disappeared. He looked down again at the medal. He could feel his neck growing. Yes, his head was climbing up and up, up to heaven like the Tower of Babel. His forehead reached the clouds. His long arms gradually rose like the wings of a bird poised for flight.

'It is a long time before the pot where the goat is cooked loses the smell,' he said to himself. Who said that the Mekas were finished? Was there not one of them, himself, Meka, the one African of Doum decorated by the Chief of the white men? Yes, he was known in Timba, his name had crossed the seas and flown over the mountains and come to the ear of the great Chief of the whites, who had sent another great Chief to decorate him at Doum. The whole world knew this, the whole world had seen how the very hand of the High Commissioner had pinned the medal on to his chest.

The great Chief of the whites, together with his second in command and M Fouconi and his assistant, stood in the middle of the courtyard, facing Meka. M Fouconi beckoned the interpreter that Meka had met a few days before in his office. The African interpreter, his pith-helmet in his hand, ran over to Meka and told him that the Chief of the whites invited him to drink and to eat for the whole day and the drinking was to begin at the African Community Centre. Meka tossed back his head to indicate assent. The interpreter told him to go over and stand with the officials and M Pipiniakis. Meka with his head held high went across the courtyard and, not deigning to stand beside the Greek, took up position by the side of M Fouconi's assistant.

The bugle sounded. The soldiers began to march off to the sound of the *Marche Lorraine*. They turned their heads sharply towards the great Chief of the whites who had brought his hand up to the peak of his kepi.

Deeply impressed, Meka watched with bulging eyes the fine rifles that passed to and fro in front of him. Who could resist the sons of Japhet? He thought of his old kaffir musket. To think his father had wanted to fight it out to the end against the whites with that! He looked for the smoke bomb which Ignatius Obebé had talked about, but no one of the soldiers was carrying the great black ball which his imagination pictured. Meka began to count the rifles in his mind. He lost count, tried to begin again, lost count again. Then he thought about the gorillas, the unclean creatures that devastated the banana groves. If he was given one of these rifles being wasted here – just one – the gorillas would know who they had to deal with. He made up his mind that he would ask the great Chief of the whites for a rifle. What would it cost him to make a present of just one of them? The idea grew so in his mind that he began to look from the great Chief of the whites to M Fouconi and then back. He caught a withering look from the assistant. Meka moved his lips and took a step forward. The assistant signalled to him with a sharp gesture to step back. Meka felt a great throbbing in his feet. He passed his hand over his face. The assistant shrugged his shoulders and took no more notice. Meka's throat was constricted. He brought his heels together and leant forward a little to watch the last of the rifles disappearing. When he stood up again he caught another withering glance from the assistant. Meka felt his urgent need return.

Kelara had watched her husband presented with his medal through eyes damp with joy. When the white man shook Meka's hand she thought her heart would stop beating.

'There's somebody,' they were saying. 'You can't say we haven't got a great man at Doum.' Then some troublemaker said, 'I think they ought to have covered him in medals. That would have been a bit more like it! To think he has lost his land and his sons just for that . . .'

That was the false note that quenched all Kelara's enthusiasm. It was then that she knew that her sorrow was still sharp and that nothing could ever make up for the loss of her two sons. She unknotted her neckerchief and pushed it into her mouth so that she could not cry.

'What's wrong with the old woman?' someone asked. 'Is she ill?'

A woman held her by the shoulders. Kelara started to weep with all her heart on the woman's shoulder, and the woman started to weep with her. The men turned their eyes away.

'What can be the matter with the old woman?' they asked again.

Kelara could feel the lump that had come up into her throat dissolving away as she went on weeping. When she felt it had disappeared she thanked the woman who had given her support. Then she stood on tiptoe to see into the courtyard where the march past was now coming to an end. She saw her husband, his head gleaming in the sun, grin foolishly at the Chief of the white men. Something happened inside her which she could not understand. Meka seemed to her like someone she had never seen before. Could that be her husband who was grinning away over there? She looked down at the pair of old slippers wrapped up in a newspaper that she was holding under her arm. Then she stood up on her toes again. The man laughing over there had no connection with her. She felt frightened at herself. She rubbed her eyes and looked at Meka again. The corners of her mouth dropped in a grimace of contempt. She forced her way through the crowd till she reached a gawky youth whose hand she seized. He looked at her open-mouthed in astonishment.

'It was you who spoke just now,' she said to him. 'Thank you. The Holy Spirit spoke through your mouth.'

The young man was going to protest, then he changed his mind and passed his hand over his lips.

'Good God,' he said out loud. 'What was it I said then?' 'You want to know?' said his neighbour, a short young man who could easily have been taken for Chinese. 'It was you who made the old woman start crying just now . . .'

When the gawky young man turned round in his horror to apologize to Kelara she had disappeared.

'I don't understand,' he said. 'Was she the wife of the chap they've just given the medal to over there?' he asked his neighbour.

'She may well be, because she started crying when you said he ought to have been given lots of medals. How did you know that he had lost his land and his sons for the medal they gave him?'

'The Commandant was saying that last night to M Pipiniakis when they were talking over dinner. You forget I am the Commandant's houseboy . . .'

The two young men fell silent.

On the veranda outside M Fouconi's office, Meka was the only black and khaki spot amongst the white suits of the Europeans of Doum. He kept forcing himself to smile to attract their attention. Every now and then a white hand passed over his head or by his ears before making a perfunctory gesture of admiration at the medal hanging on his chest. He was pleased to notice that no one else among the whites was wearing a medal like his. He had given Father Vandermayer the broadest smile he could manage when the priest had tapped him on the shoulder and said with a smile at the corner of his mouth that he was now a most important person.

Meka did not know how he came to be standing outside the circle the Europeans had made round their Chief. His fellow Africans were already dancing in the courtyard. The drumming had begun after the end of the march past.

Meka did not know who to ask when they were to go to the African Community Centre. He went and tapped Father Vandermayer on the shoulder. The priest shot an angry glance at him and waved him away sharply with the back of his hand. Meka, quite bewildered, brought his hand up to his chin and opened his mouth like a fish. No, he could not believe it. Father Vandermayer could not be giving him an answer like that.

Meka moved a few steps away and leant up against the wall. He stretched his legs and put his hands on his hips. He tossed his head several times and then held it still. His mouth hung open with his astonishment like the mouth of a strangled animal. He stared down at the floor in stupid fascination as if the cement had the eyes of a snake. He was no longer watching the group of white men and only the murmur of their conversation reached him. Where was it he had heard whites talking like that without understanding what they said and without seeing them? He put his head in his hands and began to press on his temples as if he wanted to force the fleeting recollection out of the chaos of his memory. He frowned and then his face relaxed. He remembered. It was when he had been listening to a gramophone! He closed his eyes and dismissed Father Vandermayer, M Fouconi and the great white Chief from his thoughts.

At that moment someone tapped him on the shoulder. Before he opened his eyes, Meka felt it was Father Vandermayer. He recognized his way of tapping the faithful on the shoulder when he passed behind them on Sunday taking the collection.

'Have you got sleeping sickness?' he asked him in bad Mvema.

He started to laugh but the laugh froze on his lips. Meka had just given him the first angry look he had ever given in his life.

'Are you ill, have you got a pain?' stammered Father Vandermayer.

'No, Father, I am rather tired,' Meka lied.

'You'll feel better later on, at the Community Centre,' said the priest and gave Meka's ear a tug.

'Yes, Father,' said Meka.

Father Vandermayer when he rebuffed Meka realized too late that he had carelessly let his claws show and he wondered if Meka had noticed. He wanted to reassure himself, and, noticing Meka was no longer at his heels, he had gone over to talk to him. He was soon reassured. He noticed nothing in Meka's face, and went back to the others.

At last M Fouconi mentioned the reception. The circle of Europeans opened to let the High Commissioner pass. When Meka noticed, he stood up and straightened the tails of his jacket. The High Commissioner went down the steps and smiled at him. The whites got into their cars. Father Vandermayer invited Meka to get into the back of his van though there was no one with him in the cabin. The High Commissioner's car started first. M Fouconi's followed, then Gullet's, then Father Vandermayer's. Meka sat down on a case of communion wine and took off his shoes.

*   *   *

On certain rare occasions in his hut Meka would wake up slowly and gradually, drifting back into consciousness. There was no chance of waking up like that now. Suddenly he found himself flung down under the bench. Plunged in darkness, the Community Centre was under the onslaught of the first storm at the end of the dry season.

Everything was creaking and whining in the wind and the thunder. It sounded as if thousands of bucketfuls of water were being poured down on to the ancient tin roof, flattening it out with their impact. Slats, joists, rafters, were all giving way above Meka's head. He wondered if perhaps this was the end of the world. A flash of lightning rent the darkness and the crash of thunder that followed shook the ground under Meka's buttocks. He felt everything leap in his stomach. He had no idea how he came to be lying on his back in empty space with his arms flailing in the darkness to find something to hold on to. He tried to get up but another crash of thunder flung him down on to the ground. He rolled over like a rabbit and then he found himself on the bench again. Lightning and thunder followed one after the other like flashes from a blazing fire, overlapping in the disturbing speed of their succession. Meka crossed himself and his hands began to lift the bench up over his head. He swung it about in front of him. There was a crashing of metal and breaking bottles which was soon lost in a peal of thunder even more shattering than the first one. Meka crossed himself again.

Frantically he got to his feet and began to move forward. In a flash of lightning he caught sight of the huge French flag fluttering over the platform. Water was swirling everywhere. Meka could feel it round his ankles. He tried to tuck up the bottoms of his trousers but as he stood on one foot he lost his balance and went down like a log into the pool that was swirling round his feet. When he got up he found that the tin roof was almost touching his head. He gave a wild scream and plunged forward into the darkness.

Was he going to die like a porcupine, alone in this enormous trap with no way out? His hands began to explore the corrugations of the roof. At last his fingers met with the door hinges. He felt round the edges of the door itself and then pulled it. The whole building swayed. Meka stretched his arm up above his head. He shuddered when he felt the roof against his fingers and his blood drained away. He felt round his neck to see if he still had his St Christopher medal. He was relieved to find it was there in its place, hanging on a piece of twine from a fish-sack. In a flash Meka realized at last that he was shut in the Community Centre in a storm and that the shanty was about to collapse on top of him. But he was now quite calm. Good St Christopher was beside him.

Meka heaved at the door again with all his might. He heard the rain that had gathered up on the sagging roof smack down into the court-yard in a great sheet of water, and the wall he was leaning against began to heel dangerously over. Meka ran towards the platform. The section of wall he had been pressing on collapsed and let in a seething cascade of water. Miraculously the roof still held. The water was beginning to under-mine the end wall and that too was beginning to slant. Meka started to shout. He roared like a madman with the storm raging all around him. He never understood how he came to be in the gutter which he recognized from the sapling citronella trees, half covered by the water.

In the courtyard visibility was zero. Meka stood up. His trousers were soaked and the water was running down his legs. He was pleased to find he was barefooted. The peals of thunder grew fainter and the lightning less bright. Meka edged forward cautiously. He tested how deep the water was with his foot before he planted each step. Then he brought up the other foot from behind. At times he was going on all fours to be sure that he would not fall. When he felt large pebbles under his hands he sighed and stood up. He was on the road.

The storm had raged at Doum with a violence that had never been known before. The world that had been deprived of water for so long was now steeped and sapped and drenched and sated with it. Here and there trees struck by lightning were burning like funeral torches in the night.

The sheet of water reflecting the flashes of lightning stretched away into infinity. Meka was alone in that immense sea, without compass or lamp. The rain was still falling. Meka had long ago lost his eyebrows and the water that ran down his forehead went into his eyes. He pressed his eyelids closed and blew out the water that was running into his mouth, pouting out his lips into the shape of a duck's behind. A drum was hammering in his head. From time to time Meka punched himself on the back of the neck to settle the pain he could feel in his head. He looked back towards the African Community Centre. In a flash of lightning he caught sight of a heap of corrugated iron. His stomach began to ache with retrospective fear. It had been a near thing. He crossed himself, sucked his thumb and put off the prayer until later. He tossed his head and wondered what he was going to do to find his way across this wilderness of water where the road was completely covered. He thought of Kelara and Engamba and all the rest who were waiting for him before beginning the goat. Had his hut stood up to the storm? He made up his mind to walk straight ahead. It was growing calm all round though the sky was still laden with clouds and menacing. Meka, as he moved forward as slowly as a tortoise, was frightened the rain would start again. The storms that came at the end of the dry season always had two phases. After the first of rain and lightning a second phase followed with just rain.

Meka increased his pace. At every plop that his feet made as he pulled them out of the water or let them fall back in, they seemed held by an enormous weight. Meka lifted them up as high as he could. He found he was tiring himself out and making little progress.

'If only I could swim,' he said to himself.

But the water only came up to his calves. He had to be content with doing a kind of goose step.

'Man is a lonely creature,' he thought. How did he, a member of one of the largest families in Doum come to be all alone in the middle of the disaster that was passing over him. He tried to call to mind all the events of the day. Everything was confused in his mind. Without thinking he brought his hand up to his chest and stopped, in dismay. The medal he had been given by the Chief of the whites had gone. He looked down at the water swirling at his feet. His mind went back to the Community Centre. Had he lost his medal or had someone stolen it? He hoped it was stolen. If he had lost it there was no hope of ever finding it after such a storm. He crossed himself again and said Our Father and a Hail Mary. Then he sucked his thumb.

He thought about his medal again. But, God in Heaven, where could he have lost it? He saw himself back in Father Vandermayer's car.

'The crook!' he said, out loud. Then he said inwardly, 'O God, forgive me if that was blasphemy. I don't know what I am doing. I have lost my medal. I have lost everything ... everything. I am all alone, alone in the world.'

He continued his solitary progress through the rain. He loomed up in the glare of the lightning like a corpse raised by miracle out of the waters, a vision from the apocalypse in the midst of the warring elements.

At last Meka noticed the first huts of the location. The roofs were silhouetted against the edge of the orange sky where the lightning flickered intermittently. Meka felt a sudden flush of warmth. The St Vitus dance that had made him tremble from head to foot suddenly left him. He decided he would go and dry his clothes at Mammy Titi's.

The location was not right beside the road. It was reached down a slope and then by a path that went winding through a small copse of mango trees where there had once been a swamp.

Meka could now think of nothing else. Mammy Titi filled his whole mind. He waited for a flash of lightning so that he could take his bearings from the mango copse.

'Now what is this rotten lightning waiting for?' he complained out loud.

He was suddenly caught in a beam of light. He lifted up his arms to cover his eyes.

'Who is that messing about?' he demanded nervously.

Then, in a voice full of supplication:

'O man with the electric torch, God has sent you to me. Come and help me find the path leading to the location . . .'

The beam of light came forward. Meka could hear the water churned by boots. He tried to turn his eyes away from the blinding beam of light.

'Don't shine the light in my eyes, my friend sent by Providence! Light up God's earth so I can find my path . . . my friend, only the path . . .'

'All right, enough of that,' came a hollow voice.

Then the light went out, plunging Meka into primeval darkness.

Before he recovered from his surprise, an iron fist crashed into his stomach, winding him. Meka felt himself lifted up into the air. Was he in the claws of an eagle being carried up into the sky? The flash of lightning he had been waiting so long for revealed two dark shapes almost conical in their long capes. He tried to find the ground with his feet. He gave a guttural cry, cut off by the splash of his body striking the water. As he went under he lost consciousness.

When he came to, painfully, he was bathed in light from the torch. He could see the scarred faces of the constables above him, shouting.

'Get up, you pig! Where are your papers? Eh? Your papers? Where have you come from? What are you doing fucking around here . . . eh? Who is with you, eh? Where are the others? . . .'

Stunned by the fall and still dazed by the drink he had had and the rain which was still falling, through his confusion Meka realized at last what was happening. He got to his feet without thinking, his legs trembling, and began to search frantically through his pockets.

His right thumb got caught in the left pocket of his coat. He began to unbutton it so that he could go through it more easily. He half took it off and unbuckled the belt that held up his trousers.

His neck was crushed in a vice and he could hear bells pealing in his head.

'I hope my balls drop off if I ever had designs on your arse,' shouted the constable. 'Cover up your dirty old arse. And show me your papers!' he went on, spitting to ward off ill omen.

Meka did up his belt and buttoned his coat.

He went on with the search of his pockets, slapping himself here and there on the wet cloth as if he was having trouble with mosquitoes.

'It wasn't papers . . . that the Go-go-vernor . . . told me to bring . . . It was the medal . . . that . . . that he was bringing me,' stammered Meka, still smacking himself on this side and that.

'That's enough,' said the constable. 'What kind of a fool do you take me for, giving me all this bollocks ... You've used the storm as cover to come out and loot the European area ... Your number's up now.'

'No,' protested Meka. 'I am an elder ... The Governor is my friend ... Officer, it's only this medal ...'

'Shut your mouth, you old fool. Aren't you ashamed? These are the kind of lies a woman tells in bed.'

'I am a Christian, officer! The mouth that receives the Saviour is forbidden to lie ... officer.'

'Your mouth will receive some cat shit if you're not careful, you old tortoise ... Come on, on our way.'

Meka went as fast as he could. The constable pushed him from behind, his hand on his neck, almost running. Meka was out of breath. Now and then he gave a groan. He heard the constable panting like a long-distance runner on form. He was splattered with the water thrown up by the constable's boots.

'I can't go on,' said Meka, stopping. 'I can't ...'

He fell down into the water. The constable seized him by the collar of his coat and dragged him along for some way like an old sack.

'O man,' beseeched Meka. 'What has a man of my years done to you?'

The constable kicked him in the back. Meka gave a mournful shriek and his head dropped on to his shoulder. The constable seized his ear and shone the torch into his face. He lifted up his eyelid with his thumb. Meka blinked.

'Get up. Get up!' shouted the constable. 'Go on, move! Or do you want me to let you have it?'

Meka's head dropped down again on to his shoulder. The constable dragged him along the ground to a gutter and pushed his head down into the water that was flowing in it. Meka snorted like a dog, and rubbed his eyes. The constable let go of him. Meka licked his lips, pushed them out into a pout and blew. Using his knees and elbows he got unsteadily to his feet and nearly fell into the ditch again. The constable held him by his coat collar. Meka began to choke and gave a cry like a terrified chimpanzee. The constable loosened his hold and Meka dropped down again. Again the constable caught him by the collar of his coat.

'On your way, my good friend of the Governor!' the constable commanded, with a peal of laughter. 'Just look at the old devil! Go on, move!'

'My son,' said Meka, gasping for breath, 'you are young enough to be my son, officer,' he entreated. 'Why do you want to shed blood as old as your own father's? O officer, why do you want to bring down a curse on you and yours . . . O officer! Do my words run off you like water off a duck's back?'

'Shut up,' roared the constable, shaking him like a mango tree.

Meka staggered but made no further complaint. He tried to get out of the iron grip on the collar of his coat. When he found his efforts were futile, he stood stock-still. The two of them stared at each other like china dogs in the half darkness. The constable spat with contempt and then let go of Meka's collar. Meka craned his neck with a circular movement. The constable turned on his torch again into his face. Meka raised his hand to his eyes. The policeman switched off the torch.

'On your way, my good friend of the Governor!' he said, pushing Meka in front of him.

He accompanied the words by making the great beam of light burst over Meka again, holding the torch over his head. For a moment they marched in silence. Now and then a flash of lightning revealed them, one behind the other, Meka conducting his monologue to himself and waving his arms.

'Officer, O my son,' he called. 'Listen to me just one last time! I am not a prowler, my son!' he droned. 'A Meka has never been a thief! I went to be given the medal of friendship, officer! Only the medal of friendship . . .'

'. . .'

'I am a man among the men of Doum, O child of the rising sun who does not know me! O officer I went to be given the medal of friendship . . .'

'You're getting on my nerves,' the constable flared up. 'You keep your moaning till you see Gullet!'

'Can't we possibly come to some agreement, my son?' asked Meka without turning round. 'Why are you so determined to hand me over to those foreigners? O my son, why are you so determined to hand me over to them? My words run off . . .'

'Will you shut your mouth?'

Meka fell silent and then lifted up his arms.

They came to the charge office. The constable gave a violent pull at a door with a strip of light coming from underneath and flung Meka into the room.

The African police sergeant sleeping with his mouth open on a table next to a tilley lamp woke up sharply and swore. Meka stepped backwards in fright. The constable who had brought him in shut the door, pushed Meka out of his way and came to attention in front of the sergeant. The sergeant gave him a fascist salute and ordered 'At ease'. The constable went over and laid his cape on the table where the sergeant was opening a book. He raised his eyes over the lamp to where Meka was standing, turned them to his colleague who now and then wiped his thumb across his forehead, then lowered them to the book. Finally he gave his subordinate a look of enquiry.

'Nothing much,' said the subordinate, turning to Meka and waving him forward with his hand. 'Go on,' he said to Meka who was shuffling forward with his arms crossed over his belly like a sheep being driven in the rain.

When Meka was in the light, the constable leant over to his chief who was listening with his chin in his hands propped up on his elbows over his book.

'Loitering with suspicious intent,' said the constable turning round automatically towards Meka. Then leaning over once more to his chief, 'No lights, no papers . . . nothing . . . he'll have to see Gullet . . .'

The sergeant raised his eyes from the book, looked down again at it and raised them again towards his colleague.

'That's a bugger, isn't it? We don't want this filthy old sod dirtying up the cell now it's just been painted . . .'

He got up and leant against the table facing Meka.

'Where are you from?' he asked him.

'From . . . from . . .' Meka began, licking his lips.

'He says he's a friend of the High Commissioner,' the constable explained, 'and he lost the medal he gave him and he's a real genuine Lord . . . this one!'

The two men looked at Meka in silence. He dropped his eyes like a shy girl. The policemen burst into laughter. Meka gave a start.

'Your name?' the sergeant asked.

'Meka . . .'

'Meka!' repeated the constable.

The sergeant went back to his seat behind the desk. He shrugged his shoulders, then he dipped his pen in the inkwell. He made sure the pen was between the first and second fingers and nicely resting against the ball of his thumb. He leant over his head towards his right shoulder and stuck out his huge tongue like a dog about to copulate. His subordinate watched him in wonder, a smile of blissful admiration across his face. The sergeant once more raised his eyes above the lamp.

'Meka eh?' he repeated as if to himself.

'Meka,' his assistant confirmed.

The sergeant placed his left hand flat on the table and then bent over until his chin touched it. His tongue swelled visibly. He raised his left hand which began to describe circles in the air like a bird of prey before it swooped down on to the blank page.

'Meka . . .' he breathed again.

'Meka,' said the constable who was leaning over his chief. The sergeant's hand was wriggling on the book.

The same movements had to be gone through several times when Meka gave his christian name, Laurence, which he pronounced 'Roron' and which the sergeant wrote Roro at the dictation of his assistant.

'Good,' said the two policemen together, giving each other congratulatory glances.

The sergeant took a bunch of keys out of his drawer. His assistant picked up the lamp and went to open the door. It was still raining outside. It was a fine rain falling like a cloud of pins as it crossed the halo of light round the lamp.

'Rain for the witches,' said the constable as he set out.

'Forward,' shouted the sergeant to Meka.

Meka began to fall over himself as he tried to take the step from the constable in front with the light. The toes on one foot knocked against the other heel. He gave a great skip like a shooed cockerel, to try and close the gap that had widened out between himself and the constable in front.

'The man is mad,' said the sergeant.

His assistant turned round and lifted the lamp up to the level of Meka's face. Meka turned his face away into the area of darkness.

'This way,' shouted the constable.

They went round the veranda and stopped outside a little door made out of pieces of wood from a wine-case. The constable held the lamp for the sergeant who bent down over the padlock. He opened the door wide. Meka went forward to the threshold and then turned round to the policemen.

'God keep you!'

The constable flung a kick at him which knocked him off balance and he fell inside. The door slammed on his heels. Meka was once more in the primeval dark. He went forward with his arms out in front of him like a man walking in his sleep until he felt a wall at the tips of his fingers. He leant up against it and then slid down to the floor. He wiped his hand over his face, then he clapped his hands with surprise and stroked the corners of his mouth. He remained like this trying to accustom his eyes to the darkness. A mosquito buzzed round his ears.

Lost in his thoughts Meka made no move. He had never before come face to face with himself like this. He did not know how to seize the thoughts and images that were springing in his head. For a long while he stayed with his chin cupped in his hand, then suddenly he shouted.

'My God!'

He passed his hand over the top of his head and over his cheeks. He could hear drops of water rattling down on to the cement. He gave a long sigh and at the end of it he murmured 'My God' again. He stretched out his arms and shook his head from one side to the other. Then he clasped his head in his hands. He felt how tired he was. Everything was getting on top of him and thrusting him down into the darkness, the deafening mosquitoes, the bare room, cold as a morgue, where he could feel himself freezing into a corpse. Above all, the events of the day, throwing up such images that he felt he was drowning in them. He lay down on the floor to ease his lumbago.

'The shame of it,' he said out loud. 'The shame . . .'

He got up and leant against the wall, then he let himself slide down again on to the ground. He stretched out his legs.

'Poor us,' he said.

Outside a night bird called. Meka felt an immense wretchedness. The bird's mournful cry brought to his mind his bamboo bed and the great fire that Kelara would build on rainy nights. At such times he loved to listen to the patter of the rain on the raffia roof while his eyelids gradually drooped with sleep. He would slip his arm beneath Kelara's neck and she would snuggle down her plaited hair into the hollow of his shoulder. Tears came to his eyes.

'Poor us!' he moaned again. 'Poor us . . .' he repeated, catching his breath.

He reached out for a shoulder in the darkness as he always did when he wanted to share some confidence, but the movement made him lose his balance.

'Man is all alone in the world!' he said to himself, wedging his buttocks against the wall as best he could.

He took his head in his hands. How could he, the descendant of the great Mekas, 'The-stock-unshakable-beneath-the-storm', the 'River-without-fear-of-the-forest', the 'Pythons', 'Rocks', 'Cotton-trees', 'Elephants', 'Lions', the son of men who had never bowed to another man's strength, how could they treat him like this, as if he had been . . . he did not know what.

Meka was a prey to conflicting thoughts. He savoured in advance the

excuses that the policemen would make in front of Gullet. He imagined
the scene. He would be dragged in front of the white men as people in
his place always were. He would hold his head down for a moment to
create a better effect of surprise – then he would fix his look like a
dagger in the white man's face. Gullet would blanch. Ah, the poor constables – what would they clutch at ... mumbling their excuses. But
would he, Meka, accept them? Their contempt for him had been inex-
cusable, grotesque. Basically, since the time of Jesus himself, the police
had always been degenerate dogs. And today they still have no talent
for telling a God or an honest man from a bandit. Bah, what contempt-
ible creatures they were! It was no good bearing a grudge. Meka tried
out in the darkness the generous gesture he would make with his hand
to forgive them, while at the same time in his heart he was consigning
them to the devil.

The contempt for the constables which his sense of his own innocence furnished him, restored his calm. But God, what was the use of
being innocent and humble in this world where virtue and honesty no
longer paid? Where man had become as impersonal as a grain of sand
in the desert? Meka felt very old. But, God knows, he wasn't in the
cemetery yet! When he was young his shoulder blades had never been
forced by the strength of another man to touch the dust and that was
something he would make clear to the constable. He went towards the
door of the cell. Surprised to find it locked, he showered kicks against
it.

'Slaves of the uncircumcized!' he howled. 'Open up, open up. See the
real Meka! ... Swine! Dare you face me? My shoulder blades have
never been forced into the dust by the strength of another man. Sons
of whores!'

As he was delivering this speech, Meka moved to and fro in the
darkness. He put one knee on the ground, stretching out his right arm
towards his unseen opponent as he used to when as a young man he
challenged to a wrestling bout. He moved his shoulders and gave a
great cry to raise the corrugated iron roof. He burst into a demented
laughter making his body shudder and then he began to hurl insults at
the constables again.

This went on till he felt the beads of sweat standing on his face. Then
he noticed that his clothes had dried. He wanted to go on shouting but
his voice had gone. When he spoke he sounded like those lepers with
faint voices like the noise of air sweeping through a gaping hole.

He muttered a few more insults at the constables then he stopped,
frightened he might lose his voice altogether. He crouched down on his

heels and then dropped down on to the cement floor. The coolness made him feel better.

'Swine,' he whispered again.

He fell asleep thinking that he would knock down the first constable who opened the door next morning.

Meka was ashamed when he realized how soundly he had slept.

'The body does not belong to us . . .' he said out loud. 'Poor us.'

He was relieved to find his voice had come back. It must have been quite late in the morning because the daylight coming through cracks in the door and the space between the corrugated iron roof and the walls of the cell was enough to light the room. Meka saw that it was completely bare. The walls had been repainted to cover up the obscene drawings. Meka could make them out underneath the thin covering of whitewash. So this was it, the cell at the police station! A cage for an animal. They couldn't even provide a stool for the prisoner to sit on. Meka felt something come up to his throat. His eyes seemed to burn. He had to take hold of himself or he would have fallen on to his knees. He rolled up his trousers and the sleeves of his khaki jacket. He began to make loosening up movements like a boxer before the bell goes. His bones began to crack. Then when they had stopped he went over and put his eye to one of the cracks in the door and waited.

Meka's heart beat loudly when he heard someone working the lock outside. He stepped back, realizing in panic that he had nothing prepared to say to Gullet. As the door opened, Meka was leaning against the wall, with his arms crossed over his chest.

The constable, whom Meka recognized by his enormous size, looked at him in amusement and then lumbered towards him. Meka tried to side-step but his whole body seemed held down by a huge weight. When the constable got within range he seized Meka by the collar of his coat.

'Outside,' he shouted. 'To see Gullet.'

Meka felt himself shaking from head to foot. As in a dream he seized the constable's arm, yes, in the same way he would grasp the head of a porcupine he found half dead in one of his traps . . . He felt his fingers sinking into the man's soft flesh like the flesh of a ripe avocado pear. The constable leapt back with the pain and shook himself free. Meka made the very most of his victory. He put on a terrible look though in his heart he would have been happy enough to leave things where they stood – and anyway this great lout could easily have the best of it. Nevertheless, he placed one knee on the ground and challenged the huge constable to wrestle with him.

'Last night you were the stronger because I did not understand!' he said. 'Now, if your bollocks are not made of sand, let us settle the matter here, without witnesses . . .'

The constable was puzzled what to do. He took a step towards Meka who backed away while the constable himself took three steps backward. Meka called him a child of the woman's curse. The constable blew his whistle to alert his colleagues.

Meka felt himself lifted off the ground by a whole group of red chechias, and hoisted up on to their shoulders. Someone slipped handcuffs over his wrists. He tried to shout but the honour he felt at being attacked by so many policemen at once, left him speechless. They manhandled him to Gullet's office. Gullet took out his riding-crop and laid it two, three, four, ten times across Meka's shoulders. He spat on Meka's face and then signalled the constables away.

'Who is this lunatic?' he asked.

The constable clicked his heels and brought his hand up automatically to the peak of his kepi. The ritual seemed to irritate Gullet who turned red and asked again what was going on. The constable swallowed his saliva, and composing all his venom into the look which he bestowed on Meka said, without a pause in his elliptical speech, 'He' pointing at Meka, 'nothing, no papers, no lights . . .'

Gullet went over to Meka and was slightly put out of countenance by the look of injured innocence on the face of the aged black man. He scratched his temple with the end of his riding-crop, then he sent the constables away. He tried to coax a smile from Meka by being the first to laugh. Meka remained frozen. He surveyed Gullet from his feet up to his head and then he stared into the distance. M Varini put his hand on to his shoulder. Meka lowered his head. His jaws, swollen with rage, jutted sharply out from the skin of his sunken cheeks. Gullet gave him a shake. Meka swayed then whistled with impatience through his teeth. Gullet put his hand under his chin and lifted his head but Meka kept his eyes fixed firmly on the ground. Gullet took his hand away and Meka let his head drop down on to his chest. Gullet called for an interpreter.

'What's wrong with him?' he asked.

The interpreter made a little pout of embarrassment with his lips and then shrugged his shoulders. Gullet nodded with his head and stroked his temples again with his whip, then he spoke to the interpreter. When he had finished the young man put his hand on Meka's arm. Meka moved his lips and gave him a distant glance. The interpreter was not discouraged. For a long while he translated what the white man had said to him into Mvema. When he had finished, Meka passed his hand over his lips and staring straight ahead he said to the interpreter:

'I feel very tired, so tired that I have nothing to say to Gullet. They can do what they like to me ... He asks me who I am. Tell him I am a very great fool, who yesterday still believed in the white man's friendship ... I am very tired. They can do what they like with me ...'

Meka pinched his nostrils, breathed in, then passed the back of his hand over the end of his nose. All the while the interpreter was translating M Varini was giving Meka a strange look. Now and then he glanced in annoyance at the constables who were watching the interrogation from the other end of the veranda. When the interpreter had finished, the Commissioner called the sergeant. They went into the office.

Meka did not even turn round. He was several years away back in the past. It was the time when the village of the wives that belonged to his terrible grandfather stretched over there, beyond all these white men's houses he could see in front of him. What was left of the village of the great Mekas, those who in this land were men and true men! A shadow of sadness passed over Meka's eyes. He propped his chin with his left hand.

'On this earth we have to learn to hold out,' he thought. 'Sometimes this is a difficult fate ... who would have thought that yesterday's masters would be the slaves of today? The "Mekas",' he murmured, 'the Lion-men, the Thunder-men, the Sky-men, men who were incarnations of strength and ruled the sky and the earth in this country ...'

Meka closed his eyes. He saw again his first white man. How old had he been then? He did not know how to work it out. He remembered that his mother used to take him to the river where the women of the village bathed. He was still so diminutive a man that his presence did not embarrass the naked women. His mother let him paddle near the bank where the water only came up to his ankles. Then she put him on to her back to take him home to the village.

Night fell upon Meka's memories from those years of his life. He thought of his circumcision and then of the fever that had raged in the country at the very time when his wound was healing. The drums sounded from morning until evening and from evening until morning. There was talk about the presence in the country of a phantom man. He was as white as chalk, with panther eyes and long hair like the mane of a horse. There were preparations to fight a war with him. Meka remembered the great gathering which had taken place in his grandfather's indaba hut. Spears and matchets were sharpened and assegai handles cut. Arrow heads were envenomed with strophantus. The men smeared their bodies with ointment that was to make them invulnerable. Then there was the great departure for the region of the river of the two caymans. Meka like all the other boys who had been left behind with the women took his newly acquired manhood very seriously. It amused his mother the way he came demanding his food trying to make his voice deeper by swallowing air. After the short rains, the men returned. It was a triumphal return, to the rhythm of the drums and the 'yo yo' of the women. They had caught the phantom man. They tied him up to the village palm tree.

Meka looked round and tried to see where it had been. The great canopy of verdure thrown up by the mango tree in the hospital grounds blocked his view. He closed his eyes again. Now everything was dancing in his head. The phantom man they had finished off when they discovered he was vulnerable. His skull had gone to Meka's grandfather as great chief of the Mvemas and he gave it to Meka on the day he killed his first panther.

'I am not afraid of white men!' he said out loud.

He thought about that German's skull. He had thrown it into a river the day he was baptized.

'The day I became a slave,' he said out loud.

A great roar of laughter from the other end of the veranda followed these words. Meka saw the constables holding their sides and throwing glances of amusement in his direction. He made a step towards them. The laughter froze on their lips. Meka stared at them with profound hatred then, with a long drawn-out sigh, the hatred evaporated. He looked at himself in pity, tossed his head and said,

'Poor us.'

Then he forgot them. An interpreter came and called him inside. Meka found a somewhat embarrassed Gullet who stretched out a hand to him hesitantly then changed his mind and pulled out a packet of cigarettes. Always cigarettes. He offered one to Meka and when he made no move Gullet put the cigarette into his mouth for him. He lit it.

'Smoke and don't annoy the white man,' said the interpreter. 'You can think what you like about him when you are out of here ... Don't do anything stupid – your case has all been fixed up!'

Meka's mouth trembled. His hand came up eagerly to his mouth and pushed the cigarette until he could feel it settled in the gap he had had made between his upper incisors. He sucked in his cheeks and a cloud of smoke came out through his nostrils and the corners of his mouth.

He thought of the bare room where he had spent the night, then of Kelara and the good fire in his hut.

Gullet smiled at him. He took the cigarette out of his mouth and smiled back. The white man spoke to the interpreter for a long time. When he had finished the interpreter translated.

'The white man has said a great many things and if I tried to translate them all we should be here all night. All I can tell you, is that you can go back home ... and they are going to get you another medal. You are lucky this white man recognized you, and in future remember to take a lamp when you come into town at night. That's all ...'

Gullet smiled at Meka again, who gave an awkward grin from ear to ear. Gullet stretched out his hand. Meka hesitated. He looked at his hands and at the white man's hands. He gave an embarrassed smile.

'Poto – poto,' he said looking at his hands ochre-coloured with dried mud and then at Gullet. 'I don't want to dirty the white man.'

'What is he saying?' the white man asked the interpreter.

'He says his hands are muddy,' the interpreter translated.

Léopold Sédar Senghor

In Memoriam

It is Sunday.
I fear the crowd of my brothers with stony faces.
From my tower of glass filled with pain, the nagging Ancestors
I gaze at roofs and hills in the fog
In the silence – the chimneys are grave and bare.
At their feet sleep my dead, all my dreams are dust
All my dreams, the liberal blood spills all along the streets, mixing
  with the blood of the butcheries.
And now, from this observatory as from a suburb
I watch my dreams float vaguely through the streets, lie at the hills'
  feet
Like the guides of my race on the banks of Gambia or Saloum,
Now of the Seine, at the feet of these hills.
Let me think of my dead!
Yesterday it was Toussaint, the solemn anniversary of the sun
And no remembrance in any cemetery.
Ah, dead ones who have always refused to die, who have known how
  to fight death
By Seine or Sine, and in my fragile veins pushed the invincible blood,
Protect my dreams as you have made your sons, wanderers on delicate
  feet.
Oh Dead, protect the roofs of Paris in the Sunday fog
The roofs which guard my dead
That from the perilous safety of my tower I may descend to the streets
To join my brothers with blue eyes
With hard hands.

Léopold Sédar Senghor

Paris in the Snow

Lord, you visited Paris on the day of your birth
Because it had become paltry and bad.
You purified it with incorruptible cold,
The white death.
This morning even the factory funnels hoisted in harmony
The white flags.
'Peace to all men of good will.'
Lord, you have offered the torn world, divided Spain, divided Europe,
The snow of peace.
And the rebels fired their fourteen hundred cannons
Against the mountains of your peace.
Lord, I have accepted your white cold that burns worse than salt.
And now my heat melts like snow in the sun.
And I forget
The white hands that loaded the guns that destroyed the kingdoms,
The hands that whipped the slaves and that whipped you
The dusty hands that slapped you, the white powdered hands that
    slapped me
The sure hands that pushed me into solitude and hatred
The white hands that felled the high forest that dominated Africa,
That felled the Saras, erect and firm in the heart of Africa,
    beautiful like the first men that were created by your brown hands.
They felled the virgin forest to turn into railway sleepers.
They felled Africa's forest in order to save civilization that was lacking
    in men.
Lord, I can still not abandon this last hate, I know it, the hatred of
    diplomats who show their long teeth
And who will barter with black flesh tomorrow.
My heart, oh lord, has melted like the snow on the roofs of Paris
In the sun of your Goodness,
It is kind to my enemies, my brothers with the snowless white hands,
Also because of the hands of dew that lie on my burning cheeks at night.

Wole Soyinka

from The Interpreters

Bandele paused, latch-key in hand. 'I forgot to warn you. I have a guest and you may not like him.'

'For the privilege of escaping Lagos,' Sagoe said, 'I will accept any torment. Who is he?'

'Some journalist hitch-hiking through Africa. Has the most formidable array of camera equipment I ever laid eyes on.'

'English?'

'No, German, but he thinks he is American.'

'Oh?'

'You will probably find him unbearable. I do.'

'If the worst comes to the worst I can go and stay with Kola.'

'I won't advise it. He is grown manic over the Pantheon. Quite unbearable as a social animal.'

There was a stampede of elephants on the stairs, a yell of 'that you, Bandili?' They sensed a leap from the fifth step down and a crash just behind the door. There was a few seconds' fumbling with the knob, filled with sounds which exhorted them to be patient, won't be a minute, what's wrong wirra godamn door, but the door opened suddenly, a pink oval grinned over them, a hairy pink wrench pumped their hands, slapped their backs – how ya bin you son-of-a-gun – tore the bags out of their hands – that your friend from the Foreign Office? – and shoved them into the sitting-room with a beer in each hand.

Then the same zoo rushed up the stairs bellowing, 'I had begun to think you weren't coming back tonight how did your friend like America wanna talk to the guy diree ever get to Chicago?'

'Is this a practical joke?' Sagoe demanded.

'I don't know.'

'What do you mean you don't know?' But Bandele only shrugged and sipped his beer. 'Well, this is your house isn't it? So now you keep a private jester.'

'Met him on the compound with Joe Golder.'

'And who the hell is Joe Golder?'

'Sorry, American lecturer, history. You'll run into him some time. Anyway the next thing I knew Joe Golder had made off and left that clown on my hands.'

'You invited him to stay with you?'

Bandele sadly shook his head. 'Don't remember doing that. But he's here.'

Peter came down again much in the same manner as before. This time he introduced himself formally, 'I'm Perrer. Hi!'

'Are you American?' Sagoe asked. He had no choice but to remain seated. Peter had placed both hands on the armchair rests and thrust his face right into Sagoe's. Then he busied himself mixing up all the accents.

'Yeah. Wall, not really. I'm German but I use 'merican passport. Just gonna get m'self a zrink. So soree couldn't come down wi' ze others to Lagos, burra had a date wiz a Minister. I'm a journalist, you know, reckon Bandili told you. Did you paint ze town red last night? Fabulous guy your Minister, real feller of a guy. Invired me to spend a week-end at his country residence.'

'You going?' Bandele's affected indifference amused Sagoe enormously.

'Sure, felt real honoured.'

'Which Minister?' Sagoe asked.

'It could be any. A bit of overseas publicity, gratis.'

'Until the result though, then they'll find they've been misquoted.'

'And then it's − Drive them out drive them out who the hell do they think they are how dare they abuse our sovereign integrity with neo-colonialist neo-capitalist reactionary misrepresentation deport the bastards Nigeria we hail thee . . .'

The refrigerator shuddered with unaccustomed violence and Sagoe remembered that Peter was still with them.

'Your friend's a sure funny guy. Wassat he was shouring just now?'

Sagoe spoke under his breath, 'That you seem to me a graft of emptiness on dregs of crushed Aryan bestiality.'

Peter was laughing. 'First you shout so the whole house is shaking zen you whisper so a guy can't even hear one word.'

'That's my nature,' Sagoe confessed.

'So how's life in ze Foreign Office.'

'No spies lately, how about you?'

In a way, Peter reminded him of Chief Winsala, the way he laughed. 'Bandili, your friend is just aboure funniest guy I seen in Africa. You reckon I'm a spy, Bandili?'

'No, I don't think you are a spy, Peter.'

'He ain't like you. Bandili is so solemn but your friend is just aboure cat's whiskers. Couldn't guess in a hundred years he worked in ze diplomatic service.'

'I admire your perception. I don't work in the Foreign Office.'

'Bandili, dig that, ain't he just about ze . . .'

'You were mistaken, Peter, this is Sagoe and he works on a newspaper.'

'But I thought you wuz expecting your friend from the Foreign Office.'

'His plane arrived late. He will be here later.'

Sagoe was puzzled. He looked at Bandele but was silenced with a signalled promise of a later explanation.

'So you're in ze profession!' And he walked over and pumped his hand. 'Well I must confess I really feel at home now.'

Bandele winced.

'Damn your instant implication of life-long familiarity,' Sagoe muttered, turning his face away as the compost vent of Peter's mouth hit him fully. He pushed his way up saying, 'I'll just go up for a wash.'

'How we spending tonight, Bandili? Let's go and celebrate your friend's acquaintance as a fellow-journalist.'

'Actually, I've been asked to some sort of party.'

'Very good. Ve all go.'

Bandele looked very sad. 'Ah, you don't know our families here. It is really a family thing you see.'

'So you take me, huh? I am vun of ze family. I feel I am a Nigerian. I really feel at home you know zat? I don't feel no different from nobody. Already I make so many friends wiz people in ze street, eat at ze roadside shacks just like a common Nigerian.' He stopped, seeing Sagoe take the back-door out. 'Where's your friend going? Hey, that ain't the way to the bathroom. You wanna go upstairs.'

'It's OK.' Bandele patiently explained. 'He only uses the shower, in the boy's quarters.'

'Gee, that's a reel guy, your friend. A reel guy. You know I like ze sort of guy who don't go for no ceremony. Ha, Bandili, I gorran idea. First we go to zis party, zen we go to some dive and look up some tarts, what you say?'

'Sure, Peter.'

Peter, after experimenting variously, settled on the whisky and thrust the bottle in his mouth. 'Just whar I like about Yankees. You know when I go to nightclub here people always looking at me cos I drink from bottle. Americans don't waste no time on glass, zey all zrink from bottle.'

Bandele sighed, mentally writing off the bottle because he would not offer what was left of it to anyone he called a friend. Sagoe had come back into the house muttering, 'That damn fool didn't let me remember to take soap and towel.'

Before he reached the top of the stairs, Peter was after him. Too late Sagoe tried to lock himself in the bathroom but the key had fallen to the floor. Desperately, since the door was now sealed with Peter's wide frame, he turned into the cupboard and made to begin shaving. Furiously he lathered his chin and upper lip so he would not have to open his mouth, wondering had the fool overheard him at last?

'Say, thought you might like a swig while you're shaving. Don't you wanna swig?'

Sagoe shook his head.

'What's zis? Ah, after-shave lotion. Ho ho whisky much better for rubbing on ze skin, you gorner have a drink? Whas merrer c'mmon let's get high. I always get high before I meet my family. Family's always square you know. Reel square.'

'WILL YOU TAKE THAT BOTTLE FROM MY FACE!'

Bandele chuckled to himself and braced for Peter's descent.

'Say, your friend's a sure touchy guy. What's eating him?'

'Ask him.'

'I guess I just don't know what he got so sore about. What the hell, enh? I just offered him a zrink zat's all.' He helped himself to another mouthful. 'You gonna drink, Bandili?'

Bandele shook his head.

'C'mon man, let you and me git reel high.'

'I'm already on beer.'

'Zat's okay, you zrink some visky and chase it wiz beer, yes? C'mon guy whas marrer wiz everyone?'

He thrust the bottle in Bandele's hand and Bandele took it but not quite. The bottle crashed to the floor and Bandele returned calmly to his beer.

Peter was up in a broad flash. He picked up the mop and stopped in the doorway of the bathroom long enough to say 'Your friend sure acts crazy. What's he gone and wasted good liquor for?' He sounded truly aggrieved and began to mop the liquor, incessant in ideas for painting first the town, then the night itself, red.

In the garage Bandele stopped. 'You are sure you want to go to the party?'

'Anything to get away from Peter. God, in five minutes that man reduced me to an apprehensive jelly.'

'OK, let's go.'

'What will he say when he finds we are gone?'

'Oh he'll find us an excuse. He's pretty thick-skinned.'

'What was that business about planes?'

'Only to get rid of him. I said a friend who had been on foreign service in Canada was returning with his family and would be staying with me.'

'Is Egbo coming?'

'He is hardly out of here now. Some little girl has really done for him.'

'I don't believe it.'

'You'll see for yourself.'

'No, I don't believe it.'

The drive was choked with cars at the big party and Sagoe said, 'Let's return the car and walk back.' Bandele shook his head.

'The dogs will bark at us. Or bite if they think we are stewards.'

'Yes, I gather they are snobs. What do they do to cyclists?'

'Depends. Stewards get by. Two short barks for lecturers; it means — Commies.'

'I am impressed.'

In the dashboard glow, Bandele's face was dry and straight. 'That is nothing. If you drive any of the bigger models they lie on the road and let you kill them.'

A buzz of white, genteel laughter and character slaughter welcomed them from the drive and they entered the house of death. From the direction of the punch bowl, a shrill voice — it was a strange dialect of some British tribe — 'and then she developed a sudden interest in the madrigal group, so John said, better see what's going on.' General titter, then a deep voice intoning, 'I did think her departure to London was very sudden,' and right on cue again, measured titters.

'Will we ever get through to the bottles, think you?'

'We only need push slightly and they'll withdraw.'

'Wait a minute. I see black faces — are they Nigerians?'

'Appearances deceive, come on.'

Among the bowls of tit-bits — groundnuts, popadums, meat-on-the-stick, and the inevitable olives, Sagoe saw a bowl of fresh fruits and made for it shouting, 'To hell with patriotism, Bandele, there is no fruit in the world to beat the European apple.'

'You are deluded,' Bandele said, 'but go find out for yourself.'

Sagoe returned in a fury. 'What on earth does anyone in the country want with plastic fruits ... hey ... hey, wait a minute Bandele wait a minute....' He was only now seeing the decor of the room and his tongue went click-clicking as he spun slowly in a circle.

'What is the matter? Oh, still on about the fruits?'

'To use Mathias's favourite expression, O-ko-ko-ko!'

From the ceiling hung citrous clusters on invisible wires. A glaze for the warmth of life and succulence told the story, they were the same as the artificial apples. There were fancy beachhat flowerpots on the wall, ivy clung from these along a picture rail, all plastic, and the ceiling was covered in plastic lichen. Sagoe had passed, he now noticed, under a special exhibition group of one orange, two pears, and a fan of bananas straight from European wax-works.

'I feel let loose in the Petrified Forest. What's the matter with those who live in it?'

'Nothing.'

'Have they petrified brains to match?'

From the area of the truffles, 'I tell you I had to give up my leave on her account. Nephritites simply cannot stand Africans. She's such a sensitive cat. Who was to look after her?'

Bandele gently removed Sagoe's fingers from his arm. 'I heard. I don't need a tourniquet.'

'But did you hear? I mean, did I hear aright?'

'Yes, yes, just face the drinks table.'

'But who is the black fool listening so sympathetically. Who is the bellboy in the tuxedo?'

'Don't talk so loud. That is the new Professor. It's his party.'

'... I tell you she positively breaks out in rashes. Simply allergic to Africans. Oh she is such a dar ... ling.' And again the Professor nodded with understanding.

'But if she were talking to a fellow white I would understand....'

And gradually, beginning from his fingertips Sagoe felt a strange excitement. A crawling sensation over his skin of a dubious and dangerous anticipation.

A woman approached. 'I think,' Bandele began, 'this is where you pay for your drinks. You should have put on a tie.'

'What do you mean?'

'The hostess approaches. Good luck.'

'Good evening Bandele,' the woman said, 'I didn't see you come in.' And the excitement grew until Sagoe found he needed a pee.

'I was very late, I'm afraid. I have only returned from Lagos.'

'You mean you drive on that road at night? It is very dangerous, you know ... those madmen. I always make my husband take the driver if he simply must travel at night.'

'I was determined not to miss your party,' Bandele said, and Sagoe nearly dropped his drink.

'Isn't it sweet of you to say that. Who is your friend?'

Sagoe sharply forestalled him. 'We only met on the steps, didn't have time to introduce myself. I am Edward Akinsola, you must be the hostess,' humming inside him ... bells on her fingers, Big Ben on her toes, and she shall have BO in spite of her rose ...

She extended a hand – gloved. Gloved elbow length. 'How do you do? We haven't met before have we?'

'No I don't think so.' Sagoe took the glove ... what have you got inside it, woman, a slithery fish?

'You must be new in college, of course.'

'I have just arrived from America.'

'A-ah, the States. That explains it, of course.' Sagoe stared and waited for her to explain what explained what, and she obliged. 'Americans are so informal, aren't they?'

Sagoe, caught off-balance, felt outraged. But she beat him to a possible retort asking, 'Have you started lecturing?'

'No, I have been doing some research' ... and to begin with, research me why your bulbous naval sprouts an artificial rose ...

'I forgot, lectures are over in fact. Mostly exams and things at the moment.'

'Indeed,' said Sagoe, 'exams and things.'

She smiled sweetly, 'Anyway you will need the time to settle down first. Always a difficult thing to settle down after one's student days I am sure. I always think it is terrible for students to be put straight to lecture, very difficult to re-adjust. Bandele, bring him to us for tea won't you?'

'With the greatest of pleasure, Mrs Oguazor.'

'Did you manage to find something to eat, by the way? It was only a buffet supper. If you hurry you might get some ...'

... the plastic apple was nice thank you ... but Sagoe only simmered, silenced, and to make it worse, Bandele was chuckling as the woman turned her back and left.

'What the bloody hell do you find to grin at?' Sagoe exploded.

'You. That was touché.'

'I don't see what was so bloody touché about it.'

'Don't feel so bad. You didn't do too badly yourself, only, for people like that, you really have to be prepared.'

A concentration of clucking in one corner of the room, just by the stairs. All the women had somehow sifted together and stood waiting for something. Sagoe turned to Bandele to ask if the party was over when the professor himself approached them.

'I thought Ceroline was here.'

'She was a moment ago.'

'Oh der, end the ledies are wetting for her.'

Just then Mrs Oguazor herself emerged from a group and came to the professor.

'Ceroline der, the ledies herv been wetting for you.'

'I know. I was just looking for you to tell you we must go upstairs. Will you handle things at this end?'

'Ef cerse der.'

'Ah I see you've met the *new* lecturer' – and Sagoe distinctly perceived the exchange of understanding – 'I have asked Bandele to bring him to tea; he is not yet used to things here.'

From the marionette pages of Victoriana, the Professor bowed. The contempt in his manner was too pointed for any error, and it was with the greatest difficulty that Sagoe refrained from looking down to see if his fly was unbuttoned.

'Cem en der,' and the Professor took his good lady's hand, 'we mesn't keep the ledies wetting.'

Caroline accorded Bandele another teaspoon smile and they watched her diminish in little rustles.

'I told you, you should have put on a tie.'

'Have I disgraced you?'

'Oh yes you would have done, irreparably. But you forget you told the lady that I didn't know you.'

'Of course. Just as well. I have a sixth sense for these things. Thought I'd better not risk your reputation.'

'It's ruined, don't you worry. The politeness is the barest they can manage for me.'

'Why do you bother to attend their party, then?'

'But don't you enjoy just watching people sometimes, especially when you know they can't stand the sight of you?'

'That's a queer taste.'

'Not so queer as theirs. Why did they invite me?'

'If I may presume to say so, there didn't seem much strain between them and you.'

'That is what is known as civilization. We are all civilized creatures here.'

The hall was clear. The women crowded the foot of the stairs, awaited the final summons for ascent. The men, house-trained and faultless, had created a Men's Corner at the opposite end of the room. A few did require manoeuvres by the professor, but his suggestions were imperceptible. Coffee came and cigarettes were counter-offered. By tacit understanding, their backs were turned on the stairs until such time as the women would have completely disappeared. It was all so gracefully managed that Sagoe was lost in admiration. The Professor was whispering to them that the ground-floor lavatory was all theirs, but Sagoe had found it much earlier. Excitement loosened him in short drips like a dog, and in some strange perverted manner, he felt a tingle of excitement fan out in him until it seemed some event must happen suddenly or he would die of heart failure.

The stairs movement took unnecessarily long, sabotaged by the efforts of a young girl in the middle of the floor, patiently explaining a point of disagreement to two wildly gesticulating gloves. Some moments earlier she had been engaged in animated conversation with some male guests, but they made a graceful departure when Mrs Oguazor appeared and coughed lightly behind them – no more word was needed. The girl was however ignorant of signs. And when Mrs Oguazor finally explained the point, her reply was:

'Oh later perhaps, thank you Mrs Oguazor.'

The interval had grown quite embarrassing before Sagoe caught the first words from the pair.

The girl was saying, 'But I don't feel like going.'

And the hostess, her sweetness dissolving slowly down her face, 'Mrs Faseyi, you are keeping the others waiting.'

The girl's voice remained a patient whisper. 'I assure you I don't want to go upstairs.'

'My dear, you are being very awkward. All the ladies retire upstairs at this point. They are waiting for you dear.'

'But I don't want to go.'

'These details of common etiquette cannot be really strange to you. And if they are, simply watch the others and follow their example.' She had grown more terse.

'I used the ground-floor toilet about ten minutes ago. I don't feel like going again so soon afterwards.'

'The point is not whether or not you . . .' Her voice pitched suddenly high and she caught herself, glanced quickly round. The few men who had looked round quickly obscured recognition with huge puffs of smoke. Sagoe cast aside all sense of decency and moved nearer to eavesdrop, while the women turned positive backs on the girl's disgrace.

Mrs Oguazor tried syrup once again. 'My dear, the point is this, all the ladies have to go upstairs. Perhaps you'd like to adjust your make-up or . . .'

'But I don't use make-up.'

'Surely you will want to freshen up, Mrs Faseyi. And anyway if you don't come, you'll be left alone with the men.'

'Oh I don't mind at all.'

'You are being impossible, Mrs Faseyi. And from you of all people. I don't understand why you choose to upset everyone in this manner.'

Her eyes opened wide. 'I have upset someone?'

'Now come on, that's a good girl.' Commanding now, she took her arm. 'Come along now.'

The girl arrested her rush by placing a friendly hand on Caroline's shoulder. 'You take the others. But don't leave me alone too long.'

This should have been the end, and a few days before it would have been. But this was her first social evening as the Professor's wife, and the scene — it could no longer be disguised — had become public. And she, a rare species, a black Mrs Professor was faced with the defiance of a young common housewife, little more than a girl, in her own house, publicly, and the code of etiquette was on her, Mrs Oguazor's side!

'You will come with us at once,' said Caroline, 'or don't ever expect to be invited to my house again.'

And the girl said simply, 'Oh, I understand that.'

It was the women who came to the rescue. Mrs Oguazor was prepared now to leave, but the hall had lengthened in the meantime and the distance was bare and endless to where they were herded. Across this desert loped salvation, the gaunt Mrs Drivern, wife of the gynaecologist.

'I think we've waited long enough, Mrs Oguazor.' She seized the grateful woman by the glove, threw a proud hump at the outcast and trooped ahead of forty-odd moral supports to the forced sanctuary of supped ladies.

Sagoe said, 'Is the girl's husband here?' And when Bandele nodded he asked, 'What do you bet I pick him out first time?'

'Nothing. That would be no guess.'

Sweat had broken free on the neck of a husband. Nothing kept him earthed but the desperate wish that the floor might open and swallow him. His motions became palsied and his palms clammed on a cigarette until it snuffed out.

'He'll take off,' Sagoe said. 'The earth won't swallow him so he'll take off. On the wings of his bow-tie.'

'He is already framing his apology. I know Ayo.'

And they heard his glass rattle on a table, and Mr Faseyi squared his back, turned to reveal the resolution of a man on trial, dissociation from a wife's conduct – by instant reparation.

Simultaneously, Bandele and Sagoe set off for the floor centre.

'You have to live with them. Better keep out.' And he firmly pushed Bandele back.

But even Sagoe was too late. Kola was just coming in with Egbo when the scene began and had remained watching from the door. They saw him walk briskly to the girl who stood so starkly isolated, talk briefly to her and then begin quite crazily to do a slow High Life to the ballet music playing softly from hidden loudspeakers. Sagoe retrieved his glass, saying with mock disgust, 'This place is crawling with Sir Gala-hads.'

The record was Popular Pieces from Famous Ballets and the pair merged their slow high life to the contribution from Swan Lake. In the corner Faseyi sweated, thrown, irresolute. This husband would wait but a tightening of the back warned him of a watchful Professor and he stepped forward.

'Fash!' It stopped him. He turned and was relieved to find that it was only Bandele. 'Ah, hello, sorry just leaving.'

'With the dancing just beginning?' And then Bandele produced his brainwave. 'Or do you have to go and lock in the boys?'

'Enh. Sorry ... I ... what did you say?'

'Stop pretending. Everyone knows you've got the warden job in Shehu Hall.'

'Enh, what's that? Enh? Where did you hear this?' He became a rotor dog, a wet bone at both ends of a whistle. 'You mean you heard something ...'

'Oh come off it, Fash ...' And then the record was snapped off. The Professor gravely laid the pick-up aside, wasting no glance on the dancers' profanity.

Sagoe was not drunk but he felt that excitement again. The Professor was returning to his group, the dignity of his home restored, protected in an armour of righteousness.

'Jolly good.' Above the hush Sagoe's voice rang out startling, 'Let's have a juju or a twist instead.'

It halted the Professor in his stride and the Men's Corner went silent with indignation. Glasses stayed in the air as when the toastmaster has fallen flat on his face. It was the silence that follows a bounced cheque, the silence – felt Sagoe – of a makeshift voidatory.

The Professor moved at last, his face set so that each guest began to ask his neighbour, 'I hope it wasn't you who brought him,' and sighed, disappointed that the candidate had not lost his chance of nomination to some committee.

By all appearances however, J. D. Oguazor was dismissing the whole episode from his mind. A new Professorship called for new virtues, like — magnanimity. His face appealed for calm, dignity and restraint in face of barbarous provocation. The company responded, the chatter was slowly resumed. Egbo joined Kola on the floor and Sagoe followed almost immediately, but the husband drew Bandele back, began to question him about the wardenship. All rumour, Bandele insisted, but rumours from important quarters.

Finally he invited Bandele to lunch.

Lecturer Grade III Adeora managed to discover where the President of Guinea had lunched when he visited the university, then recounted an intimate conversation they had together shortly after that lunch. 'Yes yes. Had lunch with him. Capital fellow.'

Nnojekwe asked the Professor for fatherly advice on when he should take his annual leave, then praised the brass chandeliers on the four walls. 'Chandeliers?' asked the Professor. 'Oh, oh yes,' Oguazor, scared to be ignorant, failed to perceive the trap. 'Very expensive they are bet Ceroline wanted them so badly.'

And Nnojekwe drew him out a little further, then returned to his group to transmit Oguazor's latest.

From Dr Lumoye, '. . . this is really confidential, you know, but did you know one of the girls is pregnant?' Gasps of horror. 'Second year student, came to me in my clinic and asked me if I would help her. Man, that kind of thing I don't do, that's what I told her. I advised her to wait out the remaining weeks and go home and let her parents handle it.'

'That's the last thing she'll want. Most of them can't expect any sympathy from their family.'

'Well she won't get *that* kind of sympathy from me I tell you. I'm not risking seven years for someone else's pleasure. If I tasted of it myself I would at least have something to show for it . . .' And the laughter rose genteel above the champagne bubbles.

Professor Singer was playing with an ash-tray and Oguazor beamed on him. 'Do you like that?'

'Rather nice, oh yes indeed, rather nice.'

'Got them for my wife's birthday. Six of them. And those chandeliers on the wall.'

'Sorry . . . er . . . what did you say?'

'The brass ones. Useful things to herve around the house. I am a rather prectical man with presents. And Ceroline is very fend of chende-liers.'

Professor Singer spent the rest of the evening trying to locate brass chandeliers on walls.

In the house of deaths where brains were petrified for Dehinwa's wardrobe handles, Sagoe looked up again and discovered clusters of green grapes and black draped from wall brackets and dripping with the shine of evergreen synthetic leaves.

Dr Ajilo denied that he took prostitutes home. Never further than his garage, he swore, but Oguazor was just behind him, and he was not amused.

'Those madrigals. Useful grounds, you know, then the husband began to suspect the late rehearsals . . .'

'They *say* Mr Udedo can't even pay his electricity bills. What does he do with his money?'

'Who is Salubi going with these days? That boy is morally corrupt I tell you. He doesn't even keep off the students.'

'Wen of these days,' Oguazor was saying, 'the Senate will charge him with meral terpitude.'

A scarf of a man aimed himself at Bandele and found himself alone with Sagoe. 'Hold him off if you can,' Bandele muttered, dissolving instantly in the crowd. Sagoe was now fully in the power of his excite-ment. He achieved the weightlessness of a true Voidante after an enema – the company was castor to a Voidante psyche.

'You must be the turnip,' was Sagoe's salute.

'I beg your pardon?'

'The turnip. The turnip is missing. I've seen apples and pears. Even plastic mistletoes although I won't ever look that way if I see Ceroline standing under it. Would you?'

'I beg your pardon.'

'I said, are you the turnip?'

'Who are you, I don't believe I understand you.'

'You don't? Don't you speak English?'

'Ha ha. I should think I do indeed. English all the way and not ashamed of it.'

'In that case I beg your pardon. Wrong person.'

'That's all right. I did think it was all rather strange. My name is Pinkshore.'

'Pinkshawl?'

'No. Pinkshore, ha ha. Are you new in college?'

'Yes and no. I am the Professor's son-in-law.'

Sagoe felt his duty was now ended, Bandele had safely disappeared and he lost interest in the man. But Pinkshore now appeared to adopt him, following him every step around the hall. At first he thought he had acquired cultivation value as the professor's son-in-law, but this was a mistake. Pinkshore knew all about the professors and deans and registrars and the chancellors vice pro and real and senate councillors and chairmen and their families down to the most intimate detail and he knew the simple fact that Professor Oguazor had three sons and one five-year-old daughter only and the daughter gave him much sorrow and pain because he could not publicly acknowledge her since he had her by the housemaid and the poor girl was tucked away in private school in Islington and in fact was Oguazor's favourite child and the plastic apple of his eye ... so it was obvious to him that Sagoe was an impostor who had come to steal the silver and it was a good thing to perform small services for this new black élite which he secretly despised but damn it all if the asses are susceptible to fawning and flattery let's give it them and get what we can out of them while the going is good.

So Pinkshore stuck to Sagoe and there was no dodging him. He became quite an obsession and Sagoe ran out of the most sadistic schemes for getting rid of the plague.

And suddenly Pinkshore appeared to wilt. An animal noise came from his throat and his eyes popped in alarm. He retreated three rapid steps, bumping into a small gathering and Sagoe gathered his senses back to the immediate and understood why. In his hand was another of the apples and his hand was pulled back to send it after its brother. Vaguely he recalled that his hand had gone through a similar motion within the past ... but time was now diffused for him – he could not recall the actual start to the ejection act. Two bright refractions indicated the flight of Pinkshore's glasses and the Shawl curved to pick them up. Before he straightened the apple was through the window and Sagoe picked up a pear from the next wall fruit-bowl. Pinkshore reeled, drunk on astonishment as Sagoe from whisky and euphoria.

'What ... what the devil do you think you are doing?'

'Feeding the dog.'

'Are you trying to be funny? That was the Professor's property you threw out of the window.' Sagoe sent out the pear.

'Are you mad? What right have you to throw away those things?'

'What things?'

'The decorations. And don't pretend you don't know what I'm talking about.'

'They are fruits – not decorations.' And he threw out the bunch of bananas.

'Stop it or I'll report you to the professor.' And Pinkshore moved in on him.

'If you come nearer, I will call in the dog.'

'Don't try to clown your way through this.'

'Clown? So that's all it seems to you. Look out if you like, only watch out for the tip of your nose. He's savage.' He decided to throw the bowl as well but the hostess was upon him now. He raced her to the first words, and won.

'Before the party ends, may I offer my congratulations to you for the appointment of your husband to a professorship?'

'That is kind of you but would you mind telling me . . . ?'

'I see now why it's a tuxedo party. That kind of event deserves nothing but mourning dress.'

'Just tell me who you are and why you have been throwing the decorations through the window.'

'But I told you, madam, I am the UNESCO expert on architectural planning.'

'Frivolity,' and she gave the dead stare, 'does not amuse me.'

'He must be drunk, Mrs Oguazor,' said Pinkshore.

'That is a lie, you anaemic Angle.'

'To what department do you belong, sir?'

'Architecture.'

Very sharply she retorted, 'There is no department of architecture in the university.'

'I am hardly surprised madam. Just look at the buildings, enh? Work of amateurs!'

'Will you please . . .'

'Of course your own house is very charming. Obviously an outside job.'

She swung on starch and Sagoe knew she was looking for her husband. For Pinkshore it implied a sentence of failure, and a situation like this seemed built for him. He planted his indefinite frame before Sagoe and began, 'Look here, my friend. I think you're a gate-crasher.'

'Of course he is!' and she swung back.

Suddenly Sagoe asked, 'Do you keep hedgehogs?'

Pinkshore retreated in fright. 'Because' – and his smile was benign – 'my neck is tickling from poisonous spines.' He looked round the guests studiously, nodding each time with discovery.

Pinkshore whispered, 'We had better get help, Mrs Oguazor. I think he's mad!'

'Ha you think so, enh!' His snarl was manic, straight from the last bullet of the 46th floor last-stand films. Pinkshore yelled aloud and fifty heads turned in their direction. Sagoe saw the Professor apologizing his course through glass and smoke and he began to consider retreat.

'On second thoughts, madam,' he bowed. 'I will retrieve your plastic cornucopia. If this butler of yours is right and they are decorations, the dog would not have touched them. He's a real choosy bitch.' And before Mrs Oguazor could guess his intentions, he raised her hand and kissed it.

Oguazor arrived just then. 'Congratulations, Prof,' he fawned on him. 'Many happy returns of today.' Sagoe hesitated, then decided his host was not really of ministerial rank and so he wouldn't kiss his hand. He contented himself with two vigorous pumps of Oguazor's hand. And he bent with a speed which surprised himself, sniffed the plastic rose which decorated Mrs Oguazor at the navel and sprang up again holding his nose to heaven in aromatic bliss.

'Like real, Caro. Like real.' And he shot from the room like mad.

He walked rapidly, half-expecting some form of pursuit but unable to tell why. A neighbouring dog began to bark and he stopped. His heart was pounding and the excitement was not quite over. He began to retrace his steps, making no resistance at all to the madness that urged him on. Round the back of the house, squeezing between the shrubbery that fenced off Oguazor's home, he slipped suddenly but recovered, looking down he saw the cause, it was one of the plastic lemons he had thrown out. Sagoe picked it up. He skirted the house bending low in the shadows until he found the window. They were all there, undoubtedly they were discussing him. Pinkshore leant out from time to time to see if any of the fruits were lying about in the garden. Sagoe closed his eyes saying, Pinkshore, really you shouldn't tempt me. And he counted five to give him what he called a sporting chance. But Pinkshore stood there still, a little to one side now, saying something to the Oguazors. The fruit was light and Sagoe crept nearer saying, Winds be still ... and flung the lemon. It took Pinkshore full on the mouth, soft, wet from the grass and sudden. His brain spinning, instant solutions found mysterious terror – witch-moth, bat shit, murder, knobkerry, death, Africa at night.... Pinkshore, ignorant of the fact, levelled up with his assailant by passing out on his hosts.

Calvin C. Hernton

The Distant Drum

I am not a metaphor or symbol.
This you hear is not the wind in the trees,
Nor a cat being maimed in the street.
It is I being maimed in the street.
It is I who weep, laugh, feel pain or joy.
I speak this because I exist.
This is my voice.
These words are my words, my mouth
Speaks them, my hand writes —
I am a poet.
It is my fist you hear beating
Against your ear.

A. L. Young

Birthday Poem

First light of day in Mississippi
son of labourer & of house wife
it says so on the official photostat
not son of fisherman & child fugitive
from cotton fields & potato patches
from sugar-cane chickens & well-water
from kerosene lamps & watermelons
mules named jack or jenny & wagonwheels,

year of meaningless farm work
work Work WORK WORK *WORK* —
'Papa pull you outta school bout March
to stay on the place & work the crop'
– her own earliest knowledge
of human hopelessness & waste

She carried me around nine months
inside her fifteen year old self
before here I sit numbering it all

How I got from then to now
is the mystery that could fill a whole library
much less an arbitrary stanza

But of course you already know about that
from your own random suffering
& sudden inexplicable bliss

Ngugi Wa Thiong'o

from A Grain of Wheat

In the days when European and Indian immigrants wrestled to control Kenya – then any thought of a black person near the seat of power was beyond the reach of the wildest imagination – Mr Rogers, an agricultural officer, travelling by train from Nairobi to Nakuru one day, saw the thick forest at Githima and suddenly felt his planning mind drawn to it. His passion lay, not in politics, a strange thing in those days, but in land development. Why not a Forestry Research Station, he asked himself as the train rumbled towards the escarpment and down to the great valley. Later he went back to Githima to see the forest. His plan began to take shape. He wrote letters to anybody of note and even unsuccessfully sought an interview with the Governor. Mad they thought him: science in dark Africa?

Githima and the thick forest, like an evil spirit, possessed him. He could not rest; he talked to himself about the scheme; he talked about it to everybody. One day he was crushed by a train at Githima crossing, and he died immediately. Later, a Forestry Research Station was set up in the area, not as a tribute to his martyrdom, but as part of a new colonial development plan. Soon Githima Forestry and Agricultural Research Station teemed with European scientists and administrators.

It is said that the man's ghost haunts the railway crossing and that every year the rumbling train claims a human sacrifice from the Githima settlement; the latest victim was Dr Henry Van Dyke, a fat, drunken meteorological officer, who had always sworn, so the African workers said, that he would kill himself if Kenyatta was ever set free from Lodwar and Lokitaung. His car crashed into the train soon after Kenyatta's return home from Maralal. People in Githima, even his enemies, were dismayed by the news. Was this an accident, or had the man committed suicide?

Karanja, who worked at Githima Library dusting books, keeping them straight in their shelves and writing labels, remembered Dr Van Dyke mostly because of a strange game he sometimes played: he would come up to the African workers, put his arm around their shoulders and then suddenly, he would strike their unsuspecting bottoms. He used to let his hand lie on their buttocks feelingly, breathing out alcohol over the shoulders of his victims. Then unexpectedly he would burst into open and loud laughter. Karanja resented the laughter; he never knew whether Dr Van Dyke expected him to join in it or not. Hence Karanja always settled into a nervous grin which made him hate Dr Van Dyke all the more. Yet the news of the man's death, his car and body completely mangled by the train, had made Karanja retch.

Karanja picked a clean stencil from a pile on the table and started writing labels. The books recently bound at Githima belonged to the Ministry of Agriculture, Nairobi. Soon Karanja's mind lost consciousness of other things, Uhuru or Dr Van Dyke, and he concentrated on the label in hand: STUDIES IN AGRONOMY VOL –. Suddenly he felt a man's presence in the room. He dropped the stencil and swung round. His face had turned a shade darker. He tried, with difficulty, to control the tremulous pen in his hand.

'Why don't you people knock at the door before you rush in?' he hissed at the man standing at the door.

'I knocked, three times.'

'You did not. You always enter as if this was your father's thingira.'

'I knocked at this door, here.'

'Feebly like a woman? Why can't you knock hard, hard, like a man circumcised?' Karanja raised his voice, and banged the table at the same time, to emphasize every point.

'Ask your mother, when I fucked her—'

'You insult my mother, you —'

'Even now I can do it again, or to your sister. It is they who can tell you that Mwaura is a man circumcised.'

Karanja stood up. The two glared at one another. For a minute it looked as if they would fall to blows.

'You say that to me? Is it to me you throw so many insults?' he said with venom.

Mwaura's lower lip fell. His stomach heaved forward and back. His breathing was quick and heavy. Then he seemed to remember something. He held his tongue.

'Anyway, I'm sorry,' he suddenly said but in a voice edged with menace.

'So you ought to be. What do you want here?'

'Nothing. Just that Thompson wants to see you, that is all.' Mwaura went out. Karanja's mood changed from tension to anxiety. What did Thompson want? Perhaps he would say something about pay. He dusted his khaki overall, passed a comb through his mole-coloured hair and hurried along the corridor towards Thompson's office. He knocked boldly at the door and entered.

John Thompson, the Administrative Secretary, raised a tired face from a mass of paper on the table.

'What is it? Why do you people knock so loud?'

'I thought, I thought you sent for me, sir,' Karanja said in a thin voice, standing, as he always did before a white person, feet slightly parted, hands linked at the back, all in obsequious attention.

'Oh, yes, yes. You know my house?'

'Yes, sir.'

'Run and tell Mrs Thompson that I'll not be coming home for lunch. I am going – eh – wait a minute. I'll give you a letter.'

John Thompson had, over the years, developed a mania for writing letters. He scribbled notes to everyone. He rarely sent a messenger anywhere, be it to the Director, to the stationery office for paper, or to the workshop for a nail or two, without an accompanying note carefully laying down all the details. Even when it might be easier to see an officer personally he preferred to send a letter.

Karanja took the note and lingered for a second or two hoping that Thompson would say something about the pay increment for which he had recently applied. The boss, however, resumed his blank stare at the mass of paper on his table.

John Thompson and Mrs Dickinson used Karanja as their personal messenger. Karanja accepted their missions with resentful alacrity: weren't there paid messengers at Githima? Mrs Dickinson was the Librarian. She was a young woman who was separated from her husband and she made no secret of living with her boy friend. She was rarely in the office, but when she was in, men and women would flock to see her and laughter and high-pitched voices would pour out all day. An enthusiast for the East African Safari, she always took part, co-driving with her boy friend, but she never once finished the course. Her missions were the ones Karanja hated most: often she sent him, for instance, to the African quarters to buy meat for her two dogs.

Today as he rode his creaking bicycle he was once again full of plans: he would certainly complain to John Thompson about these trivial errands. No, what Karanja resented most was not the missions or their triviality, but the way they affected his considerable standing among the other African workers. But on the whole Karanja would rather endure the humiliation than lose the good name he had built up for himself among the white people. He lived on that name and the power it brought him. At Githima, people believed that a complaint from him was enough to make a man lose his job. Karanja knew their fears. Often when men came into his office, he would suddenly cast them a cold eye, drop hints, or simply growl at them; in this way, he increased their fears and insecurity. But he also feared the men and alternated this fierce pose with servile friendliness.

A neatly-trimmed hedge of cider shrub surrounded the Thompsons' bungalow. At the entrance, green creepers coiled on a wood stand, massed into an arch at the top and then fell to the hedge at the sides. The hedge enclosed gardens of flowers: flame lilies, morning glory, sunflowers, bougainvillea. However, it was the gardens of roses that stood out in colour above the others. Mrs Margery Thompson had cultivated red roses, white roses, pink roses – roses of all shades. Now she emerged from this garden of colour and came to the door. She was dressed in thin white trousers and a blouse that seemed suspended from her pointed breasts.

'Come into the house,' she idly said after reading the note from her husband. She was bored by staying in the house alone. Normally she chatted with her houseboy or with her shamba-boy. At times she quarrelled with them and her raised voice could be heard from the road. Both boys had now left and it was during these few days that she had come to realize how they had been an important part of the house.

Karanja was surprised because he had never, before, been invited inside the house. He sat at the edge of the chair, his unsteady hands on his knees, and idly stared at the ceiling and at the walls to avoid looking at her breasts.

Margery felt a sensual power at the fear and discomfiture she inflicted on Karanja. Why did he not look at her? She had often seen him, but never thought of him as a man. Now she was suddenly curious to know what thoughts lay inside his head: what did he think of the house? Of Uhuru? Of her? She let her fancy flow. She warmed all over and stood up, slightly irritated by the thrill.

'Would you like some tea, coffee or anything?'

'I – I must go!' Karanja stammered out his thoughts.

'Sure you don't want some coffee? Never mind Mrs Dickinson,' she said, smiling, feeling indulgent, almost glad of a conspiracy.

'All right,' he said edging deeper into the seat with eyes longing for the door and the hedge beyond. Even now he had no courage to lean back and be comfortable. At the same time, he desperately wished one of the workers was present to see him entertained to coffee by a white woman, the wife of the Administrative Secretary.

In the kitchen, Margery played with pots and cups. Although she was still ashamed of the thrill, she would not let it go. She could only remember once before when she had experienced a similar flame. That was the day she danced with Dr Van Dyke at Githima hostel. This was soon after the Rira disaster. She was attracted, at the same time disgusted, by his drunken breath. When later in the evening he took her for a drive, she submitted to his power. She let him make love to her, and experienced, for the first time, the terrible beauty of a rebellion.

Waiting in the room, Karanja found his nervous unease replaced by a different desire. Should he ask her, he wondered. Maybe she would give him what he really wanted: to hear her contradict rumours that the Thompsons would be flying back to England. Many times Karanja had walked towards Thompson determined to ask him a direct question. Cold water lumped in his belly, his heart would thunder violently when he came near the white man. His determination always ended in the same way: he would salute John Thompson and then walk past as if his business lay further ahead. What Karanja feared more than the rumours was their possible confirmation. As long as he did not know the truth, he could interpret the story in the only way that gave him hope: the coming of black rule would not mean, could never mean the end of white power. Thompson as a DO and now as an Administrative Secretary, had always seemed to Karanja the invincible expression of that power. How, then, could Thompson go?

Margery came back with two cups of coffee.

'Do you take sugar in your coffee?'

'No,' he said automatically, and knew, at the same time, he lacked the courage to ask her about the rumours. Karanja loathed coffee or tea without lots of sugar.

Margery sat opposite Karanja and crossed her legs. She put her cup on the arm of the chair. Karanja held his in both hands afraid of spilling a drop on the carpet. He winced every time he brought the cup near his lips and nostrils.

'How many wives have you?' she asked. This was her favourite question to Africans; it began the day she discovered her latest cook had three wives. Karanja started as if Margery had tickled a wound that had only healed at the surface. *Mumbi.*

'I am not married.'

'Not married? I thought you people – Are you going to buy a wife?'

'I don't know.'

'Have you a friend, a woman?' She pursued, her curiosity mounting;

her voice was timbred with warmth. Something in the quality of her voice touched Karanja. Would she understand? Would she?

'I had a woman. I — I loved her,' he said boldly. He closed his eyes and with sudden, huge effort, gulped down the bitter coffee.

'Why didn't you marry her? Is she dead or —?'

'She refused me,' he said.

'I am sorry,' she said with feeling. Karanja remembered himself and where he was.

'Can I go now, Memsahib? Any message for Bwana?'

She had forgotten why Karanja had come into the house. She re-read the note from her husband.

'No, thank you very much,' she said at the door.

It was almost twelve o'clock when Karanja left Thompson's house. The wound that Margery had tickled smarted for a while. Then gradually he became exhilarated, he wished Mwaura had seen him at the house. He also wished that the houseboy had been present, for then news of his visit would have spread. As it was, he himself would have to do the telling: this would carry less weight and power. Being nearly time for lunch-break, he went straight to the eating-house at the African quarters, thinking about his visit and the bitter cup of coffee.

The eating-house was called *Your Friend Unto Death*, in short, *Friend*. The stony walls were covered with grease, a fertile ground for flies. They buzzed around the customers, jumped on top of the cups and plates and at times even made love on food brought on the table. Plastic roses in tins decorated each creaking table. The motto of the house was painted in capitals across one wall: COME UNTO ME ALL YE THAT ARE HUNGRY AND THIRSTY AND I WILL GIVE YOU REST. On another part of the wall near the cashier's desk hung a carefully framed poem.

> Since man to man has been unjust,
> Show me the man that I can trust.
> I have trusted many to my sorrow,
> So for credit, my friend, come tomorrow.

Friend was the only licensed eating-house at Githima.

There Karanja found Mwaura. It was not good to create enemies, Karanja always told himself after alienating any of the other workers.

'I am sorry about the incident,' Karanja quickly said, an affability that didn't come off. 'I hope you'll take it as a little *shauri* between friends. You see, some people don't understand that the work we do, you know, writing labels for all those books of science, requires concentration. If somebody flings the door open without a warning, it upsets you and you ruin the letters. I tell you, if you knew that Librarian woman as well as I do – you think she separated from her husband for nothing – Waiter, two cups of tea, quick ... Now, what news from Rung'ei?'

John Thompson – tall, a leathery skin that stuck to the bone – did not go to Nairobi, but remained at Githima during the lunch-hour, going through motions of working: that is, he would stand, go to the cabinet by the wall, pull out a file and return to the table, his face weather-beaten into permanent abstraction, almost as if his mind dwelt on things far away and long ago. His thin hands and light eyes went through each file carefully before returning it to the cabinet. Once or twice he sat up and his finger played with a few creases crowded around the corners of his mouth.

In turn, Thompson contemplated the clean blotting-paper on the table, the pen and pencil rack, the ink-bottle, the whitewashed office walls and the ceiling as if seeking a pattern that held the things in the room together: but his mind only hopped from one thought to another. He then took the day's – Monday's – issue of the *East African Standard*, the oldest daily in Kenya, and leaned back on the chair. Glancing through reports on Uhuru preparations for Thursday, Thompson winced with a vague sense of betrayal. He could not tell what it was in the paper which since internal self-government in June, caused this feeling – whether it was in the Uhuru news, which he already knew, or in the tone, a too-ready acceptance of things. Once he saw the picture of the Prime Minister on the front page: he could not look at it twice, but hurried on to the next page: afterwards he felt ashamed of this reaction, but he could not bring himself to look at it again. Thompson already knew the Duke of Edinburgh would deputize for the Queen. Any news on Uhuru always reminded him of this knowledge. No matter how he looked at it, Thompson was pinched by sadness at the knowledge that the Duke would sit to see the flag lowered, never to rise again on this side of Albion's shore. This sadness was accentuated by his mind racing back to 1952 when the Queen, then a princess, visited Kenya. For a minute, Thompson forgot the newspaper and relived that moment when the young woman shook hands with him. He was then District Officer. He felt a thrill: his heart-beat had quickened almost as if a covenant had been made between him and her. Then, there, he would have done anything for her, would have stabbed himself to prove his readiness to carry out that mission which though unspoken seemed embodied in her person and smile. Recalling that rapture, Thompson involuntarily pushed away the paper and rose to his feet. There was a flicker in his eyes, a watery glint. He walked towards the window muttering under his breath: 'what the hell was it all about!'

The momentary excitement died and a hardness settled in his belly. He leaned forward, his eyes vaguely surveying the scene: in front of him lay the low corrugated-iron roofs of the three laboratories – one for plant pathology and forestry, one for soil-physics and the other for soil-chemistry. To the left, hot-houses were scattered about in groups of two or three. He watched Dr Lynd, a plant pathologist at the station, cross the tarmac road; soon she disappeared behind the hot-houses; a few seconds later her dog, a brown bull-mastiff with black dewlaps, dashed from the laboratories and followed her. To the right, he could just see the library: a group of Africans lay on the grass below the eaves. Everything was so quiet, Thompson reflected, now looking from the green grass compound to the chemistry-block, the nearest laboratory. Test-tubes upon test-tubes were neatly arranged by the glass window. Would these things remain after Thursday? Perhaps for two months: and then – test-tubes and beakers would be broken or lie unwashed on the cement, the hot-houses and seed-beds strewn with wild plants and the outer bush which had been carefully hemmed, would gradually creep into a litter-filled compound.

The bull-mastiff emerged from the other side of the chemistry-block, sniffing along the grass-surface. Then it stood and raised its head towards the library. Thompson tensed up: something was going to happen. He knew it and waited, unable to suppress that cold excitement. Suddenly the dog started barking as it bounded across the compound towards the group of Africans. A few of them screamed and scattered into different directions. One man could not run in time. The dog went for him. The man tried to edge his way out, but the dog fixed him to the wall. Suddenly he stooped, picked up a stone, and raised it in the air. The dog was now only a few feet away. Thompson waited for the thing he feared to happen. Just at that moment, Dr Lynd appeared on the scene, and as the dog was about to jump at the man, shouted something. Thompson's breath came back first in a long-drawn wave, then in low quick waves, relieved and vaguely disappointed that nothing had happened.

He left the office and walked across the grass compound towards the library where a small crowd of Africans had gathered. Dr Lynd held her dog by the collar with the left hand and pointed an accusing finger at Karanja with the other.

'I am ashamed of you, utterly ashamed of you,' she said, putting as much contempt as she could into her voice. Karanja looked at the ground; fear and anger were visible in his eyes; the sweat-drops had not yet dried on his face.

'The dog – dog – come – Memsahib,' he stammered.

'I would never have thought this of you – throwing stones at my dog.'

'No stones – I did not throw stones.'

'The way you people lie —' she said, looking round at the others. Then she turned to Karanja. 'Didn't I catch you holding a stone? I should have allowed him to get at you. Even now I've half a mind to let him —'

At that point John Thompson arrived at the scene. The Africans gave way, Dr Lynd stopped admonishing Karanja and smiled at Thompson. Karanja raised his head hopefully. The other Africans looked at Thompson and stopped murmuring and mumbling. The sudden silence and the many eyes unsettled Thompson. He remembered the detainees at Rira the day they went on strike. Now he sensed the same air of hostility. He must keep his dignity – to the last. But panic seized him. Without looking at anybody in particular, he said the first Swahili words that came into his mouth:

'I'll deal with this.' And immediately he felt this was the wrong thing to have said – it smacked too much of an apology. The silence was broken. The men were now shouting and pointing at the dog: others made vague gestures in the air. Karanja watched Thompson with grateful eyes. Thompson quickly placed his arm on the woman's shoulder and drew her away.

He led her through the narrow corridor that joined the library block and the administrative building, without knowing where he was going. Everything seemed a visitation from the past: Rira and the dog. Dr Lynd was talking all the time.

'They are rude because Uhuru is coming – even the best of them is changing.'

He wanted to tell her about the dog but somehow found it difficult. He knew he ought to have done something. What if Karanja had been touched by the dog? As the Administrative Secretary, he was supposed to deal with staff–worker relations; and he had received a number of complaints about Dr Lynd's dog from the secretary of the Kenya African Civil Servants' Union (Githima branch). They had now come into a big tree-nursery surrounded by a wire-fence. They sat down on a grassy part. He wanted to tell her the truth – but he would have to tell her about his own paralysis – how he had stood fascinated by an anticipation of blood.

'Actually, it was not the boy's fault . . .' he started. 'I saw the dog run towards them.'

Like many other Europeans in Kenya, Thompson had a thing about pets, especially dogs. A year ago he had taken Margery to Nairobi to see *Annie Get Your Gun* staged at the National Theatre by the City Players. He had never been to that theatre before – for nothing really ever happened there – he always went to the Donovan Maule Theatre Club. The road from Githima to Nairobi passed through the countryside. It was very dark. Suddenly the headlights caught a dog about to cross the road. Thompson could have braked, slowed down or horned. He had enough time and distance. But he held on the wheel. He did not want to kill the dog and yet he knew he was going to drive into it. He was glued to the seat – fearing the inevitable. Suddenly there was a scream. Thompson's energy came back. He braked to a stop and opened the door and went out, taking a pocket torch. He went back a few yards; there was no dog anywhere. He looked on either side of the road but saw no sign of the dog – not even a trail of blood. Yet he had heard the thud and the scream. Back in the car, he found Margery quietly weeping. And to his surprise, he too was shaking and could not comfort her. 'Perhaps it's under the car,' she said. He went out again and carefully peered under the car. There was nothing. He drove away sadly; it was as if he had murdered a man.

He had relived the chilling scene the moment he saw the bull-mastiff run towards Karanja; the incident was still close to the skin as he tried to tell Dr Lynd what had happened – the difficulty lay in separating what had occurred outside his office on the grass – only tell her that – from what had gone on inside him.

To his surprise and extreme discomfort, he saw that she was weeping, and looked away: the dog was wandering among the young trees; it stopped beside a crowd of camphor trees, raised its hind leg and passed water.

'I am sorry,' Dr Lynd said, suppressing a sniff, holding a white handkerchief to her eyes. She was a grey-haired woman with falling flesh on her cheeks and under her eyes. She daily flitted about the compound – between the hot-houses, the laboratories and the seed-beds – a solitary being, like a ghost.

'Don't let it worry you,' he said, his eyes vaguely following the dog.

'I tried not to, but – but – I hate them. How can I help it? Every time I see them I remember – I remember –'

He fidgeted on the grass, felt his ridiculous position in relation to this woman from whom he wanted to get away now that the urge to tell her about the dog had faded. But Dr Lynd was in that mood – a sudden upsurge of pure holy self-pity – when one feels closer to another person, even to a stranger, and ready to confide in him one's innermost dreads and burdens. So she told him about the incident that had plagued her life, had shamed her body. She had lived alone, at Muguga, in an old bungalow overgrown with bush on all sides to the roofs. She had loved the house, the solitude, the peace. It was during the Emergency. Many times the DO warned her to leave the lonely place and go to Githima or Nairobi where she would be sure of protection and security. She would not hear of it: the stories of women murdered in their remote farm-houses did not frighten her. She had come to Kenya to do a job not to play politics. She liked the country and the climate and so had decided to stay. She had never harmed anybody. True, she often scolded her houseboy but she also gave him presents, clothes, built him a little brick house at the back, and never worked him hard. He was a small Kikuyu man from Rung'ei who had apparently been a cook or something during World War II, but had been without a job for a long time before he came to her. Between the houseboy and the dog had developed a friendship which was very touching to see. There came one night, it was so dark outside, when the boy called her to open the door rather urgently. On opening the door, two men rushed at her and dragged her back to the sitting-room, the houseboy following. She looked to him for help, but he was smiling. She waited for them to kill her, for after the initial shock she had resigned herself to death. But when she saw what they wanted with her, she felt terribly cold all over. People say that women faint on such occasions or else struggle. She wished she could faint or die there and then. But that was the terrible part, she saw everything, was fully conscious... Later two men were arrested and hanged; the houseboy was never caught. She had to buy and train another dog (the first one was poisoned by the houseboy on that night). She had never been able to outlive the heavy smell, the malicious mad eyes of those men – no – no, she would never forget it to her dying day.

Thompson looked at her, recoiling from her voice, from her body, from her presence. Both left the field, and took different paths, almost as if they were ashamed of their latest intimacy. He felt rather than knew the fear awakened in him. In the office, he tried to suppress the low rage of fear, but only thought of the dog. And he remembered the other dog as the headlight caught its eyes. What happened to it? What would have happened if the bull-mastiff had jumped on Karanja and torn his flesh? The hostility he saw in the men's eyes as he approached them. The silence. Sudden. Like Rira. There the detainees had refused to speak. They sat down and refused to eat or drink. Their obduracy was like iron. Their eyes followed him everywhere. The agony, lack of sleep, thinking of how to break the silence. And in the dark, he could see their eyes. In the men at the library, he had recognized the eyes, the same look.

John Thompson had worked as a District Officer in many parts of Kenya. He worked hard and his ability to deal swiftly and effectively with Africans was widely recognized. A brilliant career in the colonial administration lay before him. During the Emergency he was seconded to detention camps, to rehabilitate Mau Mau adherents to a normal life as British subjects. At Rira, the tragedy of his life occurred. A hunger-strike, a little beating and eleven detainees died. The fact leaked out. Because he was the officer in charge, Thompson's name was bandied about in the House of Commons and in the world press. He had suddenly become famous. A commission of inquiry was set up. He was whisked off to Githima, an exile from the public administration he loved. But the wound had never healed. Touch it, and it brought back all the humiliation he had felt at the time.

As he now stared at their eyes, he saw in them a new and terrible significance: would he have had to endure another inquiry, this time under a black government, had anything happened to Karanja?

He could not work and yet the afternoon passed quickly. Maybe he would come back tomorrow to finish this job. He shut the window and again relived the scene and his fear. At the end of the corridor, Karanja waited for him. What did he want? What did he want?

'Yes?'

'I took the letter.'

'So?'

'I want to thank you.'

Thompson remembered his lie; he stared at the boy and passed on. On second thoughts, he called Karanja.

'About that dog—'

'Sir?'

'Don't worry about it, eh? I'll deal with the matter.'

'Thank you, sir.'

And Thompson went away raging within. Did he have to pacify Karanja? What have we come to!

He felt tears at the edges of his eyes. Blindly he rushed to the car.

Evan Jones

The Song of the Banana Man

Touris', white man, wipin' his face,
Met me in Golden Grove market place.
He looked at m' ol' clothes brown wid stain,
An' soaked right through wid de Portlan' rain,
He cas' his eye, turn' up his nose,
He says, 'You're a beggar man, I suppose?'
He says, 'Boy, get some occupation,
Be of some value to your nation.'

I said, 'By God and dis big right han'
You mus' recognize a banana man.

'Up in de hills, where de streams are cool,
An' mullet an' janga* swim in de pool,
I have ten acres of mountain side,
An' a dainty-foot donkey dat I ride,
Four Gros Michel, an' four Lacatan,†
Some coconut trees, and some hills of yam,
An' I pasture on dat very same lan'
Five she-goats an' a big black ram,

'Dat, by God an' dis big right han'
Is de property of a banana man.

'I leave m' yard early-mornin' time
An' set m'foot to de mountain climb,

---

* janga: a crayfish, found in some of the rivers of Jamaica.

† 'Gros Michel' (pronounced 'grow mee-shell') and 'Lacatan' are two varieties
of bananas.

I ben' m' back to de hot-sun toil,
An' m' cutlass rings on de stony soil,
Ploughin' an' weedin', diggin' an' plantin'
Till Massa Sun drop back o' John Crow mountain
Den home again in cool evenin' time,
Perhaps whistling dis likkle rhyme,

(*Sung*) 'Praise God an' m' big right han'
I will live an' die a banana man.

'Banana day is my special day,
I cut my stems an' I'm on m' way,
Load up de donkey, leave de lan'
Head down de hill to banana stan',
When de truck comes roun' I take a ride
All de way down to de harbour side –
Dat is de night, when you, touris' man,
Would change your place wid a banana man.

'Yes, by God, an' m' big right han'
I will live an' die a banana man.

'De bay is calm, an' de moon is bright
De hills look black for de sky is light,
Down at de dock is an English ship,
Restin' after her ocean trip,
While on de pier is a monstrous hustle,
Tallymen, carriers, all in a bustle,
Wid stems on deir heads in a long black snake
Some singin' de songs dat banana men make,

'Like, (*Sung*) Praise God an' m' big right han'
I will live an' die a banana man.

'Den de payment comes, an' we have some fun,
Me, Zekiel, Breda and Duppy Son.
Down at de bar near United Wharf
We knock back a white rum, bus' a laugh,
Fill de empty bag for further toil
Wid saltfish, breadfruit, coconut oil.
Den head back home to m' yard to sleep,
A proper sleep dat is long an' deep.

'Yes, by God, an' m' big right han'
I will live an' die a banana man.

'So when you see dese ol' clothes brown wid stain,
An' soaked right through wid de Portlan' rain,
Don't cas' your eye nor turn your nose,
Don't judge a man by his patchy clothes,
I'm a strong man, a proud man, an' I'm free,
Free as dese mountains, free as dis sea,
I know myself, an' I know my ways,
An' will sing wid pride to de end o' my days

(*Sung*) 'Praise God an' m' big right han'
I will live an' die a banana man.'

Aimé Césaire

from Return to My Native Land

And I, and I,
I who sang with clenched fist.
You must be told the length to which I carried cowardice.
In a tram one night, facing me, a Negro.
He was a Negro tall as a pongo who tried to make himself very small on
a tram seat. On that filthy tram seat he tried to abandon his gigantic
legs and his starved boxer's trembling hands. And everything had left
him, was leaving him. His nose was like a peninsula off its moorings;
even his negritude was losing its colour through the effects of a perpetual tanner's bleach. And the tanner was Poverty. A great sudden
long-eared bat whose claw-marks on that face were scarred, scabby
islands. Or perhaps Poverty was a tireless workman fashioning some
deformed cartridge. You could see clearly how the industrious malevo-
lent thumb had modelled the lump of the forehead, pierced two tunnels
– parallel and disturbing – through the nose, drawn out the dispropor-
tion of the upper lip, and by a masterstroke of caricature had planed,
polished, varnished the smallest, neatest little ears in all creation.
He was an ungainly Negro without rhythm or measure.
A Negro whose eyes rolled with bloodshot weariness.
A Negro without shame, and his big smelly toes sniggered in the deep
gaping lair of his shoes.
Poverty, it has to be said, had taken great pains to finish him off.
She had hollowed the eye socket and painted it with a cosmetic of dust
and rheum.
She had stretched the empty space between the solid hinge of the jaws
and the bone of an old, worn cheek. On this she had planted the shiny
little bristles of several days' beard. She had maddened the heart and
bent the back.
And the whole thing added up perfectly to a hideous Negro, a peevish

Negro, a melancholy Negro, a slumped Negro, hands folded as in
prayer upon a knotty stick. A Negro shrouded in an old, threadbare
jacket. A Negro who was comical and ugly, and behind me women gig-
gled as they looked at him.
He was COMICAL AND UGLY.
COMICAL AND UGLY, for a fact.
I sported a great smile of complicity ...
My cowardice rediscovered!
I bow to the three centuries which support my civil
rights and my minimized blood.
My heroism, what a joke!
This town suits me to perfection.
My soul is supine. Like this town, supine
in the dirt and mud.
This town, my face of mud.
I demand for my face the dazzling prize
of being spat upon!
Being such as we are, can the rush of virility, the limb
of victory, the large-clodded plain of the future, belong
to us?
I prefer to admit that I have babbled generously, my
heart in my brain like a drunken knee.

My star now the funereal hawk

And on this ancient dream my cannibal cruelties:

(bullets in the mouth thick saliva
our heart daily bursts with meanness
the continents break the frail moorings of isthmuses
lands explode along the fatal division of rivers
and now it is the turn of these Heights
which for centuries have stifled back their cry
to quarter the silence
and the people
courage leaping
and our bodies dismembered
in vain by the most refined tortures
a hotter-headed life spurting from this dung
like a bullock's-heart tree unexpected among decaying bread-fruit!)

On this ancient dream within myself my cannibal cruelties

Destiny was calling me
and I hid behind a stupid vanity:
here's a man forced to the ground, his feeble defences scattered,
his sacred maxims trampled underfoot, his pedantic declamations
farting through every lesion
here's a man forced to the ground
and his soul is naked
and destiny triumphs as it looks upon
this once defiant soul
moulting in the ancestral mud-pit.

I say that it is well so.
My back shall make a victory out of its whipping sores.
I shall trim my natural obsequiousness with acknowledgements of
    gratitude
and my enthusiasm will outclass the silver-braided
flummery of that postillion in Havana, lyrical baboon,
pimp of the splendours of servitude.

I say that this is well.
I live for the greater flatness of my soul
for the great limpness of my flesh.

Peter Blackman

from My Song is for All Men

My song is for all men Jew Greek Russian
Communist pagan Christian Hindu Muslim Pole Parsee
And since my song is for all men
More than most I must state a case for the black man.

I have wandered with the Men of Devon over the Devon hills
Conned thought with Milton where low voices drift
through time buoying music over death and forgetfulness
I have wandered beyond to distant Caucasia
Skirting my wonder of blood wined in the beauty
Of green mountains hemmed by blue waters on Georgia's coast
I have listened to debate in London and Moscow
Prague Paris and many another town
I have heard statement confused or insistent
patient or fretted facing a claim
And ever the claim was the same
'This is my own' the voices repeated 'my hands have built it. It is my
    very own. Show us your fruiting.'
Let me then bring mine own
This is mine own. I state a claim for the black man

I am the black man
I hide with pigmies in the hot depth of the forest that is Africa's girdle
I am the Zulu striding hot storm over the brown whispering veldt
that rides in my blood like a battle
I am the Ashanti I fold my strength in the beaten gold
of a stool shaped for immortals
I am the Nilotic standing one-legged for my rest
I am the Hyskos escaped out of Egypt and become king of Ruandi
I am the miner baring the wealth of South Africa
I hold the fate of the world in my hands in the uranium pits of the
    Congo

I am no more the man of Zambesi than I am the man of Limpopo
I am no less the man from the mountains of Kavirondo than I am the
      warrior bred of the Masai
I am as much Ibo as I am Yoruba
I am all that is Africa I reach out to embrace those who have left me
I dig cane-holes in hot West Indian islands
I run donkeyman on trampships plying from Cardiff
I wear a red cap on all North American railroad stations

I bring rough hands calloused in the tumult of weariness
Strong-boned not given to prayer force strained to hard bruising
Bearing rough burdens to enrich men in England America France
      Holland Brazil. I work for my bread.

A woman comes with me long-limbed high-bosomed proud of
      countenance
She walks abroad her presence dressed
Fluent of Earth and love
Sweet as the fresh-rained corn at early morning

Eyes soft as mountain lakes deep-shaded
O'er shot of sunshine truant midst the reeds
At hide and seek with laughter supply flung
The music of her motion

Sweeter is this purple grape
Than Pompadour's wild roses
Wild-eddied leaps life's promise
Strong
In the rivers of her keeping

The Black woman brings her beauty
I shall sing it
Bid every nation know
And worship it
With her at my side I measure all things
She is the source of my pride from her stem all my creations

Sembene Ousmane

from God's Bits of Wood

Among the strikers there were some few who secretly went back to work. They rose very early and did not return to their homes until after nightfall. Tiémoko had recruited a group of commandos to take care of such men, and the 'renegades', as he referred to them at meetings, were dealt with harshly. This collective action made the strike-breakers more wary and discouraged others from joining them, but there was, nonetheless, one case which caused considerable commotion and provoked extremely varied reactions, depending largely on the age, the sex, or the particular situation of those who were involved. It was the case of Diara, the ticket collector.

When Diara's trial was held in the union building, the meeting hall was filled to overflowing and had lost its customary aspect – there were several women present, and this was something entirely new. Diara himself was seated at the centre of the stage, alone, and without even a table before him. His head was bowed so deeply that all that could be seen was his forehead. He seemed to have shrunk – actually to have shrivelled up somehow – giving the appearance of a piece of meat that had been set out here to dry. His back was bent beneath the weight of his humiliation, and his arms hung limply at his sides, grafted to his shoulders like lifeless stumps.

Seated at a table to his right were Konaté, the secretary of the Bamako local, and the regional director from Koulikoro. With them was Sadio, Diara's son, and facing them, aligned on a bench, were the eight jurors. The hall itself was so crowded that those who had been unable to find a place were jammed into the door and the windows, as they had been on the night the strike was called. But the atmosphere this night was frigid, and not a sound disturbed the silence.

Diara, the ticket collector, was accused of *dynfa* – a Bambara word that was seldom used any longer, but which meant nothing less than treason: betrayal of one's own people. This was serious enough in itself, but in addition there was the fact that this was the first time that anyone there – in the hall or up on the stage – had taken part in a trial.

Subconsciously they were torn between the feeling of brotherhood that each of them had for the others – including the accused – and a vague memory of what was meant by the law, which they knew only from fragments of stories they had heard. Because of this conflict of emotions, they had a curious feeling of having been removed from their natural element, but the very newness of being forced to make a decision of this kind for themselves had sharpened their interest and their curiosity. There were some of them who realized that, for the first time, they were being called upon to play the role of a man – of their own man.

It was Tiémoko, who was the official record-keeper for the local strike committee, who had insisted on holding the trial, and everyone knew that the idea for it, and even the manner in which it was being handled, had come from a book in Ibrahim Bakayoko's library. Konaté was presiding, and he began by exhorting everyone who would have something to say to do so without hatred or malice towards Diara.

Standing up, with one hand still resting on the table, he said sorrowfully, 'I have no need to tell you that this affair is disagreeable for all of us.' Over his shoulder, he glanced at Sadio, the son of the accused, who seemed as broken and unhappy as his father, and then he continued. 'Until this moment, we have punished strike-breakers simply by beating them, and, as you know, there are two who are still laid up as a result. I went to see them before coming here. That is a sorry business, because we all have wives, and mothers and fathers, and children.

'But now there is the case of Diara. Diara voted for the strike, and like ourselves he received his proper share of relief, but then he moved over to the side of our enemies. Now it is up to you to speak. Everything you say will be carefully noted, and then your judgement will be carried out by men who will be appointed for that purpose.'

Normally, when Konaté had finished speaking, he was always loudly applauded, but this time everyone was so conscious of the gravity of the matter that no one moved. For a moment there was utter silence in the hall, and even among the crowd at the door and the windows, and then a voice called out, 'Why don't we ask Tiémoko to begin?'

'If Tiémoko wishes to begin, I am willing,' Konaté said.

Tiémoko was seated in his customary place in the third row. He rose heavily, his bull neck seeming even more massive than usual. The sweating in his palms bothered him, and he folded his arms across his chest. Before speaking, he flicked his tongue over his lips, and his strong, white teeth bit down on them, hard. He knew very well what he must do, but his tongue rebelled against it. 'Ah,' he thought, 'if Bakayoko were here in my place, he could make them understand, right away!'

The eyes of everyone there went from Tiémoko to Diara, and from Diara back to Tiémoko. Diara's appearance troubled them. Where was his normal dignity, his splendid bearing? Deep lines, like scars, ran down from the bridge of his nose and circled the corners of his mouth, his eyes were glassy, and the tight skin around his nostrils was grey. Their hearts constricted at the sight of him, as if they were in the presence of a dying man. And Sadio, watching his father, felt that he, too, was dying, slowly and painfully. There was no hatred or bitterness in him, towards anyone, but just a sort of dazed incomprehension. He would gladly have taken his father's place and had even asked to be allowed to do so. Now he had a feeling of being lost, and like the sacred dancers of some parts of Central Africa he 'buried his countenance in his soul'.

In the silence which followed the moment when Tiémoko rose to his feet, the same voice which had called for him to begin was heard again. 'Well, Tié,' it said, 'we are listening,' and another voice said, 'Yes, go ahead, speak.'

And at last Tiémoko was able to open his mouth. 'I promised you,' he said, 'that we would take care of any renegades, and we have done it. But, is beating people really a proper way to convince them of anything?'

It was a big question he had asked, and since no one ventured an answer he went on, 'I know that some men are like mules, and sometimes you have to hit them just to make them move, but this kind of beating is no real solution, especially when we are all together in this thing, when we are all sharing the same hardships. Why, then, must we judge Diara, and why should I be here to judge him, when you all know that Diara is my uncle? If I ask why to this, then I must also ask why to the whole question of the strike, and the white men, and the machines.'

The words came to him with such difficulty that he seemed to be moaning rather than speaking.

'What I have to say is very difficult for me. If Bakayoko were here, he would have understood me and helped me to make you understand. As it is, I will have to go back to the beginning of this story of the renegades . . .'

This is the story Tiémoko told of what had happened.

About ten o'clock one morning, when the strike had been going on for several weeks, the strikers had all come to the union office in a state of great confusion. Every one of them had received an order drafting him back to work on the railroad. It seemed like an actual mobilization order, and they had no idea of what to do. Konaté had done his best to calm their fear and told them to leave the draft orders with him. Two days later, Tiémoko, recording the orders, discovered that five of them were missing. It could mean only one thing – the five men who had received those orders had deserted their comrades. The idea of a punitive expedition came to him at once and was readily accepted by the strike committee; all the more readily because, at that particular time, about twenty of the strikers had just been jailed.

The first two strike-breakers were trapped in the Place Maginot, almost in front of the police station. There was a brief scuffle, and then the men of Tiémoko's commando group had taken them to their own homes and administered their rough form of justice.

Two of the others were caught later, but Tiémoko decided that their punishment should not take place in the relative privacy of their homes; he wanted to make a public example of them. He chose a dead-end street between the statue of Borgnies-Desborde and the church for the purpose, and when his men had done their work the two deserters were forced to keep to their beds for several days. But from that time on the battle lines were drawn between Tiémoko's commando group and the authorities.

Since that day, Diara had been escorted everywhere he went by five policemen. His two wives lived at some distance from each other, and whenever he stayed with one of them both the commandos and the police were on guard outside. Tiémoko had placed men all around the station, and he scarcely slept himself, but he was forced to watch helplessly as Diara came and went. Returning to the union office empty-handed after one such vigil, he had been enraged to learn that Diara had begun forcing the wives of the strikers to leave the train whenever they attempted to visit one of the neighbouring towns.

Tiémoko began reinforcing his group of volunteers. Konaté, who had other things on his mind, was of no use to him in this, but he did enroll his young cousin Sadio, Diara's own son, who joined the commando group out of a spirit of adventure and without knowing much about what it was doing.

A short time after this, the one train that ran every week was forbidden to the wives of the strikers, but the European employees and the soldiers who were functioning as mechanics and station masters were careful not to molest or annoy anyone. As for Diara, he was still the only Sudanese who was working on the line. When Tiémoko thought about it he became so furious that, if he had been face to face with his uncle, he might have killed him. Sadio still played his part in the commando group and did as he was ordered, but without much conviction. He was well aware that his father was behaving badly towards his comrades, but he thought that they would never go so far as to beat him.

At last Tiémoko could stand it no longer and decided to risk pursuing his quarry into the station itself. He told his cousin to wait for him in front of the Chamber of Commerce and started off by himself. The streets that led to the station were swarming with people. Automobiles and carts were parked at every corner, and a long line of women was waiting patiently in front of the big general store owned by the Lebanese. Some children were playing in the shade of a huge flame tree, and emaciated dogs ran in and out of the crowds, growling angrily at everyone.

To reach the station, it was necessary to pass through a barbed-wire fence guarded by infantrymen and sailors. There was just one opening, scarcely wide enough for two people to walk abreast. In the courtyard behind the fence a group of legionnaires lounged about, laughing and joking. As Tiémoko went through the entrance he put his hand up to his face, as if he had something in his eye. He had no wish to be recognized by the militia-men.

Covered with sweat, he came at last to the central hall of the station, where a vast crush of people was gathered, waiting hopefully for a train that might never come. Every corner of the hall was crowded with men, women, and children, seated on the ground or resting on whatever baggage they were carrying – boxes and cases of every size, rolls of clothing, animal skins or matting, sacks of dried grass and herbs. A fearful stench filled the air and flowed out of the waiting-room, on to the covered porches and the tracks, where still more people waited. The walls and floors were covered with dripping, spreading stains of spit, dyed red from the chewing of cola nuts, or black from plugs of tobacco. Clouds of flies swarmed over gourds which still held some remnant of food and clustered around the sandals which were scattered everywhere, as if waiting for their owners to return. The station looked like the camp of a conquered army, carrying with it its plunder, its wounded, its dead, and its limitless vermin.

Tiémoko was too preoccupied with the angry mission which had brought him here to pay much attention to the spectacle. He glanced briefly at the closed and barred service doors and the deserted ticket booths and then went over to a woman who was bouncing a baby on her knees.

'Woman,' he said, 'do you know if the train from Kati has arrived?'

'Yes, it has, and it left again a few minutes ago.'

As she was speaking, he heard someone call, '*Hé*, Tié!' and saw a man he knew leaning against one of the ticket booths. The man straightened up and said to the people who were standing around him, 'He's one of the strikers.'

When they heard this, a little circle of curious people formed around Tiémoko.

'Brother,' the man went on, smiling, 'when is this strike going to end?'

'I don't know,' Tiémoko answered. 'Perhaps tonight, perhaps tomorrow.' He knew very well that there was no chance of the strike ending, either that night or the next day, but he was beginning to be a little alarmed at seeing himself surrounded like this. He tried to slip away from the crowd but to no avail.

'Do you work here?' one of the men asked. He was a big fellow, tall and straight as the trunk of a tree.

'Yes,' Tiémoko replied.

'Well, then, tell us what this strike is all about. Don't you ever think about people like us, who have to stay here and wait a week or more for a train? Look here – this is my daughter ...' He took a pretty girl of sixteen or seventeen by the hand and pushed her forward. 'She was supposed to join her husband at Tamba-Counda, and now she is just waiting, like all the rest of us ...' His arm made a sweeping gesture towards the throng in the hall. 'Everyone says that you don't want to go back to work. Do you think the trains belong to you? They don't – no more than they did to your fathers – but you decide to stop working, just like that, without thinking about other people. And yet you workmen, of all people, should be satisfied with what you have. You don't have to worry about drought or rain or taxes, and you don't have any expenses. Why should you prevent these farmers from going where they want to go?'

The man had seized Tiémoko by the shoulder, like a father reprimanding a child. He had the air of someone who was accustomed to giving orders. A little skull cap of cotton, set on the back of his head, left his enormous forehead free of any shadow, and his eyes were clear. For a moment he was silent, and then he said, 'Look at all of these poor people! One train a week, and that one is like a jungle! And on top of that, most of them have had nothing to eat for days.'

'Neither have we,' Tiémoko said. 'We have had nothing ...'

'If you have nothing, it's your own fault,' the man said, 'and it's as it

should be. Some of you are in prison, and that is as it should be, too.'
He lowered his voice. 'You should tell your comrades to go back to
work.'

'I will tell them – but let me go now please. The "soldiers" don't like
to see us here.' By 'soldiers' Tiémoko meant the militia-men, because
he had recognized that this man must be a retired watchman. He was
beginning to feel very uneasy and had even forgotten why he had come
to the station. 'If they should spot me, I'll be good for a trip to jail
myself.'

The woman to whom he had first spoken rose to her feet, holding the
baby in her arms. 'Let him go,' she said. 'He's not the only one who has
stopped working, and he can't make the trains run again all by himself.'

'You don't know anything about men like him. In my day we used to
throw them all in prison. I probably should call a watchman now.'

'Don't do that, Uncle,' the woman implored.

Tiémoko felt the hand on his shoulder relax its grip, and without
waiting for any further discussion he made his way hurriedly through
the crowd. But he didn't breathe freely again until he was past the
barbed-wire fence and out of reach of the soldiers.

Lost in his thoughts, he walked right by Sadio at the corner where he
had told him to wait.

'Tié!' Diara's son called. 'I was beginning to get worried.'

Tiémoko gestured to the young man to follow him and walked on
silently, his head bowed. A horde of conflicting sentiments and confused ideas seemed to be doing battle in his mind. At Bakayoko's urg-
ing, he had done a great deal of reading, and he had not always
understood what he read, but now a single phrase came back to him,
and he murmured it half aloud, as if he were intoning a prayer.

'It is not necessary to be right to argue, but to win it is necessary
both to be right and never to falter.'

'Are you reciting the Koran?' Sadio asked, in astonishment.

Tiémoko seemed not to have heard him and went on repeating the
phrase like a litany. He could not remember clearly where he had read
it, but he did remember what Bakayoko had said about it.

They crossed the park in silence, and then Tiémoko said suddenly,
'Let's go to Bakayoko's house.'

'What for?' Sadio asked. 'The others are waiting for us.'

'You don't want them to beat your father, do you?'

'That's a hell of a question!'

'Well, then, come with me, before it's too late.'

Tiémoko had remembered where he read the phrase that had come to him like a ray of light in the darkness, and now he was in a hurry. As they walked he explained briefly why he had been delayed in the station.

'I don't see the connection between that and going to Bakayoko's now,' Sadio said.

'You will see. This strike is like a school, for all of us. We have punished some people for what they have done, but is that a good thing?'

'I don't know, but in any case they haven't gone back to work.'

'Right; they haven't gone back. But is that enough, for the future?'

'Are you asking me that?' Sadio said, completely baffled.

Tiémoko himself was tormented by his inability to explain this phrase which resounded so clearly in his ears and seemed so true to his mind.

'Look, Sadio, your father is my father's brother; you are my cousin. Your honour is also mine; your family's shame is my family's, and the shame of our whole country, the dishonour of all of our families together. That is why we cannot beat your father.'

'I knew that you were a friend, and not just a relative.'

'Don't speak too soon. We won't punish my uncle as we have punished the others, but suppose we should decide to try him, before all of the workers?'

'What! Have you lost your mind? Do you know what you are saying? My father — there, in front of everyone — and everyone insulting him, disgracing him! I'd rather die than....'

'It's not a question of dying, cousin. It's a question of learning, and of winning. It's a question of doing what is right, and of doing it as men should.'

They had arrived at the compound of the Bakayokos as they spoke, and after the customary greetings had been exchanged Tiémoko addressed himself to Fa Keïta, who had been talking quietly with old Niakoro.

'I came to borrow a book,' he said. 'Ibrahim told me that I might use them when I needed them.'

'What my son has is yours,' Niakoro said.

'I will ask his daughter to help you,' Fa Keïta added, and called, 'Ad'jibid'ji, Ad'jibid'ji!'

Then, speaking to Sadio, he asked, 'And your father, is he well?'

'God be thanked,' Sadio answered, frowning, 'God be thanked, he is well, Fa Keïta.'

'*Hé*,' Niakoro said, 'you are Diara's son? *Hé*, how the children grow up! To think that I knew your grandparents. The Diaras are people of a good line. Come closer, and let me look at you.'

Sadio bent over a little, and the old woman put her hand up to touch his cheeks and his forehead, and the contact of her fingers against his skin made her realize again how old she was.

Ad'jibid'ji came out to the veranda where they were gathered, and Fa Keïta said, 'Tiémoko has come for some books.'

'Only one, Fa Keïta; there is just one that I need.'

The child showed no pleasure at the sight of Tiémoko. She had seen him only three times since the beginning of the strike, but on each of these occasions she had been aware of a surge of anger she could not explain, even to herself.

'Yes, Grandfather,' she said. 'Father told me he might. Follow me, Tiémoko.'

Sadio remained with the two old people and, as Ad'jibid'ji watched, Tiémoko rummaged through the shelves in the main room of the house. He had to search for a good ten minutes, but at last he pulled out a volume wrapped in blue paper.

'May I see what you are taking?' Ad'jibid'ji asked.

He showed her the title, and she read it aloud, '*La Condition Humaine*'.

She had read the book, without understanding it, and she couldn't help wondering if Tiémoko would understand. She took an index card from a little cardboard box and studied it carefully. 'Every time you take a book you don't bring it back until five or six months later. I hope you won't keep that one for ever.'

'What?' Tiémoko demanded. 'Does your father keep a record of everyone who borrows his books?'

'Books are rare, and expensive, and *petit père* spends all of his money buying them. But if it makes you feel any better, Konaté has six of them, including one he borrowed twelve months ago.'

'He's the person I want to see about this book.'

'Well, perhaps if you read it together it will go faster.' There was a note of sarcasm in Ad'jibid'ji's voice, but Tiémoko seemed not to notice.

When he went out to the veranda again, Assitan approached him. 'We haven't seen you in a long time, Tiémoko. Since Ibrahim left we never seem to see anyone.'

'Ah, woman, we have a lot to do . . .'

'What?' Fa Keïta asked. 'Chasing after your own uncle?'

'We are doing it for the good of everyone, Fa Keïta; and we will have need of you in the days to come.'

'Of me? After the way you treated me at the union hall the last time? And you, especially! What will you need me for?'

'For this matter of my uncle. When he is taken, which will be soon, we are going to try him.'

Keïta's eyes opened very wide, and the ritual scars seemed to bite deeper into his face. Old Niakoro looked terrified. For a moment she remained open-mouthed in astonishment, and then she said, 'You are not a bearer of good news, Tiémoko. Sadio, what do you think of this?'

'What can I think?' the young man answered, close to tears. 'I don't agree, but it isn't up to me.'

'Tiémoko,' the old woman said, 'have you thought about this? You are not *toubabs*! How can you judge a man who is respected by everyone?'

'Everything we need is in this book,' Tiémoko said.

'That book was written by the *toubabs*,' Fa Keïta said scornfully.

'And the machines were built by the *toubabs*! The book belongs to Ibrahim Bakayoko, and right here, in front of you, I have heard him say that neither the laws nor the machines belong to any one race!'

'The *toubabs* do all kinds of things that humiliate and debase us, and now you want to do the same.'

'There is no law in this book that you would refuse to admit. It's not an unbreakable set of rules, it's . . . it's a way of thinking.'

Tiémoko was unable to explain what he really meant. His face twitched with the effort of concentration, and little streaks of red appeared in his eyes.

'In any case, don't count on me,' Fa Keïta said. 'And when it is really a case of your uncle, and not of a character in a book, you will not do it.'

'If it was my own father, I would do it, Fa Keïta; I swear it on the tomb of my ancestors! And if it were you, Ibrahim Bakayoko would do the same thing.'

All of the contradictory emotions he felt were still revolving in Tiémoko's head, like the humming of a motor he could not stop. He succeeded in controlling himself, however, and cut short the conversation.

'I hope that you will pass the night in peace,' he said. 'Come, cousin.'

And he went out, followed by the dazed, unhappy Sadio.

'I am going to put all of those books in the fire,' old Niakoro said, as soon as they were out of hearing.

'No, Grandmother!' Ad'jibid'ji cried. '*Petit père* would not like that!'

'There would be no point to it,' Fa Keïta said. 'It would change nothing.'

'But think of it! To allow the honour of such a good man to be dragged through the mud – a man of such a good family! It is the *toubabs* who are to blame for this. These children will never have white hairs – our world is falling apart.'

'No, woman; it was your son who said, "Our world is opening up".'

'Wait until that one comes back . . . I may be old, but I will know what to say to him. Who would have thought that we should live to see such things?'

Niakoro's hands were trembling, and she was forced to cling to the old man's arm as she rose, but then she pulled herself erect, turned, and went into the house. Behind the door there was a staircase of hard clay which led up to the terrace. Ad'jibid'ji was already climbing the steps, skipping up lightly, two at a time.

Still followed by Sadio, and cloaked in his new resolve as if by a protective armour, Tiémoko went directly to Konaté's house. Konaté had a diploma from the school and was the best educated of all the men on the committee, but at first he did not understand what Tiémoko meant and could only think of the necessity for avoiding arguments among themselves.

'No,' said Tiémoko, who was sitting on a strip of matting. 'We cannot be held back by that. After the trial is held, everyone will understand, and they will know that they must not go back.'

Konaté was afraid that such a move would destroy the unity of the strikers, which thus far had been very well maintained. He was perplexed, and to gain time he said, 'Why don't you leave the book with me, and tomorrow I will tell you what I think we should do.'

'No, Konaté, no! You won't find in this book what you think you are going to find. It's up to me to convince you, and if I don't succeed . . .'

The secretary of the union was growing more and more uneasy. He tried another argument. 'I'm not the only one to be consulted, you know. We would have to have a meeting of the local committee. There is one scheduled for day after tomorrow.'

'No!' Tiémoko was risking everything now, in the hope of gaining everything. 'We must have the meeting tonight. We can call it for seven o'clock.'

And so the meeting had been held that same night, with everyone on the committee present, and only one question before them – the case of Diara. But Tiémoko found himself alone with his conviction, faced with eleven worried and hesitant men. To judge another man this way was not a part of their prerogatives, and the strangeness of the idea made them uncomfortable and uncertain. Tiémoko spared no effort to convince them. He had eaten nothing since early morning, but the intensity of his emotion had put his hunger to sleep.

'It is not because I ask it that you must decide,' he said, 'but because this case of Diara must be made to serve as an example.'

'It may be that you are right,' Konaté said, 'but suppose the others do not support us? What do we do then? The whole success or failure of the strike may hang on this decision. The risk is great, and I ask all of you to think about it very carefully.'

The twelve men broke up into little groups to discuss the matter, speaking sometimes almost in whispers, and sometimes in vehement exclamations. The primary obstacle to any decision was their fear of not being upheld by the rest of the strikers. Tiémoko went from one group to another, repeating his arguments, trying to communicate his own conviction to them, and although his phrases were broken and often confused there was no mistaking the depth of his feeling.

At last one of the men said, 'Tell me, Tié, why do you attach so much importance to this trial? Is it to prove that you are a leader, or just because you have said that it must take place?'

'Neither,' Tiémoko replied. His face was dripping with sweat, and his nerves were stretched to the breaking point. 'Neither the one nor the other. I don't have to look for a motive for something that is a motive itself. I want us to move forward to a point where it will no longer be necessary to punish men as we have in the past.'

'That is all very well,' Konaté said, 'but right now we couldn't try Diara if we wanted to. He is constantly guarded by the police.'

'I know, Konaté — he is protected as well as the governor in his residence. But if you leave it to me, you will have him here before you, very soon.'

And in the end Tiémoko had won, through simple obstinacy and the fatigue of the others. One of them spoke for all the rest. 'Very well, Tié,' he said. 'You have convinced us. We will go along with your idea.'

A few minutes after this, Tiémoko set out for his own house. The ground beneath his feet was still warm, although it was three o'clock in the morning.

As he walked, he considered all of the points of the plan he had in mind, and a sense of exultation swept through him. For the first time in his life, an idea of his was going to play a part in the lives of thousands

of others. It was not pride or vanity he was experiencing, but the aston-
ishing discovery of his worth as a human being. Walking very straight
in the deserted street, he began singing aloud an ancient Bambara
hymn to the founder of the empire of Mali, the *Soundiata*.

All the next day he didn't leave his house. His wife, a pretty little
woman with high cheekbones and slender features, told everyone who
came to the door, 'He spent the night with a book.'

Towards evening, Konaté came to see him.

'Are you ill, brother?' he asked.

'No, I have been studying. You know, when this strike is over we must
organize courses in reading. This book is very complicated, and I am
not sure that I agree with everything the author says.'

'After what you told me yesterday? Are you going crazy, Tiémoko?'

'Crazy? Oh no, don't worry about that! By the way, can you get me
three policemen's uniforms for tomorrow?'

'Policemen's uniforms? What for?'

'To catch my uncle!'

'*Hé*, Tiémoko, you are a surprising man!' Konaté said.

When he received the uniforms, Tiémoko gave two of them to men
he had chosen carefully and kept the third for himself.

The next morning, very early, they had gone to Diara's house, arriving there well before the real policemen.

. . . . . .

The audience in the union hall had listened to Tiémoko's story in total
silence, and in telling it he had recovered some of his normal self-
assurance. Before sitting down, he summed up the case against his
uncle.

'Diara is a worker, like all the rest of us, and like the rest of us he
voted for the strike – for an unlimited strike, until we won what we were
asking for – but he has not kept his word. He got help from the union,
enough to live on, as we all did, and he has used it, but he has not
repaid any of it since he went back to work. But more than this, he has
informed on the women who are supporting us so valiantly, and he has
forced them to get off the trains whenever they have tried to use them.
That is why I wanted some of the women to be here today, although
there were a lot of people who didn't agree with that idea.

'That is all I have to say, and now it is up to others to say what they
think. But let no one forget that while we are talking here, many of our
comrades are in prison.'

When Tiémoko sat down, the silence was so profound that it seemed almost as if the big meeting hall had suddenly emptied. Diara had drawn his legs back under his chair and sat so stiffly he might have been made of stone. Looking at his father, Sadio saw that his eyes were empty of all feeling, lost in a far away past where there was no strike, no place of judgement, and no accused.

Suddenly a woman's voice was heard. 'I would like to say . . .'

Several irritated voices called, 'Quiet!'

'Who spoke down there, at the back?' Konaté demanded.

'It's one of these silly women!' someone said.

'But I told the women to come,' Tiémoko said. 'They have important things to say. Come forward, Hadi Dia.'

A woman with heavily tattooed lips and a face criss-crossed with scars rose and walked to the front of the hall. For an occasion such as this, she had obviously thought it a good idea to put on all of the best clothes she owned. Tiémoko made a place for her beside him on the bench.

'Hadi Dia,' he said, 'tell everyone now what you have already told your neighbours. You can speak here without fear and without shame.'

The woman had a hare lip, and when she opened her mouth to speak the people nearest her could see the gaps between her teeth. 'It was the other day . . . that is, it was about two weeks ago . . . I was with Coumba, her sister Dienka, and the third wife of . . . of . . .'

'The names are not important. Go on.'

'We took the "smoke of the savanna" to go to Kati. Diara asked us to show our tickets, and when we got to Kati he came back to us with a *toubab* soldier. He said something to him in the *toubab* language, and the soldier took away the tickets we had to come back, but he didn't give us back the money for them. I told the whole story to my husband when we got home.'

'Hadi Dia, is all of what you have said true?' Konaté asked.

'Ask Diara.'

'All right, Hadi Dia, you may return to your seat. And you Diara, have you anything to say?'

The accused remained motionless and silent, while the woman went back to her own place. It was the first time she had ever spoken at a meeting of the men, and she was filled with pride. Another, older woman went up to speak, going this time directly to the stage. Her name was Sira, and she spoke rapidly and confidently.

'With us, it was on the way to Koulikoro – you all know the place where the train goes up a little rise between here and Koulikoro – he stopped the train and made us get off. Eight women alone, right in the middle of the brush! I tell you, he is nothing but a slave of the *toubabs*! Tiémoko is right – he should be crucified in the market place!'

'Thank you, Sira,' Konaté said, 'but you should tell only what you have seen. Go back to your seat.'

Two more women came forward and told of happenings that were more or less similar to the first ones, and after that there was a heavy silence in the hall. The idea of women addressing a meeting as important as this was still unfamiliar and disturbing. The men gazed absently at the stage, waiting for something to happen, their glances wandering from Konaté to Diara, and then to the unhappy figure of Sadio.

Suddenly a masculine voice said, 'I would like to speak,' and a towering, muscular workman got to his feet. His head was curiously shaved so that his hair formed a ring around his skull, and he seemed uncomfortable in his feast-day clothing. Everyone recognized him immediately as the first man who stopped work after the strike was called, and there was a murmur of approval from the audience. He was sure to have something to say, and it was right that he should speak.

He began by giving an account of his own actions during the strike, and of those of the men in his group, and only when he had completed this did he come to the case of Diara.

'Diara has behaved badly towards all of us,' he said. 'Yes, as God is my witness, he has done wrong. I am as sure of that as I am that some day I will be alone in my grave. When I told the men who worked with me to put down their tools, they did it as if we were all one man; and here today we are all still agreed to go on with the strike. But you, Diara – you are one of our elders; you should have guided us and helped us. Instead, you took the side of our enemies, and after you had betrayed us you spied on our women. We are not ashamed to admit that it is the women who are supporting us now, and you have betrayed them, too. For my part, I say that we should put Diara in prison – yes, that is just what we should do – put him in prison.'

'Brother,' someone in the hall said, 'you know that the prison belongs to the white men.'

'I know that, but we can build one!'

'And where would we get the money? We don't even have enough to feed a prisoner – not to mention that the *toubabs* would never let us do it anyway.'

'Everything you say is true, man – I know as well as you that the *toubabs* have stolen all of our rights, even the right to have a prison of

our own and punish our own; but that is no reason to defend a traitor!
If we can't put Diara in prison, we can at least do what the Koran
teaches us to do – we can have him scourged!'

The man had begun to shout, and the muscles of his face and neck
were contorted with anger. 'We should decide right now how many
lashes he will receive and who will be appointed to carry out the judgement!'

He sat down again, still muttering aloud, 'You are a traitor, Diara, a
traitor, a traitor!'

There was a turbulence of voices in the hall; everyone seemed to
want to speak at once. Some were in favour of flogging, while others still
thought that a means of imprisonment should be found, and one man
said that Diara should be made to turn in all the money he had
earned to the strike committee. Theories and ideas went from bench to
bench, and all sorts of advice were hurled at the members of the jury.
In the midst of the uproar, only the accused remained motionless, as if
he were not even present in the room. Once or twice, as the hearing
went on, he had asked himself, 'Why *did* I do it?' and the question
disturbed him, because he could not provide an answer. Surely it had
not been because he wanted money or jewels or fine clothes, richly
embroidered and starched? Had his pride made him seek the stimulant
that comes from holding power over others? He saw himself again,
giving orders to the women, with the policemen at his side. Had it been
the taste of flattery that had separated him from the others, or the
sense of well-being that comes with a full stomach? Or had it been
simply the cold emptiness of his own kitchen? The questions mingled
and blurred in Diara's mind and then disappeared completely, leaving
him alone again before the crowd in the hall, his eyes wide open but
unseeing, his lower lip trembling.

Fa Keïta, the Old One, had been present throughout the trial, with
Ad'jibid'ji sitting quietly beside him. He had been asked to be a member of the jury, but he had refused because he had not believed, until
the last minute, that the young people would actually carry out such a
plan. Now he rose slowly to his feet.

'I have a few grains of salt to contribute to the pot,' he said, and
then added, glancing in Tiémoko's direction, 'if, that is, you are willing
to accept my salt.'

Konaté said, 'Whatever you have to say, Old One, will be listened to
with both ears.'

'A long time ago,' Fa Keïta said, 'before any of you were born, everything that happened happened within a framework, an order that was

our own, and the existence of that order was of great importance in our lives. Today, no such framework exists. There are no castes among people, no difference in the quality of grain or of the bread that is made from the grain; there are no weavers, no artisans in metal, no makers of fine shoes.

'I think it is the machine which has ground everything together this way and brought everything to a single level. Ibrahim Bakayoko said to me, not long ago: "When we have succeeded in stirring up the people of this country, and making them one, we will go on and do the same thing between ourselves and the people on the other side of the ocean." How all this will come about I do not know, but we can see it happening already, before our eyes. Now, for instance, Tiémoko has had this idea, which he took from a book written in the white man's language. I have seen more suns rise than any of you, but this is the first time in my life that I have seen a ... a ... What is it called, child?' he asked, leaning towards Ad'jibid'ji.

'Tribunal, Grandfather.'

'A tribunal,' Fa Keïta repeated tonelessly. 'And I think that Tiémoko has done well. We all wanted the strike; we voted for it, and Diara voted with us. But then Diara went back to work. You say that he is a traitor, and perhaps you are right. If we are all to win, then we should live as brothers, and no one should go back unless his brothers do.

'I have heard you calling for punishment, but I know that you will not kill Diara. Not because some of you would not have the courage or the will, but because others would not let you do it, and I would be the first of them. If you imitate the hirelings of your masters, you will become like them, hirelings and barbarians. For godly men, it is a sacrilege to kill, and I pray that God will forbid such a thought to take root in your minds.

'You have spoken also of flogging, of beating Diara. The child who is scated beside me is punished that way very seldom, although my father beat me often, and the same thing is probably true of most of you. But blows correct nothing. As for Diara, you have already beaten him – you have struck him where every human worthy of the name is most vulnerable. You have shamed him before his friends, and before the world, and in doing that you have hurt him far more than you could by any bodily punishment. I cannot know what tomorrow will bring, but in seeing this man before me I do not think that there is one among us who will be tempted to follow in his footsteps.'

In the stillness, some of the women could be heard sniffling, trying to hold back tears.

'And now,' Fa Keïta said, 'I apologize for having abused your kindness. Diara, lift up your head. You have been the instrument of destiny here — it was not you who was on trial; it was the owners of the machines. Thanks to you, no one of us now will give up the fight.'

The old man looked around him for a moment and then left the hall in silence. Ad'jibid'ji remained seated on the bench.

Tiémoko had listened avidly to Fa Keïta's words, but even as he told himself, 'This is what I should have said,' he was angry with the Old One. He had moved the crowd with his gentle words and the calmness of his voice. 'I should have struck harder,' Tiémoko thought, 'and answered him firmly. He has beaten me now, because I don't know enough about these things, but it will be different next time. I must write to Bakayoko tonight.'

All of the earlier heat of argument seemed to have vanished from the hall. Men and women looked at each other furtively, and then one by one they began to walk silently towards the door.

While all of this was taking place, the eight members of the jury had not said a word. Now one of them rose and put on his cap, and two others followed his example. Konaté took the director of the Koulikoro committee by the arm, and the two men walked off together, conversing in lowered voices. Tiémoko himself started towards the door, and, as he passed the bench where Ad'jibid'ji sat, regarding him with a mixture of curiosity and dislike, he thought, 'There is more in that child's head than in all the rest of this hall.' His irritation with Fa Keïta had turned against himself, and the line of his jawbone hardened. 'It isn't a question of being right,' he muttered furiously, it's a question of winning!'

Soon after he had gone, there were just three people still in the meeting hall: Diara, his son Sadio, and Ad'jibid'ji, sitting quietly on her bench. Diara was unable to rid his mind of the thought of the woman Hadi Dia. He had held the votive lamb at her christening, and today she had denounced him; she had insulted him in public, and he knew that a wound like this would never heal. Sadio was still slumped in his chair. His fingers toyed mechanically with the papers scattered on the table, and tears ran down his cheeks. He was conscious that, from this day forward, his father could be reviled and insulted by anyone, perhaps even beaten, and he would have no defence. And he knew that wherever he himself went, people would look at him and say, 'Your father is a traitor'. Not one of the men in the hall, not one of his friends, had even spoken to him before he left. He was alone, desperately alone. He looked up towards the door and saw Ad'jibid'ji, who seemed to be following the silent drama on the stage with a kind of sadistic pleasure. Her eyes remained fixed on Sadio for a moment, and then turned to Diara, as if she were engraving the scene on her mind and wanted to be sure she missed nothing. From the intensity with which she regarded Diara, she might have been listening for the sound of his tears.

At last, Sadio got up and moved across the stage towards his father. A feverish trembling racked his slender body, and he seemed unnaturally tall beside the broken figure in the chair. He opened his lips to gulp in air, wanting to speak, and then he just fell to his knees at his father's side. Diara bent over the figure of his son and cried aloud, like a child who has just been punished.

· · · · · ·

In all this period, there was one group in Thiès that lived entirely apart, separated from both the workers and their wives and the closed circle of the company itself. It was the group of the apprentices, and because of them a series of momentous events was building up at the very moment when the deceptively calm city seemed just to be sinking deeper into the apathy caused by the strike.

Magatte, Doudou's apprentice, had rapidly become the unquestioned leader of the little band. There were twelve of them, of whom the youngest was fourteen and the oldest seventeen. In the beginning, the strike had seemed to them to be just a sort of prolonged holiday; the older people appeared to have forgotten them completely, and they savoured their freedom as if it were a new and exciting game. Then, as money ran out and the days grew harsh, it occurred to their families that they could be useful, and they were sent out to search for chickens that had wandered off or to pick the 'monkey bread' of the baobab trees, the only fruit available at that season of the year. For a time it amused their elders to see them running and jumping from one compound to another, ferreting out anything that was edible and happy with the task; but soon there were no more chickens to be recaptured, and even in the ravine which led to the airfield the baobab trees had been stripped of their fruit. Every morning then their shouting and running through the courtyards was broken up with cries of, 'Go and amuse yourselves somewhere else!'

On the outskirts of N'Ginth, the largest suburb of Thiès, there was an old baobab tree standing by a path that led into the fields. Its enormous trunk was completely hollow, and its leafless branches made it look like some gigantic old woman waving her arms in the air. No one knew exactly how old it was, but it was certainly the oldest tree in the district. The moment the apprentices discovered it they knew that this would be their future home. They scraped out the inside of the trunk to form a secret hiding place and built an elaborate ladder of huge nails up the side of the tree. They would sit in there for hours, talking or sleeping, but one of them was always on guard, astride a great branch just outside the entrance. Their discussions were invariably concerned with the same subject – the films they had seen in the days before the strike. They told the stories of every one of them over and over again, but never without feverish interruptions: 'You're forgetting the part where ...' or, 'No, that's not the way he killed the Indian!' Next to Western films, war films were their favourites. Sometimes, as a change from their enforced inactivity, they played war games themselves. The old baobab became the enemy, and they bombarded it with stones, but after a time this became too simple and they turned their attention to the swarms of little snakes and lizards in the fields around them. Occasionally they had killed as many as a hundred of them in a single day. They would gather the dead animals together in one place, shouting to each other with each new addition to the pile, 'That one didn't say his prayers today!' for they had always been taught that any serpent who neglected his daily prayers would die before the night.

One day, when they were playing idly with a hedgehog in the field beside the baobab tree, Souley came and sat down beside Magatte.

'We ought to have some slingshots,' he said.

Magatte chewed thoughtfully on a blade of grass. 'Where would we get the rubber to make them?'

Séne, the son of Séne Maséne, joined them, carrying the hedgehog, which had curled itself into a spiny little ball. 'It's a good idea,' he said. 'We should have some slingshots.'

'I saw some inner tubes for bicycles at Salif's,' Gorgui said, scratching his egg-shaped head. He still had a bad case of ringworm, and his forehead and the back of his neck were painted blue again.

'Automobile inner tubes would be better,' Magatte said.

'Maybe we could find some at Aziz's shop. He has a truck.'

'That's true – I saw it last week in the court behind his shop.'

'But how could we get in?' Séne asked, rolling the hedgehog about in the palm of his hand.

'Put that animal down,' Magatte said, chopping at his wrist. 'We have to make a plan.'

The hedgehog fell to the ground and vanished almost instantly, and the apprentices gathered in a circle around Magatte. Their conference went on all through the afternoon.

The next morning they set to work on the execution of their plan. The shop of Aziz the Syrian was located on one of the corners of the Place de France, and behind the shop was a large courtyard surrounded by a bamboo fence. Magatte opened a small gap between some of the stalks and peered through. The truck was standing in the centre of the yard.

'I'll go in, with Souley and Séne,' he said. 'Gorgui, you stay in front of the shop and watch out for Aziz. If you see him coming this way, you whistle to warn us. The rest of you keep an eye on the square.'

'Look out,' one of the boys said suddenly, 'there's a policeman now.'

The group promptly improvised a noisy game to distract attention from Magatte and his two assistants, who were cutting a space in the bamboo wall large enough to pass through. The policeman, however, was watching the passers-by in the square. His red *tarboosh* was set precisely above his ears and he carried his heavy night stick with military precision. A band of noisy children was of no interest to him. At last he walked off, and the game subsided as quickly as it had begun.

Magatte finally succeeded in cutting through the wires that held the bamboo stalks together and crawled into the courtyard, motioning to his two lieutenants to follow him.

'There's no one here,' he whispered hoarsely.

'I'm scared,' Séne said.

They made their way slowly across the courtyard, walking on their toes and holding their arms tautly at their sides, like tightrope walkers. The wheels of the truck, an ancient Chevrolet, had been dismounted, and the chassis rested on some large wooden cases, serving as blocks. They had almost reached it when the sound of an opening door made them hurl themselves to the ground. They scrambled on their stomachs into the shelter of the cases.

Aziz's wife had come out on the porch at the back of the house. She was wearing no veil, and in the shelter of a flimsy mosquito net she began to take off her clothes. When she was completely naked she began to bathe her body with a glove of towelling material. The colour of her skin, which was as white as chalk, was not the least of the surprises to the frightened boys. They were observing her every movement, in silent astonishment, when they heard a warning whistle, followed almost immediately by the sound of Aziz's voice, talking to his wife from the interior of the house. The conversation seemed to last for an eternity, but finally the woman put on her robe and went back inside.

Gorgui breathed a sigh of relief. 'There's an inner tube in there,' he said, gesturing to the driver's compartment of the truck.

Magatte opened the door on their side of the truck, seized the rubber tube, and dropped back beside the others. 'Let's get out of here,' he said.

The three lithe little bodies never stood up from the dust of the ground until they reached the fence. Séne, who was last, kept glancing fearfully over his shoulder, but the porch was empty.

A half hour later the whole group was gathered again beside the baobab tree. They set to work in an atmosphere of lazy triumph, and that day the anatomy of the Syrian woman replaced the films as the topic of discussion.

The following morning a band of light-hearted apprentices went hunting, armed with brand-new slingshots and little balls of lead. Hummingbirds were the targets of their first expedition, and then it was the turn of the lizards again. Anything that showed itself in the grass or moved in the wind was fair game. At the slightest movement or sound, a dozen projectiles were zeroed in on the suspected enemy. By noon they had collected several crows, two magpies, and a bird none of them could identify.

'We have to learn to shoot these things properly,' Magatte said.

'Yes, general,' replied the eleven soldiers of an army whose lowest-ranking member was a lieutenant.

The dead birds were hung from the branches of the baobab, and stones and lead pellets began whistling through the air in an organized drill. Each time a goal was scored, the victor marked a stripe on his naked arm with the point of a charred stick.

At night they would return to their homes tired but happy. Their parents, preoccupied with their own troubles, paid no attention to their wandering, and since they got their own meals out at their tree no one even bothered about feeding them. Sometimes they would be seen with the groups of the other children, but they rarely took part in their games any more. They wore the slings around their necks as though they were strings of prayer beads and behaved like guardians of a secret which had set them apart from ordinary humans.

One day, however, Dieynaba, who had noticed their constant absences, stopped her son as he was on his way to join the others.

'Where are you going, Gorgui?' she demanded.

'I'm going to look for Magatte, Mother.'

'What do you do all day, you and the others?'

'Nothing much – we usually go walking in the fields.'

'Well, instead of wandering around doing nothing, like a bunch of dumb animals, why don't you do your wandering in the *toubabs*' district? Some of them have chickens running around loose ...'

It took Gorgui a minute to realize what his mother meant, but then he went off like a shot and didn't stop running until he reached the baobab tree. The idea of raiding the chicken coops of the white men took their breath away at first, but the more they thought about it the more exciting it became.

'Do we go, general?'

'We go, soldiers!'

The first expedition was so successful that they didn't even have to use their slingshots. They were back at home before noon, and each one of them was carrying at least one or two chickens. They were overwhelmed with praise for their daring, and their chests swelled proudly above the sharp-boned cage of their ribs. From that moment on they had found a new reason for their existence.

Each morning one of them would go out on a scouting trip, and that night the whole band would pay a visit to the selected spot. On their return, the women would be waiting and sometimes would even come out to meet them, crying, 'Our men are back!' Thus exonerated from any feelings of guilt, they redoubled their zeal in the hunt and only the failure of a mission caused them any misgiving.

Following their success with Dieynaba's idea, Penda conceived another one. She summoned the apprentices to her cabin, and, when they came out after a long conference, their faces were marked with the expression of men who have embarked on a serious venture. Penda herself was carrying two large cloth bags. Dieynaba was sitting alone in the courtyard at the time, puffing at a new mixture of leaves in her pipe. She couldn't help smiling as she watched the little band walk off in the direction of the shop of Aziz, the Syrian.

The shopkeeper's father-in-law was stretched out on a chaise longue, sleeping, and Aziz himself was dozing behind the counter, occasionally inhaling deeply from a Turkish water pipe. The early afternoon heat seemed to have overcome him completely. Penda had chosen her time well. She went into the shop with her 'crew', as she called the apprentices, close on her heels.

Without moving an inch, Aziz said, 'What do you want?'

Acting as if she had already made her choice, Penda indicated a pile of cloth on the shelf behind the counter.

'The print?' Aziz said, turning his head, but without removing the tube of the water pipe from his mouth.

'No, the one next to it.'

'The muslin?'

'Is that really muslin?'

'You can see for yourself, woman!'

While this dialogue was taking place, the 'crew' had wasted no time. Three of them stood behind Penda, forming a screen, and behind them Magatte had pierced a hole in one of two enormous sacks of rice that stood between the glass doors of the shop. Into the opening he thrust a long tube whose other end he had placed in one of the bags Penda had been carrying. 'Well?' the Syrian said.

'No – don't bother getting up – but, tell me, is the muslin really good quality?' Penda glanced over her shoulder in time to see one of the boys dash off, with a well-filled bag on his shoulder.

The shopkeeper looked at her irritably, and the water in the bowl of his pipe gurgled as he inhaled again. 'Look, if you don't want anything, at least don't bother me.'

Séne had noticed that the shrinking sack of rice was beginning to fall off balance, and he gestured frantically. Penda took a few steps backward.

'Well, never mind about it. I just wanted to know how much it cost.'

'I don't sell anything at this hour. Come back at two o'clock,' Aziz said.

Penda had reached the door safely. 'He doesn't want to sell anything now,' she said. 'Let's go, children.'

It was high time. Just as she spoke, the sack of rice collapsed completely and fell over on its side. The band scattered through the alleys like a flight of quail.

The rice lasted for two days of a feasting and gaiety they had almost forgotten, but the exploit of Penda and her 'crew' was talked about for a week, and the Syrian shopkeeper was the butt of all kinds of jokes. After that, however, Penda seemed to lose interest in the apprentices; she had other ideas in her head now and was working to create a 'committee of women'. So the boys went back to the baobab tree, the hedgehogs, and marksmanship drills and boredom.

They had tasted the bitter fruits of danger and now nothing else had any flavour.

But one night, destiny, which has an infallible sense of timing, called out to them again.

The shadows were lengthening on the ground as the sun went down. From somewhere in the distance the mournful notes of a bugle could be heard, signalling the changing of the guard. The apprentices were walking across the field of the watchmen's camp in the twilight. No one paid any attention to them, and at the end of the field they came to the district administrator's house, standing in the centre of a well-tended garden. Not far from them some automobiles were parked beside the gateway.

Souley, the smallest of the group, was swinging his slingshot back and forth in his hand. Suddenly he stopped, picked up a stone, and placed it carefully in the leather sling. The rubber strips on either side stretched taut, the stone whistled through the air, and a headlight on one of the cars shattered noisily. For an instant the other boys were dumbfounded, but only for an instant. Then they began searching through their pockets, and the air was filled with the whistling of stones and pellets of lead, and the explosion of headlights, windshields, and windows. The watchmen came running out of their tents to see what was happening, but the band had already scattered. An hour later the windows, the showcases, and even the electric light bulbs of the station were serving as targets.

They had found a game to replace all the others. They waited until darkness had enlisted on their side, and then, moving in little groups to throw the guards and the soldiers off their track, they invaded the European quarter. Hidden behind the trunk of a tree, flattened against a wall or crouched in a ditch, they adjusted their slings, fired, and vanished into the shadows. Everything that shone in the night was a target, from windows to lamp posts. At daybreak the bulbs and the glass might be replaced, but it was a wasted effort. The following night the ground would again be littered with sparkling splinters.

They even pushed their luck so far as to attack the police station. Some of the older people did not approve of this latest manifestation of the 'crew's' activities, and there were even parents who forbade their sons to go out on the expeditions, with the result that General Magatte's army was reduced to seven soldiers. Others, however, could not help thinking that every window that broke, every light that went out, helped to establish a kind of balance: they were no longer alone in carrying the burden of the strike.

As for the Europeans, the feeling of constraint and uneasiness they had known for weeks gave place to panic. The patrols on the streets were reinforced, but, in spite of this, fear was an unwelcome guest in every house in the quarter. It was not so much the stones or the little balls of lead themselves as the thought of those black bodies slipping through the shadows that transformed every home into a fortress as soon as darkness came. Native servants were sent home, and men and women went to bed with weapons at their sides. At the slightest sound, nervous fingers reached out for the trigger of a pistol or the stock of a rifle. And, in the meantime, the members of the 'crew', exhausted from their work, slept the sleep of the just.

In between their nocturnal expeditions, they had acquired the habit of practising their marksmanship constantly, since they were determined to remain masters of their craft. Anything, living or dead, that could serve as a target was put to use. It was as a result of this that one evening, as they were wandering along the siding which connected with the main line from Saint-Louis, little Kâ, the youngest of the group, happened to notice a lizard basking in the last rays of the sun. His sling was already in his hand, and the child pulled back slowly on the rubber bands, sighted through the branches of the stick, and fired. The lizard leaped slightly and fell over on its back. They saw its little white belly twitch for a second against the crushed stones between the rails and then lie motionless. A second lizard thrust his nose from behind the wheel of a car and arrowed in the direction of a near-by wall. Seven projectiles instantly smashed into the dust around him or clattered against the rail he had leaped.

It was at this moment that Isnard appeared from behind the same car that had sheltered the lizard. His hand went to his pocket, and three shots rang out. Little Kâ received the first bullet and dropped without uttering a sound. Séne fell while he was still in the act of turning around, and the other children fled, screaming. Isnard's arm was trembling, but he continued firing until the magazine of the revolver was empty. One of the last bullets struck Gorgui in the leg, and he collapsed in the middle of the tracks.

For a moment Isnard just stood there, dazed, his arm still stretched out in front of him, holding the smoking gun. Then, with a mechanical gesture, he put it back in his pocket and began to run towards the European quarter, muttering breathlessly to himself, 'They were shooting at me! They were shooting at me!'

Magatte ran straight to the union office to tell the men what had happened. Breathless, his lips trembling, his eyes swimming with tears of shock, he tried to explain how he and his comrades had been hunting lizards when Isnard had suddenly appeared with a revolver, fired on them, and killed them all. At his first words everyone in the office moved out to the street, where there would be room for the others to join them. Lahbib and Boubacar, Doudou and Séne Masène, the father of one of the dead boys, were there already. They were joined almost immediately by Penda, who had taken to wearing a soldier's cartridge belt around her waist since she had been made a member of the strike committee.

The news spread like fire through the courtyards of the district, travelling from compound to compound and from main house to neighbouring cabins. Men, women, and children flowed into the streets by the hundreds, marching towards the railroad yards. The crowd swelled at every step and became a mass of running legs and shouting mouths, opened on gleaming white teeth or blackened stumps. The headcloths of the women fluttered convulsively, and a few lost scarves floated above the crowd for a moment before falling and being trampled in the dust. The women carried children in their arms or slung across their backs, and as they walked they gathered up weapons – heavy pestles, iron bars, and pick handles – and waved them at the sky like the standards of an army. On their faces, hunger, sleeplessness, pain, and fear had been graven into the single image of anger.

At last the crowd arrived at the siding, and the bodies of the two dead children were wrapped in white cloths, which were rapidly stained with blood. Gorgui was carried away, weeping and moaning, and the long cortège turned in the direction of home. This time the women were at its head, led by Penda, Dieynaba, and Mariame Sonko. As they passed before the houses of the European employees, their fury reached a screaming peak; fists were waved and a torrent of oaths and insults burst from their throats like water through a shattered dam.

In front of the residence of the district administrator the two corpses were laid out on the ground, and the women began to intone a funeral dirge. Watchmen, soldiers, and mounted policemen were hastily summoned and formed a protective cordon around the house. When the last mournful notes of the dirge no longer hung in the air, the entire crowd simply stood there silently. But the silence was heavier with meaning than the oaths or the clamour: it was a witness to the unlit fires, the empty cooking pots, and the decaying mortars, and to the machines in the shops where the spiders were spinning their webs. For more than an hour they stood there, and the soldiers themselves remained silent before these silent people.

At last the cortège formed up again, but the ceremony was repeated, and the bodies of the children laid out, four times again – in front of the station, in the suburbs of N'Ginth and Randoulène, and in the market square in the heart of Thiès.

It was not until almost nightfall, when the mass of this human river was already indistinguishable from the shadows, that the funeral procession ended and the remains of the two children returned at last to their homes.

Three days later, the directors of the company notified the strikers that their representatives would be received.

·   ·   ·   ·   ·

The villas of the European employees of the company stood in a district, well outside the city proper, which Lahbib – without knowing quite why – had once christened 'the Vatican'.

The houses themselves were all alike, with prefabricated roofs, well-kept lawns, gravelled walks, and porches surrounded by a low cement railing. In spite of the nearness of the railroad yards and the constant pall of smoke that hung over them, they had been painted in clear, light colours. Ivy and flowering vines climbed up the posts supporting the porch roofs, and flowers in pots or boxes ornamented the railings. In the gardens at the rear, rose bushes and borders of daisies and snapdragons made vivid areas of colour, shaded from the tropical sun by giant bougainvilleas.

Life was easy in 'the Vatican' – so easy that it became extremely monotonous, and the adults all seemed to have taken on that scowling, sullen appearance which is the hallmark of boredom. The strike, however, had changed the atmosphere considerably; a constant nervous tension hung in the air, and fear was mingled with normal irritability. The men had secretly organized vigilante committees.

The Isnards lived at No. 7, between the villas of Victor and Leblanc, and the 'old hands', as they liked to call themselves, met frequently at the supervisor's house. They came, usually, just to gossip about the general situation, to speculate on the chances for promotions or transfers, and to give out or learn whatever news there was; and in the course of their meetings they formed petty alliances and conspiracies and spread a good deal of slander. A large part of the time it was the mistress of the house who led them on.

Beatrice Isnard was well past forty, but she was fighting a desperate rear-guard action against the advance of the years. Each night she covered her face with a thick coating of fatty cream, and before the strike she had always slept on the veranda, in the belief that the freshness of the night air would keep her skin firm and youthful. She was not at all satisfied with her face; her nose was too long, and despite her creams and depilatories a fine black down persisted in reappearing on the line above her upper lip.

On the evening of the day the company had notified the strikers of the prospective meeting, she had invited Victor, Leblanc, and a newly-arrived young man, whom everyone already called Pierrot, for dinner. In the spotlessly clean and well-ordered kitchen she was grumbling irritably at the Negro cook and kitchen boy.

'You haven't even beaten the eggs yet? Well, for heaven's sake, get a move on! The dinner will be ruined.'

The second boy was setting out the silver and arranging the bottles of wine on the gleaming white cloth of the dining-room table. Through the open door the voices of the men could be heard from the living-room. They were seated around a coffee table whose highly polished wood reflected the varied colours of apéritif bottles, glasses, and packets of cigarettes.

'I don't know what happened to me – I fired without knowing what I was doing!'

For the hundredth time, Isnard was repeating the same phrase, in a nasal, almost childlike voice, as if he were trying to remember a passage from some schoolday lesson he had long since forgotten. He had been living in a sort of suspended animation ever since the night of the shooting. For twenty-four hours he had not spoken a word to his wife, and several times he had gone in search of his children, holding them close to him for a moment and staring absently into the distance. He had forbidden them to go any farther from the house than their own garden.

When he had at last told Beatrice what happened, she had simply said, 'After all, one or two children more or less won't make much difference to them. The number of children running around over there is incredible anyway ... The women don't wait to have one before they're pregnant with another ...'

But Isnard just went on muttering, 'I don't know what happened to me ... I don't know ...'

'Look here,' Victor said. 'You've got to stop thinking about that. We're all living on our nerves right now. There are times when I find myself talking to myself and saying stupid things like, "All right, go ahead – go out and get yourself killed!" The way they have of just looking at you all the time is enough to set anyone crazy. Don't think about it any more. No one saw you – it will all be forgotten.'

Pierrot, the newcomer, listened to them silently, his lips clasped firmly around a cigarette. Since his arrival he had found himself unable to avoid a kind of admiration for these 'old hands' in the colony and for the hard and thankless, but fascinating, life that must have been theirs.

Victor uncrossed his legs, leaned across the table, and poured himself an apéritif. 'You'll see,' he said to his young neighbour, 'you have to learn how to forget. Twenty years ago there was nothing here but an arid wilderness. We built this city. Now they have hospitals, schools, and trains, but if we ever leave they're finished – the brush will take it all back. There wouldn't be anything left.'

Pierrot leaned back in his chair and lit another cigarette. 'I'd like to know something about how they live,' he said uncertainly. 'I've wandered around a little in the past few days, but I haven't seen very much. In the district around the airfield the houses are nothing but rats' nests. They were swarming with vermin, and, my God, the smell . . . ! I wanted to take some pictures of a child, but his mother came out and cursed me to my face, so I didn't bother with it. I never thought Africa would be like that.'

'It's their own fault if they live in places like that. You can always take pictures of the boys or the beggars, but don't give them more than twenty francs. This part of Africa is pretty ugly anyway, though – aside from two or three cities there isn't anything of any interest in the whole of Sénégal. Now you take French Equatorial Africa – that's something else again. You'll find all the real animal life of Africa there – and the natives are a lot more peaceable, too!'

The young man refused to be discouraged. 'You could give me some tips, though. For one thing, I'd like to get to know a real African family.'

'You must have read too many books! The best thing you can do is forget that nonsense. I've been out here longer than almost anyone else, and I don't know any of them except for my servants and the men in the shop. They keep their distance, and so do we. Ask Isnard.'

But Isnard had left them, although he still sat across the table from them, his eyes half closed, staring at the wall. He had fled from everything around him, escaped from it completely, and taken shelter in a dream. It was winter, and snow lay deep on the gabled roofs of the houses and on the pine trees climbing the slope of the hills. Isnard was home again, in a little village in the Vosges. Spring came suddenly, with burgeoning flowers everywhere and the clear mountain streams running fresh again. Soon it was summer and the Bastille Day festival in the village square. The owner of the hotel brought out tables and chairs, and at night there was dancing in the open air. There were young girls – there was one young girl who left the dancing and walked off alone,

towards the viaduct. He followed her, and when he joined her she pretended to be angry and pouted a little, but her eyes gave her away ...
And then the summer had passed. The leaves from the trees covered the ground, only the pines were still green, it was the time for gathering in the honey ...

Beatrice came into the room, untying her neatly pressed white apron. 'Well, gentlemen,' she said. 'We're not very talkative tonight.'

'Oh, good evening, madame,' Pierrot said, rising politely. 'I've just been asking Monsieur Victor and your husband how I could get to know one of the native families.'

'Well, I don't advise you to do it.' The tone of Beatrice's voice indicated clearly her intention of organizing the newcomer's life in her own fashion. 'You have absolutely nothing to gain from it except lice or one of their diseases ... When you think of these half-savages going on strike! Honestly, I think I've seen everything now.'

'That's exactly what I would like to understand, madame.'

'There's nothing to understand. They are children, that's all. Somebody has put some wild ideas in their heads, but they'll see sooner or later – this strike is going to cost them a lot more than they can possibly gain from it. Just imagine – they're all polygamous, and yet they're asking for family allowances. With the number of children they have! It's incredible!'

His wife's diatribe had brought Isnard out of his trance. He swallowed a mouthful of his apéritif and turned to Pierrot. 'I've done everything I could for them. I've given my youth and health to this country of theirs, trying to do something for them; and now they are treating us as oppressors!'

'Tell him the story about your Negress,' Beatrice said, seating herself on the arm of the couch.

Isnard put down his glass and brought his eyebrows together quizzically, as though he had difficulty in remembering. 'It was one night a long time ago,' he said at last. 'I had just gone to sleep. In fifteen years in the colonies I've never seen a night like that – black as a pit and a wind that you thought would carry the huts away. In those days we didn't have these bungalows yet. Well, I had gone to bed and finally gotten to sleep when suddenly I heard someone calling, *"Missé! Missé!"* At first, I'll tell you I was scared, but as soon as I was really awake I started laughing, thinking it was just some girl for the night – they used to come around like that – and what a fool she was to be out. Well, I got up and went to the door and lit my flashlight, and what do you think I saw? A Negress, all right, but a gigantic one. I took a closer look at her and saw that she had a belly as big as a wine barrel. Then she started bellowing, "Doctor! Doctor!" in English, and for a minute I didn't know what she meant. All of a sudden she fell down on her hands and knees, screaming like a wild woman, and started to have her baby — yes, to have a baby, right there on the ground in front of me! The baby came out all right, but I had nothing to separate it from the woman's body, nothing at all. Do you know what I did?'

Pierrot, who was feeling slightly ill at the thought of the big black body opening up, and blood flowing across the ground, shook his head.

'Well, I did it with my teeth. That was the only thing I had, so I did it with my teeth.'

'Good God,' the young man murmured.

'You see what I meant?' Beatrice demanded. 'That's the sort of thing that happens in the colonies.'

At this moment they all heard a thick, slurring voice from the veranda. 'Don't believe a word of what that liar says!' It was Leblanc. He was already very drunk and almost fell as he came up the steps.

'He's told that story a hundred times, and it's the stupidest thing I've ever heard.' He pointed an unsteady finger at Isnard. 'Take a look at him. With his teeth, he says! With those store-bought teeth of his he couldn't bite into a *rum baba*! As for you, my young friend, you seem to have all the right ideas, but just wait a little while and you'll see what happens to them. And as for me, I'll tell you frankly that I don't like these blacks. They not only despise us but now they're trying to pretend we aren't even here. Do you know what we are, in this place, my young friend? We're nothing but an advance guard in an enemy country!'

Isnard, Beatrice, and Victor stared at Leblanc in disgust. They called him 'our intellectual' sneeringly, and although they continued to receive him in their homes because he belonged to their race they had nothing but contempt for him. He was an ex-student who had arrived in Africa one day 'to study anthropology'. After wandering about the continent for some time with a Haitian Negro companion, he had accepted a minor position with the company and remained in Africa ever since, dividing his time between work and drinking.

There were very few people who recognized that Leblanc's present condition was more the result of unrealized hope than of any thwarted ambition. He had tried in vain to establish some sort of friendly relationship with the Africans, but his knowledge intimidated them and his natural shyness made it difficult for them to approach him. This hostility — or rather, this lack of any response to his efforts — had gradually discouraged him, and his drinking had completed the work. He had become a narrow, bitter person, laughed at by the blacks and mistrusted by the whites.

Pierrot could not take his eyes from Leblanc's flabby, rumpled face. The yellowish, unshaven skin made him look like a plucked fowl, his eyelids drooped, and the scars of climate and alcohol had deformed and pitted his features. A heavy odour of sweat steamed from his open shirt.

The young man rose to say good night, but Beatrice stopped him. 'No, no, Monsieur Pierre – you must stay and have dinner with us. We're waiting for Edouard.'

'By all means stay then, young man,' Leblanc said, pouring himself another drink. 'Edouard is a very important man – it's a good idea to have him on your side. Believe me, in the colonies a few friends in high places are worth a lot more than twenty years of work. And tomorrow it will be Edouard who is going to represent the gangsters against the Negroes.'

Beatrice turned to him abruptly. 'Aren't you ashamed of yourself, Leblanc, acting like this? What will Monsieur Pierre think of us?'

'Ah, but that isn't the question. The question is, what do the Negroes think of us?'

'Oh, shut up about your Negroes,' Victor interrupted angrily. 'You get damned boring after a while.'

'But I'm not really the one who bores you – it's "my Negroes", as you call them. But you haven't seen anything yet. Now that those two kids have been murdered, we're going to see the hour of truth.'

'What truth, Leblanc?' asked a jovial voice from the veranda. 'Good evening, everyone.'

Edouard came into the room, carrying a large briefcase. 'Good evening, madame – Isnard, your wife is just as beautiful as ever – the heat doesn't seem to affect her at all.'

Beatrice laughed. 'And you don't change either – always the flatterer. How is your wife?'

'Still fighting with the boys, as usual, but, aside from that, everything is fine.'

'They are really becoming impossible. I . . .'

'. . . should be damned glad to have them,' Leblanc said. 'Another one of our privileges that will be hard to give up – four black servants for the price of one in Europe.'

'Be careful what you say, Leblanc – you could get yourself in trouble. It might be a good idea if you went to see Doctor Michel.'

'Oh, I know all about your Doctor Michel, and I know exactly what would happen. I wouldn't have turned my back before his telephone was ringing. "Hello, is that you, doctor? Leblanc is coming over to see you. He isn't well, and he really should be sent home ... you understand, don't you? Of course, thank you, doctor." ' Leblanc acted out the scene as he spoke, holding his glass in one hand and an imaginary telephone in the other. When he had finished, he tossed off the drink in a single swallow and collapsed against the back of his chair, as if he had been knocked unconscious. No one except Pierrot paid any attention to him.

'What news is there from Dakar?' Victor asked Edouard.

'Nothing; but they have heard the news from Thiès. They know the story of the apprentices ... and I'm to meet with the fellows tomorrow and see what they have on their chests, that's all.'

'Are you supposed to satisfy their demands or try to work out a compromise?'

'Satisfying their demands isn't possible – but we have to talk to them. They are children who want to learn to walk by themselves, and it is up to us to give them a hand.'

'You know that if they get everything they are asking for we are finished here?'

'Look, Victor, I came from Dakar with very clear instructions, and I saw Dejean before coming here tonight. We're going to try to do everything we can about the matter of salaries; for the rest, I'll see what they want and make a report, but you have to realize that the bastards have got us over a barrel. Do you know that at Bamako they picked up a man who had gone back to work, by disguising themselves as policemen? And then they held a trial, right under our noses! They're talking about it everywhere, and since it happened we haven't been able to get one of them to go back. At Dakar and Saint-Louis some of the women have been battling with the police in the streets. Then there is that story about the three million francs ... Did you know that Bakayoko, their leader, raised more than fifty thousand francs when he spoke at a meeting in Saint-Louis?'

'I thought he was at Kayes,' Victor said.

'He was, but then he came back this way. We thought he was coming here, but he stopped at Djourbel and then went to Saint-Louis. He'll be back here soon, though.'

'He's a dangerous man,' Isnard said.

'For once, you are right,' Leblanc said, opening a blood-shot eye. 'Very dangerous. But be careful – he'll be more dangerous dead than alive.'

'There's nothing more disgusting than a drunken failure,' Victor said, looking at Leblanc angrily.

'That's true; I am a failure,' Leblanc said. 'I've failed at everything, even treachery. I like the Negroes, or I used to like them — but they shut their doors in my face. I'll tell you something, though. I sent them twenty thousand francs to help out with their strike. Yes, that's right; you don't have to look at me like a bunch of dead fish — I did it. Twice, I sent them a ten-thousand-franc note.'

He got up and bumped heavily against the coffee table, causing the glasses to jump. He filled his and emptied it again with a single gulp.

'That took you by surprise, didn't it? Why, you ... I think I'll go and tell them what you are planning now. I may be a failure, but when I'm around you ... Victor, do you know why Greece couldn't defend herself against the Romans? No, of course you don't, you're much too stupid for that. All right, it's true enough that the Negroes don't like me, but it's because of you and people like you that they don't. It doesn't mean that I don't understand Africa — this trollop of a continent! Do you hear me, my young friend? If you really love Africa, she will still give herself to you — she is so generous that she never ceases to give; and so greedy that she will never stop devouring you.'

He had started towards Pierrot, but he stumbled against a chair and would have fallen if the young man had not caught him.

'Just understand that,' he mumbled. 'The Negroes hate you; that's one thing we're all agreed on. I think I'll go and see what I can do to make sure they hate you more.'

'Someone had better go with him,' Victor said.

'Right,' Isnard said. 'We'll take him home.'

They caught up with Leblanc, who was weaving uncertainly around the veranda, looking for the steps.

'I don't need you — I know what you're going to do. Let me go!'

They each took him by an arm and almost carried him away. Some children had come out to the sidewalk to see what was happening, and windows were being opened in the neighbouring houses.

Pierrot was still standing beside the coffee table, embarrassed and not knowing quite what to do. Beatrice came over to him, standing so close that her breasts brushed against him.

'It was to be expected,' she said. 'Don't let it bother you. Stay and have dinner with us — they'll be back in a few minutes. We can get better acquainted.'

Her voice hardened suddenly, and she added, 'It's what always happens to fools.'

Wole Soyinka

Telephone Conversation

The price seemed reasonable, location
Indifferent. The landlady swore she lived
Off premises. Nothing remained
But self-confession. 'Madam,' I warned,
'I hate a wasted journey – I am African.'
Silence. Silenced transmission of
Pressurized good-breeding. Voice, when it came,
Lipstick coated, long gold-rolled
Cigarette-holder pipped. Caught I was, foully.
'HOW DARK?' . . . I had not misheard . . . 'ARE YOU LIGHT
OR VERY DARK?' Button B. Button A. Stench
Of rancid breath of public hide-and-speak.
Red booth. Red pillar-box. Red double-tiered
Omnibus squelching tar. It *was* real! Shamed
By ill-mannered silence, surrender
Pushed dumbfoundment to beg simplification.
Considerate she was, varying the emphasis –
'ARE YOU DARK? OR VERY LIGHT?' Revelation came.
'You mean – like plain or milk chocolate?'
Her assent was clinical, crushing in its light
Impersonality. Rapidly, wave-length adjusted,
I chose. 'West African sepia' – and as afterthought,
'Down in my passport.' Silence for spectroscopic
Flight of fancy, till truthfulness clanged her accent
Hard on the mouthpiece. 'WHAT'S THAT?' conceding
'DON'T KNOW WHAT THAT IS.' 'Like brunette.'
'THAT'S DARK, ISN'T IT?' 'Not altogether.
Facially, I am brunette, but madam, you should see
The rest of me. Palm of my hand, soles of my feet
Are a peroxide blonde. Friction, caused –
Foolishly madam – by sitting down, has turned

My bottom raven black – One moment madam!' sensing
Her receiver rearing on the thunderclap
About my ears – 'Madam' I pleaded, 'wouldn't you rather
See for yourself?'

George Lamming

from The Emigrants

The lavatory is a place of privacy, Collis thought. You may leave the
door open, and others will pass, pretending not to see you, but no one
will enter. If the door is locked, no one will knock. In a stranger's
house, a fortnight from home, he had discovered the consoling privacy
of this place. He hadn't gone there to relieve himself, but to rescue his
sanity. He lit a cigarette and settled himself on the wooden cover of the
bowl, waiting for the right moment to re-enter the living-room where
his host was sitting.

When he arrived an hour ago Mr Pearson received him with a gracious
bow, took his overcoat, and led him straight to the living-room where
Mrs Pearson was waiting anxiously to see her brother's friend. Her
brother, Arthur, was a welfare officer in Trinidad. He had shown some
concern about Collis's immediate future in the new country, and knowing his finances and the difficulties he might encounter, he had given
him this address. Mr Pearson was a man of great influence at the Har-
greaves Ltd, where his chief business was to supervise the conduct of
the staff. He often made the choice of new applicants and told those
who were dismissed why it seemed better they should go. Arthur had
probably thought of all this when he advised Collis to see the Pearsons
as soon as he arrived.

They were fastidiously attentive. Mr Pearson had plugged the
switches and turned on an electric fire. The light was good, but Mrs
Pearson thought it would be better if she turned on the table lamp in
the corner. Collis gave them news about Arthur. Mr Pearson poured
three glasses of sherry, and they drank to Arthur's health, Collis's
success, and at Collis's suggestion, to their own prosperity.

Mrs Pearson quickly finished her sherry and asked to be excused.
She had to see about supper which would be earlier than usual. When
she had gone, there seemed nothing more to say. She had taken Arthur
with her. Collis looked round the room, trying to invent opportunities
for compliments. It was the sort of room which announced the occu-

pants' propriety. A square room with grey distempered walls, and a white ceiling marked out in squares by thin slabs of brown board. The telephone was on a shelf built into the wall above the radio, and there was a television set in another corner. A photograph of Mr Pearson hung over the mantelpiece, and above the photograph, a polished rifle suspended by thin straps of leather. This was a relic of some other time. The room seemed a persistent rebuke to the rudimentary shelter which Collis had found at the hostel. It was not only a habitation, remote and warm as the womb. It was an entire climate. The conveniences were natural elements by which the life of the Pearsons was nourished. Mr Pearson did not sit in the chair. He belonged to it. When he left it to serve the sherry, it was not only unoccupied. It became incomplete.

Mr Pearson had made no enquiries about Collis's plans, but it would seem that he had carefully chosen the people whom they would talk about. Arthur was a natural choice, not only because he was Mrs Pearson's brother, but also because he was known to them all. Later he mentioned the Redheads, a West Indian couple who had settled in England. Collis didn't know the Redheads, but since they were Collis's compatriots, the choice seemed good enough. Mr Pearson talked about them at some length. Mr Redhead was a lawyer who had spent some time on the stage, and now entertained a great deal, but Mr Pearson regretted that he had never been able to visit them in recent times. It was a pity, for Mrs Pearson had always wanted to go in the hope that there would be someone with news about Arthur. Mr Pearson poured more sherry as he spoke about the Redheads. He thought it would be a delight for Collis to meet them. Collis listened, glancing every now and again at the television set in the opposite corner. It was the first he had seen and he was hoping that Mr Pearson would offer to turn it on after they had supped.

Mrs Pearson came in once to see how they were getting on, took a glass of sherry, and returned to finish the supper. Mr Pearson never really noticed her. It was as though their behaviour followed a certain order known only to them. When they were together they functioned like things which worked according to the laws of their environment. Their behaviour was a device. The pattern was fixed, and they entered it, assuming the roles to which such a marital relationship had assigned them. Collis thought he had noticed a certain continuity in their talk. When Mr Pearson finished saying something, Mrs Pearson would add her bit, a quiet confirmation of what her husband had said. For each, the other's speech was an unconscious act of reassurance. They understood each other.

Mr Pearson had returned briefly to Arthur's work in Trindad, and in the same sweep of reminiscence he recalled his last meeting with Mr Redhead. If the evening didn't turn out to be convivial, Collis was satisfied that it would be pleasant. But he had hoped that it would be discreet at some stage to let Mr Pearson know that he was curious about the television set.

Then the telephone rang and Mr Pearson answered it. Collis felt the change which had come into Mr Pearson's voice when he replied. It was a grumble, thick and ominous. He couldn't avoid following what Mr Pearson was saying. 'He was the only one you took on yesterday.' The person at the other end was speaking again. Then Mr Pearson: 'About eleven o'clock this morning. And the police insisted on questioning the others. But why?' The other speaker was explaining the reasons for the interruption in the morning. But Mr Pearson couldn't wait to be told everything. He was continually intervening. 'Whenever I'm absent. Did the police say what happened?' The man was speaking again, but Mr Pearson couldn't wait. 'He wouldn't give any details? Were the others involved? That's what you'd expect them to say.' Mr Pearson frowned and knocked his elbow against his ribs. 'You've got his name. We'll wait and see whether the police come back. But you won't take the man back to work. Remember. I'll arrange the pay myself.' The man was saying something, but Mr Pearson cut him short. 'If he turns up send him home.' He dropped the receiver, and stood for a moment staring through the window.

Nothing was the same after that call. Mr Pearson had taken his seat, but he was more reticent. He offered Collis some more sherry but didn't pour any for himself, and a lull which threatened to be permanent had come revengefully into their talk. He made no apology for his exchange on the telephone, but suddenly he asked: 'Does Arthur like the people out there?'

The question seemed irrelevant and unwarranted, and Collis was slow to answer. He was going to ask Mr Pearson a question instead, but he had already spoken: 'I mean the native people,' he said.

'I liked him,' Collis said, raising his brows in an attitude of indifference. He didn't look for Mr Pearson's reaction, but he had suddenly felt the need to intrude on the man's secrecy. If the telephone call was responsible for the change which had come over Mr Pearson he didn't understand why in the circumstances he should have chosen to impose his mood on him. The matter was clearly one which related to Mr Pearson's work, but the unease which he had felt in Mr Pearson's presence had made him think above all of himself. He sipped the sherry, and took a glance at the television set.

'Why do so many of your people come here?' Mr Pearson asked. He had dropped his glance and steadied his hands on his knees. Collis couldn't find an answer. He thought of Arthur, and felt better. He would use that relationship as a reason for taking a plunge into Mr Pearson's thinking. They were both quiet, eyeing each other secretly and with a growing suspicion. He turned again to look at the television set, and Mr Pearson watched him in profile, wondering how well Collis knew Arthur. The telephone call seemed to repeat itself in his head as he sat back in the chair, his hands clutching his knees, and his eyes staring over Collis's head out to the fences on the other side of the street. Collis hadn't found an answer for Mr Pearson's question, but Mr Pearson seemed to have forgotten the question himself. He relaxed his hands and crawled further into his chair, an upholstered cell inseparable from the life it contained. Occasionally Collis looked in his direction and quickly took in some impression of his body in its chair. His limbs were muscular, without the organic strength of the muscle. The muscles decorated the arm like those impractical coins with which an old ex-serviceman decorates himself. His eyes sank deep under his brow, giving his nose in its abrupt ascent a positive strength. He was tall and a little narrow in the shoulders but he had a prosperous waist and his neck was meaty. He had kept his glance high over Collis's head as though it were bad manners to look the other in the face, and Collis remembered that when he had asked the last question he had spoken to some purpose. His questions were relevant. Not like Mr Pearson's, which might only have been an opportunity for testing the other's responses and making a way gradually into the other's thinking. There was a coarse certainty about Mr Pearson. He was one who quickly defined the other, calculated the responses which he should present and having done that, proceeded to make social intercourse an encounter between a definition and a response. Collis understood that he did not then exist for Mr Pearson, and he understood too that Mr Pearson didn't exist for himself. He was a fixed occasion, harmless as death until some urgency like the telephone call informed it with danger.

The room was a silent pressure. Collis noticed the small bookcase against the wall, and tried to read the titles. The books had a decorative aspect like those rare commodities that are only meant to be looked at. He could barely read the titles at the top. *David Copperfield* and *The Pickwick Papers, The Works of Anthony Trollope, Pride and Prejudice.* And the Bible. And at the bottom, laid on their sides like weary performers, were two bound collections of *Punch*. There was nothing more to see. The pressure had become unbearable. He raised himself from the chair, snapped his fingers at Mr Pearson and said: 'I'd like to go to the lavatory.'

The request had suddenly brought Mr Pearson back to a sense of the occasion. When he showed Collis the way and returned to the living room, he poured himself a glass of sherry and walked over to the window sipping it slowly. He considered again that telephone call, and wondered why these emergencies should occur when he was absent. He was not at work that morning. He didn't know the man whom the police had been enquiring about, but the foreman had said that he was one of the new ones. He had probably arrived with Collis. He sipped the sherry and thought of Collis and immediately he felt embarrassed by the silence which had separated them during the past few minutes. He looked at the chair where he had been sitting, and then at Collis's as though he were trying to measure the distance between them. He finished the sherry and put the glass on the table before walking back to the window. He stood now looking out at the street, conscious of waiting for Collis to return. Mrs Pearson came in, and noticing that Collis wasn't there, assumed where he was and returned to the kitchen. Mr Pearson had turned to see who entered, but they didn't speak. He felt the need to resume his hospitality, to continue the role in which he had received Collis earlier. But the telephone call kept coming back to mind, and then a sudden confusion invaded his thinking. He felt something like shame, a lack of duty towards Collis, and he decided to overcome the anger which the telephone had produced. He hoped that Collis would return in order to re-establish that earlier contact. He took some more sherry, and filled Collis's glass, but decided that he would wait. He returned to the chair, and thought how he might respond to Collis on this occasion.

He went out to see the time, and came back twiddling his fingers to a tune which he whistled. The light was good, he told himself, but it probably wouldn't last. This was about the time he would choose before supper for going to the garden. It was a convention which he used to emphasize the distinction between his office and his home. In spring the garden was always a promise of achievement, and he thought it was a natural opportunity for making a fresh start with Collis. After they had had the sherry he would suggest that they should look over the garden.

The flush of the bowl made him start. He went out to the passage to show Collis to the living-room, but the flush was repeated and he stepped back into the room. The recollection of the garden seemed to have steadied his anger and renewed his confidence. He stood behind the door, trying to hear Collis's footsteps in the passage. Then he opened the door and walked back to the window. Collis would find the way.

Collis flushed the bowl again. It was as though he wanted Mr Pearson to know that he was arriving. But he sat on the wooden seat and wondered what would happen when he returned to the living-room. Mr Pearson remained in the chair, preparing to meet him. Collis was thinking that it would be interesting to see his face if he told him that he had flushed the bowl for the fun of it. Or it was his way of arousing Mr Pearson from the sullen stupor in which he had left him. Then he closed the lavatory door, and walked along the passage smiling. He wanted to laugh at himself, crouched on the lavatory seat, smoking, but he remembered that Mr Pearson would not be receptive to laughter. Mr Pearson had got up and walked to the window, and when Collis entered there was still the play of a smile gradually leaving his lips. He smothered his face with a handkerchief and watched Mr Pearson's baldness, wondering what would happen.

Mr Pearson had turned in time to see Collis pursing his lips in order to suppress a laugh, and he couldn't understand what there was to laugh at. Collis noticed too the difference in Mr Pearson's manner. He had offered Collis the glass of sherry and taken his seat again. Collis sat down and they drank together.

The lavatory had certainly worked a change, and Mr Pearson was hoping that he would soon be able to make his suggestion about the garden. Collis looked prepared for anything. He sipped the sherry and looked around the room, lingering for a while on the television set. Mr Pearson waited until Collis's glance had travelled back to the chair. 'I don't know whether you like flowers,' he said, 'but I always go out to the garden at this time.' His lips were parted, and his teeth showed between the split like a rabbit's, fine and sharp, with a suggestion of interminable gnawing. Collis said he liked flowers, although he preferred them in the garden. Mr Pearson's mouth had deepened its split into a smile. There was a pause, and Collis suddenly wondered whether some new restraint was going to revive that earlier silence. But Mr Pearson didn't only wonder, his concern was gradually growing into an anxiety. He wanted to make the point about the garden, but he felt that he should offer Collis an alternative, lest it seemed that he was forcing his pleasure, as he had his anger, on Collis. But he hoped Collis would join him in the garden, because it was there that he could more easily diminish the other's recollection of the telephone call. Mr Pearson had suddenly worked up an insane enthusiasm for the garden. His talk seemed almost the direct result of a decision. He was telling Collis what seeds he found successful in the spring, and then he moved on quickly to the weather and the quality of the soil. Collis said nothing. He listened attentively and with a measure of surprise. Mr Pearson rubbed his hands and scratched the bald patch at the back of his head, and his mouth moved again, making that customary split with the lips. He seemed almost affectionate, as he rummaged for some alternative to the garden. He got up, and walked over to the table to look through the *Radio Times*. Collis hadn't given any importance to Mr Pearson's talk about the garden, but when he saw him look through the *Radio Times* he wondered whether he was going to turn on the radio, and felt a sudden disappointment. At the hostel he had to hear the radio all day. Mr Pearson had closed the *Radio Times* and returned to his chair. His fingers were making creases with the pants.

'I don't know whether you'd like to see the garden,' he said, 'it's very promising at this time of year, and as I say I go out about this time.' He pulled a handkerchief from his pocket across his mouth, and his hand fell away indifferently on the chair. 'You can see what the garden's like now, or you could look at the television.'

Collis had glanced at the television set. 'I'd like to see the TV,' he said, and for that moment his choice seemed a brutish indifference to the garden. Mr Pearson made his rabbit grin again, and said: 'As you please.' His voice was thick and dull, but Collis's eagerness to see the television had made him insensitive to the change. Mr Pearson left the chair and plugged the switches. He fiddled with the knobs and then waited for a while. Collis watched his movements, and followed the stages of the light bringing the television to life. Mr Pearson turned to see what he was doing but no word was spoken. Collis had got up, and was looking at the bookcase more closely. The television had become a kind of last event which should not be hurried. Moreover Collis was feeling that he shouldn't indulge this enthusiasm. Mr Pearson was still working the knobs. When he finished he went back to the chair, and Collis lingered by the bookcase. The television must not seem to dominate his attention. His back was turned to Mr Pearson who sat in the chair, staring through the window. The change of mood had crept over him like a solid regiment of lice. His hands reached his knees in a firm, persistent clutch, and his stare shot through the panes like a weapon violently hurled beyond the horizon of the house into the distant unseen space.

'I like what you've done to the copies of *Punch*,' Collis said. His back was still turned to Mr Pearson's chair. 'Are these old copies?' Collis

asked. He was going to take his seat in a minute. 'Or the latest?' There
was no reply. But if Mr Pearson's silence was simply awkward, what
seemed unnatural was the silence which seemed to reign over the entire
house. Collis looked to see whether Mr Pearson was ill, but the chair
was empty. The door was shut, and it looked as though it had always
been shut. He stood erect, feeling that momentary break in his thinking which brought about a complete change of feeling. He looked at Mr
Pearson's chair again, and then at the copies of *Punch*. The television
was showing a cricket match at the Oval, and a voice spoke quietly, announcing names, but Collis's response was lame. Mr Pearson's disap-
pearance was like a danger signal. Collis didn't hear him say that he
was leaving. He was sure on more careful recollection that he hadn't
spoken. He would probably be back in a minute or two. Yet he felt
undermined by his absence. The man had an uncanny way of producing
this effect of enormous distance between himself and the other. Collis
sat in the chair and looked at the television for a while, but he couldn't
follow what was happening. He was trying to understand the source of
that strange quiver which Mr Pearson had left behind him, and he felt
with each attempt how difficult it would be to communicate this failure
of understanding to Mr Pearson. He moved about you like the weather
which you might avoid, but which would not be altered by the devices
you had invented to protect yourself against it. Collis felt that he was
trapped, and the television seemed a part of that conspiracy. He
wanted to turn it off; for, like Mr Pearson, you couldn't communicate
with it. It stared at you with a ruthless persistence. With a cold, calculated arrogance it said: 'This is what you do.' He looked at Mr Pearson's
chair again, and then at the television which showed a man stalking like
a giraffe towards the wickets. His thought had returned to Mr Pearson.
He wondered whether the telephone call had renewed his sullenness.
The door opened, and he started.

'Are you all right?' Mrs Pearson asked. She was laughing like a child
who felt its guilt. 'My husband is in the garden. He didn't want to take
you away from the TV.'

'I'm all right,' Collis said. She passed the silver box with cigarettes,
but he refused.

'And supper will be ready in a minute,' Mrs Pearson said. She laughed
again and slipped out of the room.

The cricket match seemed duller than it would have been ordinarily.
Collis wondered whether he shouldn't have chosen to go to the garden.
The television was a disappointment. He got up and walked to the
mantelpiece looking at the photograph of Mr Pearson, and he got the

feeling that if Mr Pearson were present he would commit some act of violence. He would have liked to kick him in the stomach, not in anger, but as a way of evoking some genuine emotion. Only violence could make Mr Pearson feel. He looked at the photograph and clenched his fist against it as though he were going to wipe out the nose.

'Supper is ready,' Mr Pearson said, and stood within the room pointing to the door. He had come in without a trace of noise. He waited for Collis to turn from the photograph. They walked out together, not speaking, until Collis, a little confused, said: 'I like that photograph.'

'It seemed so,' Mr Pearson said dryly, and they took their seats round the table.

It seemed right that there should be silence. Collis wanted to see them both at this distance. He looked at Mrs Pearson and down at his plate. A brussel sprout had rolled off his plate and collided with a potato. Collis brought it forward and held it up on the fork. Mr Pearson concentrated on the meal. Mrs Pearson seemed to understand everything. Collis tried to see her better, as she held her head down in a silent communion with the food. He was struck now by the extreme fragility of her body. Her skin was the colour of milk with a tinge of pink on the cheeks, and her hands short and narrow came out from her sides like swollen antennae. Her face was thin and weak with the curious timidity of an animal that approached you sideways, and her eyes making circles round the plate, blue grey and liquid with the perennial solicitude of a gentle and anxious woman. Collis got a glance at the body in its chair outlined against the wall. It looked a figure of ash which could crack and dissolve by the mere suggestion of anger, but it would always by the nature to which it was condemned restore its shape and character and its fragile transparency, an object whose presence seemed also the urgent certainty of its death.

Mrs Pearson chewed leisurely like a goat half asleep at sundown. She wanted to break the silence, but Collis ate as though he were at ease, and Mr Pearson concentrated on the food with deliberate exclusiveness.

The light was thickening outside, and the trees were shaking in the wind. Mrs Pearson looked over her shoulder as though she wanted to seal a bargain with the weather.

Then she said, looking softly towards her husband, 'Did someone call this evening?'

Collis looked at Mr Pearson.

'One of the new men is in trouble,' he said, and the drop of the voice seemed final.

'Would it be one of the West Indians?' Mrs Pearson asked. The voice was laboured with concern, but Mr Pearson didn't answer. Collis announced that he would have to go immediately they were through with supper. No word was spoken; but there seemed to be an understanding that this evening had been an ordeal which was drawing to a close.

Okot p'Bitek

from Song of Lawino

My husband says
He rejects me
Because I do not appreciate
White men's foods,
And that I do not know
How to hold
The spoon and the fork.

He is angry with me
Because I do not know
How to cook
As white women do
And I refuse
To eat chicken
And to drink raw eggs
As white women do.

He says
He is ashamed of me
Because when he opens
The tin of lobster
I feel terribly sick,
Or when he relates
How, when he was in the white men's country
They ate frogs and shells
And tortoise and snakes
My stomach rebels
And throws its contents out
Through my mouth.

He complains endlessly,
He says
Had I been to school

I would have learnt
How to use
White men's cooking stoves.

I confess,
I do not deny!
I do not know
How to cook like a white woman.

I cannot use the primus stove
I do not know
How to light it
And when it gets blocked
How can I prick it?
The thing roars
Like a male lion,
It frightens me!

They say
It once burst
And the flame burnt
A goat to death!

I really hate
The charcoal stove!
Your hand is always
Charcoal-dirty
And anything you touch
Is blackened;
And your finger nails
Resemble those of the poison woman.
It is so difficult to start:
You wait for the winds
To blow,
But whenever you are in a hurry
The winds go off to visit
Their mothers-in-law.

The electric fire kills people.
They say
It is lightning,

They say
The white man has trapped
And caught the Rain-Cock*
And imprisoned it
In a heavy steel house.

The wonders of the white men
Are many!
They leave me speechless!

They say
When the Rain-Cock
Opens its wings
The blinding light
And the deadly fire
Flow through the wires
And lighten the streets
And the houses;
And the fire
Goes into the electric stove.

If you touch it
It runs through you
And cuts the heart string
As they cut the umbilical cord,
And you stand there, dead,
A standing corpse!

I am terribly afraid
Of the electric stove,
And I do not like using it
Because you stand up
When you cook.
Who ever cooked standing up?
And the stove
Has many eyes.
I do not know
Which eye to prick

* It is believed that lightning and thunder are caused by a giant reddish-brown bird that is almost identical with the domestic fowl. When it opens its wings lightning flashes and thunder is caused when it strikes with its powerful bolt.

So that the stove
May vomit fire
And I cannot tell
Which eye to prick
So that fire is vomited
In one and not in another plate.

And I am afraid
That I may touch
The deadly tongue
Of the Rain-Cock.

O! I do not like
Using the electric stove,
I cannot cook anything well
When you give me
The Rain-Cock stove.

.   .   .   .   .   .

Ocol laughs at me
Because, he says,
I do not know
The names of the moons,
That I do not know
How many moons in a year
And the number of Sabbaths
In one moon.

The Sabbath is a day
For Christians
When Protestants and Catholics shout
And suffer from headaches.

The Acoli did not
Set aside a special day
For *Jok*;
When misfortune hits the homestead
The clansmen gather
And offer sacrifices
To the ancestors:

When the rains
Refuse to come
The Rain Cock* prepares a feast.
A goat is speared
In the wilderness
And the elders offer prayers
To *Jok*.

We all know the moon —
It elopes,
Climbs the hill
And falls down;

It lights up the night,
Youths like it,
Wizards hate it,
And hyenas howl
When the moon
Shines into their eyes.

Periodically each woman
Sees the moon,
And when a young girl
Has seen it
For the first time
It is a sign
That the garden is ready
For sowing,
And when the gardener comes
Carrying two bags of live seeds
And a good strong hoe
The rich red soil
Swells with a new life.

Turning your back
To your husband
Is a serious taboo,
But when the baby
Is still toothless froth,

*The priest of rain, who presides during the ceremony for rain.

When you see the moon
You turn your back
To your husband.

If you do not resist
The great appetite
Then your child becomes
Sickly and thin
His knees become
Soft like porridge,
He will become pregnant
And the weight of his diseased stomach
Will prevent him
From standing up.

I do not know
The names of the moons
Because the Acoli
Do not name their moons.

During the *Ager* period
Millet is sown,
Just before the rains
And as they sow
They raise much dust.

When the rains return
We say
The rains have fallen
The period is called
Poto-kot
Then the millet seeds germinate.
Sometimes the rains come early
Sometimes they return late.
When the millet
Begins to flower
And the time
For the harvest is approaching
All the granaries are empty;

And hunger begins
To bite people's tummies,
This period
Is called *Odunge*,
Because fierce hunger burns
People's insides
And they drink
Vegetable soups
To deaden the teeth
Of the fire.

And as the millet
Begins to get ready for the harvest,
Some women ask,
Is this not my own garden?
They take their harvest knives
And a small basket,
They cut one head here
And another one there,
And when someone laughs,
They ask,
Whose garden have I spoiled?
So the period
Just before the harvest
Is called
Abalo-pa-nga?

The Acoli know
The Wet Season
And the Dry Season.

Wet Season means
Hard work in the fields,
Sowing, weeding, harvesting.
It means waking up before dawn,
It means mud
And thick dew.
Herdboys dislike it.
Lazy people hate it.

Dry Season means pleasures,
It means dancing,
It means hunting
In freshly burnt plains.

You hear *otole* dance drums
And funeral songs,
You hear the horns and trumpets.
And the moonlight dance songs
Floating in the air.

Youths in small groups
Go on the *apet* hunting expeditions,
Great hunters stay alone
In the wilderness
Smoking the carcass of the cob
Or the buffalo.

Others go off to Pajule
To look for bridewealth,
For if you have no sister
Then kill an elephant.
You sell the teeth
And marry a wife,
Then you call your son
Ocan, because you are poor!

Dry Season means wooing
And eloping with girls,
It means the *moko* dance
When youths and girls
Get stuck to one another!

Neville Dawes

from The Last Enchantment

Cyril Hanson arrived in Oxford two days before the start of term with a rolled umbrella, a yellow briefcase, a flat cloth cap and an Oxford accent. He was met at the station by Ramsay who had been sent to Oxford direct from Avonmouth by the Colonial Office and who had already spent nearly six weeks there. Cyril walked along the platform chatting to a white American; he was saying that he couldn't get over the rolling greenness of England and the well-kept placid bits of river they had seen after Didcot. He saw Ramsay and shouted from twenty yards off, 'Hullo, Ramsay, o' boy!' Ramsay wondered what on earth Cyril was carrying in the large yellow briefcase. The American seemed quite amazed at Cyril's personality, and Ramsay felt cheated because Cyril really looked as if he had been at Oxford for years and was a member of some newly-invented, aggressive race that would ultimately baffle the ethnologist.

Ramsay had learned by subtle indirections from the English people he met before term in non-undergraduate Oxford that a literary negro was an absurdity, a circus dog that had learned a few tricks. He had come there to learn more tricks and to study, as his father had said, everything a white man could do. What he began to doubt was the genuineness of his reactions and whether he had a right to them. There was a point on the journey from Didcot where the train rounded a gentle curve and suddenly Oxford, spires and towers, dreamed up out of the autumn mist like something in a medieval story. That moment had seemed genuine and his, something his whole colonial education had prepared him for. But never again would Oxford seem so lovely. For now, even before the real stresses of a new environment had begun, he was doubting his right to the sense of personal possession he had for the reanimation of the dead past and inert words in a book which a walk around Oxford gave.

In the taxi the American was saying, a little cynically, as it was a grey October day, 'Towery city and branchy between towers'. Ramsay thought that his own flat Jamaican voice was nearer than the American's to the tune of Hopkin's verse but he felt the American had a right to the quotation, a right that was inalienable for the American, but one to be 'given' to him, a black colonial carefully encircled by the limitations of his supposed subhumanity. He told Cyril that he had met a few West Indian and African undergraduates and Cyril replied brusquely that he had not come to Oxford to meet West Indians. Ramsay thought Cyril was trying to show the American how cosmopolitan he was and how superior to himself whose tiny shirt collar and badly-knotted tie and outsize sports-jacket gave him the general air of a stage negro. The American asked Ramsay, politely, what buildings they were passing. Though Ramsay was glad Cyril had come he resented his presence without quite knowing why. The American got out at Balliol.

'Cyril, what's the accent and the flat cap for?' Ramsay asked.

'When in Rome, o' boy, when in Rome!'

Ramsay saw him to his rooms in Brasenose College and then Cyril had to hurry off to Rhodes House.

The most depressing spot in Oxford for Ramsay was the area between the Radcliffe Camera and St Mary the Virgin's and the High. Somewhere *there*, beneath that commanding church tower he should have felt, without architectural accuracy, the Middle Ages' last enchantment and it was precisely there that Ramsay felt his own disenchantment most acutely. Everything depended on 'who' you were, the whole network of money and history that you were, or in his case, perhaps, on *what* he was. His disenchantment had begun on the first morning that he spent in Oxford. He came down to breakfast in his 'digs' in St John's Street. There were three other people at the table, a Gold Coast African who had taken his degree, an African girl and an English undergraduate who was teasing the girl. They were all talking in a friendly way. Then the English chap pointed to the girl.

'She's blushing!' he said. The laughter faltered for a second and so, recovering quickly, the English chap asked, 'But how do you know when you are blushing?' The tone of the question suggested that he really wanted to know.

'You see it in the eyes,' the Gold Coast man said easily and started talking about a Constitutional Commission that was then at work on his country's future. When the English chap had left the African said to Ramsay, 'I didn't want that English boy to get away with anything. He thinks we are fools!'

For some hours that morning he thought over the incident. Did the English chap want to be insulting, could the impotence of his language to describe the girl's reaction for both user and hearer be taken to imply inferiority; if so, why did he accept such a lame answer? Or was it simply a recognition of otherness? Ramsay saw the civility of the African's inadequate reply as the clue to the whole matter, the layers of general distrust under which real feeling was concealed, the negro's only way of grasping civilization. He was disenchanted because he saw that in the general situation of which this incident was a symptom he could be himself only cautiously, deliberately — at any rate the self which his previous education had formed and which should have found its apotheosis in Oxford. The realization came like a flash of conversion, like Paul being converted to the receiving end of persecution. He wrote to his mother and Madge and Mabel that day. He described the climate and the buildings but he couldn't tell them that the only truth he had found was that a negro's only responsibility is to *endure* and in that way he might ultimately become a man. When he told Cyril about the incident Cyril had said, 'What does it matter if you blush red or blue or black, or don't blush at all? You are too sensitive, man. Nobody hates you!'

'It isn't hate or feeling in that sense,' Ramsay said. 'It is a condition of knowing whether or not you are regarded as a man and the fear that, if you are not regarded as a man, you may not be able to prove that you are a man.'

'But I know I'm a man,' Cyril said. 'I doan' have to prove it.'

'You are exceptional, Cyril,' Ramsay said. 'The world, any world, belongs to you.'

The first undergraduate friend Ramsay made was a white American freshman, in his college, reading English. They shared an immediate and amused dislike of their literature tutor and an inability to worship old stone. Ramsay was grateful to this man because he took it for granted that Ramsay had read and understood a few books before coming to England and that there were things in England to which he had a right to object. He took tea in the American's rooms. One of the people there was a disillusioned American Rhodes Scholar from Nevada and at New College in his second year who advised them about Oxford conversation.

'Always say something surprising,' he told them. 'That's the secret of Oxford conversation. It doesn't matter how preposterous or outrageous or inaccurate what you are saying is, so long as you arrive at a far-fetched conclusion!'

Ramsay went to a few lectures on Chaucer. The lecturer was a delightful man who looked like a country squire with the same epicurean zest for Chaucer that Chaucer's Franklin had for good living. He also went to one lecture on *Beowulf* but the professor had omitted to bring his spectacles and had held his lecture notes two inches from his face. As what he could hear or follow of the professor's lecture was too abstruse, anyway, Ramsay did not return to the other lectures. Going to lectures proved that he was earning his Colonial Office keep and he felt he learned something at every lecture until his literature tutor told him that he could hardly be expected to survive in the rarefied atmosphere of English Literature. It was after Ramsay had read the tutor a bad essay written in front of a dying fire at four in the morning in the drugged mist of too much alcohol and too many unsobering cups of Nescafé — the type of essay his tutor must have heard very often. 'I don't *think* you should be reading English, you know,' his tutor said. 'Probably PPE or Law might be better. We have a black man in this college whom we have switched to a pass degree and he's doing very well now.'

Ramsay insisted that he had come to Oxford to read English and he would read English. But he stopped going to lectures altogether after that. In the mornings he would take his books and notepaper to the new library at the Union, sit in one of the deep chairs in front of one of Oxford's most comfortable fires and gradually go to sleep. He also read a lot of modern fiction on the first floor of the old library. The Union was a kind of paradise that had transcended colour, with its African librarian and Indian treasurer and yet, even there, with the leaves turning brown and falling in Frewin Hall he read:

I could hear women too, and then all of a sudden I began to smell them. 'Niggers,' I whispered. 'Sh-h-h-h,' I whispered.

It always happened that, when he had begun to feel community with a writer and enjoy a book, that contemptuous word and attitude would pull him up short. He read inattentively and got the mistaken idea that Faulkner was a negro-hater.

Then he met Guy Horne and Oxford took on a definite shape. Guy Horne first saw Ramsay as a figure, three minutes before lunch in late November, trying to huddle into itself in the single shaft of sunlight that touched, apologetically, a small area in the first quad.

Guy Horne was a classless Englishman, a product of the war and statistics and evacuated schools and levelling up, a working-class Londoner who had always spoken with an upper-middle-class accent. He had been called up in the RAF just after the end of the war and had spent his National Service in a perpetual 'gloom session' somewhere in the Middle East. He found himself in Oxford with some surprise and immediately developed an unassailable attitude to the place. He saw Oxford as a free activity theatre in which most undergraduates were acting, in the sense of endeavouring after something, truth, a Blue, a Union reputation, a College Club reputation, a First, a coffee society reputation, the OUDS, a Second, a way of making a living afterwards, a reputation for doing nothing or for knowing 'what's going on'. There were a few others who were not actors, and who felt they shouldn't really be there. They were not spectators because the actors themselves were their own audience. They were the outsiders who spent their time watching the others act or being acted to, and recording everything for private viewing but with less discrimination and sensitivity and inertia than a cine-camera. The outsider drifted cheerfully from place to place, not where the acting was most exciting but where it was most amusing. Guy Horne could sit for an hour in the morning in The Cadena, drinking one cup of coffee and listening. He lived, symbolically, out of college in his first year. He was dark-haired, very short, with a bouncy walk, had no distinction whatever and no affectations.

Guy and Ramsay became friends because (if there are ever real reasons for a friendship) they both liked frivolity, for different reasons, and hated living in England, for the same reason. Frivolity was Ramsay's best escape from his racial and political awkwardness; for Guy, frivolity was the only thing worth pursuing for any sake; and they both disliked the English climate. The first thing they spoke about was Oscar Wilde's wit and Guy was the second person in England who automatically credited Ramsay with ever having read and understood any English literature.

The outsider is *not* an outcast. He *is* invited to parties and to coffee after Hall, and in Hall he sits with the liveliest groups, even at the Boat Club table, but nobody ever expects him to throw a party or to want to be sconced. The first thing Ramsay and Guy did was to find the snippet of conversation which best defined Oxford. After listening for nearly two terms they decided that it was:

'Wher' you off to?'

'Going to listen to some Sibelius. Like to come?'

'Lahv it!'

Guy 'outsidered' everywhere. He even went to lectures and tutorials in that spirit. Realizing that their friendship was regarded by the other men in the college as an oddity, Ramsay and Guy became actors for a while. They started entering rooms with obscure Shakespearean conversation. To enter the Common Room loudly with 'I do not know

Maecenas. Ask Agrippa', was sure to turn one or two heads away from *The Times*, and going into the bar at 'The George' with, 'If we compose well here, to Parthia,' could stop the fluted faery voice that was relating what 'Nevil' had said.

The success of his friendship with Guy made Ramsay remember Dr Phillips's advice, 'Forget you are a negro and be a human being for three years.' Guy had what he would have described as an essentially 'bash-on' attitude to colour. He knew it was there but he didn't see it and he really liked Ramsay whose mind and emotions were not noticeably different from his. He genuinely despised those white people who were colour-prejudiced and even gave up an incipient friendship with a girl from St Hilda's whom he brought to tea in Ramsay's rooms because she was uneasy and excessively Christian to Ramsay. The first serious moment in his friendship with Guy was, as Guy reported it, the girl's saying that she couldn't possibly bring herself to kiss a negro. Guy's frank bewilderment, and his explanation that the circumstances of the remark had nothing to do with Ramsay personally, saved the friendship. The frivolity continued but was set in a more sombre key. Dr Phillips's remarks became an obsession for, setting aside the ignorance and ingrained insularity of a few people, it really began to seem possible in Oxford, especially when he considered Cyril Hanson.

Cyril had become an immediate success in Oxford. He was known in the Union where he spoke occasionally, and professed to put forward the 'balanced colonial viewpoint'. The other West Indians hated him and the West Africans regarded him with contempt but it didn't matter since Cyril didn't mix with them, anyway. He was very well known in his own college – the scouts liked him and the dons were aware of him. In their first year Ramsay saw very little of him: he visited Ramsay only to report news of himself. One afternoon towards the end of their first term Cyril came in to say that he had been chosen to play soccer for the University against Cambridge. He looked so remarkably fit that Ramsay felt he had to make an athletic comment.

'What position?'

'Inner left,' Cyril said, and his accent modulated back to Surrey College.

'Are you playing the "W" formation?' Ramsay said, 'W' formation having been one of Cyril's favourite sixth-form topics.

'Oh, no, the "W" formation is t-terribly out of date, o' boy.' He was Oxford again. 'We're playing four forwards up and one scheming inside man. I am the schemer.'

'Well,' Ramsay said, 'you've got your "Blue".'

'And after that *Vincent's*,' Cyril said. 'I had the secretary to tea t'other day.'

'Mrs Hanson will be very happy.'

'I've cabled her the great news. Oh, by-the-bye, have you heard? The PDP won a by-election in Clarendon. In the *country*, can you imagine that?'

Ramsay couldn't sleep at night trying to understand Cyril's significance. Cyril was so wonderfully integrated that he had even developed a stutter. True, he had been annoyed about Ramsay's tutor's remark and had encouraged Ramsay to do his best in the preliminary examination and 'show that ass', but it was a personal annoyance over a friend's discomfort. So Ramsay began writing a thesis that would clarify his own thinking. He called it, *Is the Negro a Man?*; then changed that to, *Is the Negro whose ancestors were Slaves, a Man?*; then changed it to, *Is (Can) the Negro, whose ancestors were Slaves, (be) a Man?* The first paragraphs read:

> *This is not a philosophical treatise but an attempt to define emotion precisely. It is necessary to say this because our first proposition may, very loosely, be called 'metaphysical'. Our postulate is — Man is a human existence with a purpose that is universally valid, that is, a purpose which any other human being might accept and live towards without denying his true nature.*
>
> *We must anticipate by declaring uncategorically that, historically the post-slavery Negro cannot have a Christian purpose. This statement will be demonstrated later and is put here merely as a precaution against unnecessary stalling of the discussion.*
>
> *We will try first to answer three simple questions (1) Was the Negro a Man before Slavery? (2) Was he a Man during Slavery? (3) Is he (can he be) a Man now?*

After writing these three paragraphs he put the treatise aside. He was to rewrite these paragraphs numerous times in his three years at Oxford, changing the phrasing to greater simplicity or greater elaboration, sometimes omitting the second paragraph altogether.

He felt that this treatise was a particularly vital exercise after he found that Guy was completely ignorant about the truth of colonialism. This came out during a discussion they had about the 'college Communist'. The college Communist, Sydney Bogan, was a young Englishman reading the extremely respectable school of *Literae Humaniores*.

This and the fact that he was not a Jew made it difficult for the guardians of college honour to deal with him, but he was almost an outcast and was treated with bare-teethed civility. He played a fairish game of tennis, good enough to be in the college team that went, together with the cricket team, to play the 'sister' Cambridge college. The practice is for the coach to stop at every pub on the road for drinking and good fellowship. On this journey no one spoke to the Communist at all and he stayed in the coach at each pub. Ramsay spoke to him frequently and had tea with him. He was a mild Marxist, quite undogmatic but with a passionate hatred of the Conservatives who were the ruling faction in the college. He was not a party member and he thought a revolution would be unnecessary in Britain. He had only a sketchy knowledge of colonial politics but Ramsay felt sad and frightened about this man's pariah status, a status which through any remote occurrence, such as the massacre of all the English people in Jamaica, might easily become his.

Guy, whose parents were definitely workers, had voted Labour in the first post-war general election, but he adopted the accepted attitude to the Communist and one day told Ramsay, with great delight, that in the Union the evening before Bogan had been severely heckled when making a very red speech on the motion, 'That this House deplores the colonial policy of the Government'.

'Of course, everybody knows,' Guy said, 'that the colonies are not ready to govern themselves.'

'Why not?' Ramsay asked. 'Don't *you* think I can govern myself?'

'But I don't think of you as a 'colonial' in that sense,' Guy said, and could not explain himself further.

Ramsay gave him a lurid and exaggerated account of the horrors of slavery and imperialism. Guy didn't seem to be very interested. At one point he said, 'All right, Ramsay, if you say so I believe you, but I hadn't thought British administration was as bad as all that.' And then later, when Ramsay swung into the fantasy of himself as a reformer, Guy who had a clear grasp of Ramsay's character said, 'You will never be a politician. You aren't crafty enough.' One thing that interested Guy was the account of Empire Day celebrations in the colonies. At first he didn't believe that little black children marched on that day waving little Union Jacks and singing *Rule Britannia*. The whole thing seemed extremely funny and he laughed himself into hiccups and tears; he said the English are crazy. Ramsay, who had been brought up to sing *Rule Britannia* and wave a Union Jack on Empire Day and then had grown to hate doing it saw, for the first time, because of Guy's laughter, that, beneath the insult, the Empire Day situation was extremely comic. That night before going to bed he made a note for use in his treatise:

> *Only something less than a man would willingly wave his oppressor's flag over his own enslavement and sing a song of triumph which implied that he never never never would be anything other than a slave.*

At the end of the Easter term Ramsay wrote a preliminary examination, then called 'Sections', in the subjects *Old English* and *Chaucer*. He prepared for the examination feeling hate for his tutor's remark and fear that his tutor was right. He read, by chance, the one illuminating book on Chaucer which, though it gave no new knowledge, made the poet for ever the personal possession of a remote, dispossessed, twentieth-century negro in a cold curtained Oxford room. It gave his life for a few weeks a complacent sentimentality. Then he wrote the examination and was the only candidate to get a distinction in *Chaucer*: and his language tutor, a kind portly man who expected only .05 per cent of his students to have any academic pretensions, confessed his surprise that Ramsay had very nearly got a distinction in Anglo-Saxon, too, and had written, to one particular question, the best answer the don who marked the papers had ever seen. But the exam results proved nothing to his literature tutor, who 'farmed' him out to other tutors; or to Ramsay, who kept himself pure from lectures for the rest of his time in Oxford.

He decided there was no point in striving for a 'good' degree in a world where he had no place, in using a degree to prove that he was an intelligent existence. He noted, for use in the third section of his treatise (although the first two sections had not yet been written):

> *The white world can accept the Negro only as a myth, a mythical stupidity, a mythical cheerfulness, a mythical unmorality, a mythical sexuality.*

Ramsay joined, feeling he had a right to, the English Club, and the reaction to him was either incredulousness or pity. The secretary of the club, a clever girl from Somerville, was initially one of the pitying, but she was more than that; the pity was a sublimated curiosity.

She was pretty with a black-haired gypsy look that was neither Welsh nor Jew, and her full lips disturbed him. She made him talk about his reaction to literature, some genuine quality in her manner forcing him to fight down the consciousness of pity.

'The things I like,' he said, 'give me a sense of floating and completeness at the same time but you never exhaust the book or story even, and it never exhausts you.'

'How very much that sounds like sex,' Marjorie Stannard said. The Myth, Ramsay thought. Or Freud? It always embarrassed him when a girl he didn't know spoke to him about sex in this clinical way without love or personal passion. She didn't have any suspicions about his semi-Puritan conscience, though this would not have altered the Myth, since his was a purely contemplative morality, a way of looking at an action after it had been performed.

She was very attractive in his room now that she wasn't wearing an overcoat or a scholar's gown. There were certain facts that he tried to isolate as meaningless facts – the white blouse, the line of her throat, her breasts, her fine legs towards the fire. He tried to avoid making the sexual assumptions that would link those facts together, for those assumptions belonged to another country and another time, so he plunged on.

'I can name *Tristram Shandy*, *The Heart of Darkness*, *Portrait of a Lady* (Henry James), and *The Brothers Karamazov*. Incidentally, *The Brothers Karamazov* is the best novel I've ever read. I get this sense of floating frequently in poetry but only rarely in fiction. While one is floating one keeps on asking, 'How did he manage to conceive the thing?' It's a personal reaction but I could prove that all these books get their power from perfect construction.'

He turned from the fire to which he had spoken the words and tried to remember what stupid thing he had said that could make her look at him so glassily.

'The trouble about Oxford conversation,' she said, 'is that it tends to become so impersonal, as if life was a vast abstraction.' Then, after a pause, 'Do you write, Ramsay, yourself?'

He thought of lying but instead said, 'No', quickly.

She was looking at him and smiling eagerly. That was the cue, as he understood civilized conversation, to introduce another abstraction wrapped in a surprising metaphor. He had just chosen the idea and the metaphor and was beginning to shape the sentence in his mind when she said, 'D'you know, there is something *very* silly that I very much want to do.'

'What's that?'

'I'd like to touch your hair. It *is* silly, isn't it?'

This was genuine, blurted out. She sat on the arm of his chair.

'It is very *soft!*' she said, as if Ramsay might not know, her surprised fingers still trying to believe this softness. 'It's *very* soft.'

He knew that her curiosity went further than that but he resented being humanized from a golliwog into a lover. That way he would have no validity as a person. He shook his head irritably.

'Don't you want me to do that?' she asked.

'No, no, it isn't that.' He could not say what it was and she had been very sympathetic to him. She went back to her chair and they talked about English literature.

'She *did* come here with that Myth in her mind,' he thought, while she was talking. And she thought, 'He is excessively shy and alone in this country and so *much* in need of friendliness.'

He did not go back to the English Club and he refused her invitation to tea. After two terms he did not recognize her at first when she stopped him in the street.

In their first summer term Guy and Ramsay became close friends of the Prince. The Prince was a tall elegant sober young African who had spent a few years at an English public school. He was faintly amused by Oxford and would have been an outsider if he didn't get so many invitations to tea and sherry parties. He was much more initiated into Oxford life than Guy or Ramsay. Once during Eights week, though he hadn't been to the races at all, he was invited to a party on the Christ Church barge. He got out of the Meadows by climbing into Merton Gardens and then he arrived in Ramsay's room with his speech slightly muddled and his usually correct Trilby hat at a rakish angle and he looked generally like a slightly tight ambassador. The Prince was a symbol of what Ramsay would never be. His ancestors had never been colonial slaves and though his country had been conquered in almost equal battle by a European nation it was his own. Ramsay envied him his simplicity of purpose. To the Prince questions of racial discrimination and imperialism, though extremely important, were subordinated to his personal responsibility to return and work for his people. Oxford was only a small part of his preparation for that work. Even his amused progress through the Continent during the vacations fitted in with that purpose. He did not need an abstract treatise. He was this Prince, with this royal tradition behind him, and this commitment for life. He was not pompous and he was extremely witty, especially in his own language. Guy and Ramsay knew that he would one day return in triumph beside his Emperor, as cynical to the deference he would then be given as people were now cynical about his complexion. He was completely a man and proof to Ramsay that slavery and continued domination dehumanized a people for ever. Ramsay was ashamed that he had ever enjoyed the monstrous caricature in Waugh's *Black Mischief*.

Out of his friendship with the Prince and invitations which both he and Cyril received to meet the English Queen, Ramsay got another idea for his treatise. Cyril was much more visible during summer because his cricket was not quite up to university standard. He had played well enough in the trials, though, to be made an Authentic almost immediately. He came in one day to invite Ramsay to a Drake Club dinner. The Drake Club is a collection of Commonwealth undergraduates, mostly Rhodes Scholars, who invite important public men to address them on topics 'affecting' the Empire and Commonwealth. Ramsay had the impression that it was slightly more reactionary than the Conservative Club. Ramsay was in his most sarcastic mood because Cyril evidently thought he would be honoured by the invitation.

'What the hell you joined a club like that for, man?' Ramsay asked. 'What do you do there? Sing *Rule Britannia* after dinner? Weren't you a Socialist at one time?'

'Oh, yes. 'Course. But you've got to find out what the other man is thinking.'

'You can read it in the *Telegraph*,' Ramsay pointed out.

'Well, *really*, nothing can happen to you if you have dinner at the Drake Club,' Cyril said, wearily. 'You sit beside Conservatives in Hall, 'ntchu? Come, don't be tiahsome.'

'What you mean "Don't be tiahsome"?'

'That's the way the word is pronounced here, "tiahsome" —'

'I would be contaminated for the rest of my life!' Ramsay shouted.

'My dear Ramsay, you've got some sort of inferiority complex,' Cyril said.

'OK, OK. But you don't realize that you and I *are* inferior; it's not a complex, it's a fact,' Ramsay said, to deflate Cyril a little. 'Thank you very much, Cyril, but I cannot come, I have married a wife.'

'Oh, by the way,' Cyril said getting up and striding slowly about the room, 'I'm going to be presented to the Queen on Thursday, at Rhodes House.'

'So am I,' Ramsay said.

'No. I'm perfectly sayrious.'

'So am I. At Goldsmiths' Hall in London on Tuesday.'

'In London, eh?' Cyril said very crestfallen. 'Rather a long way to go just to meet the Queen.'

'You brute! Ah catch you!' Ramsay said, and they burst out laughing. It was the laughter of Jamaica and Surrey College and for a moment they saw themselves, from outside themselves, as two perfectly ludicrous negroes in an Oxford room.

Cyril recovered his poise. 'You really mean that?' he asked.

Ramsay showed him the embossed invitation card.

'Come on, Head, let's go and have a drink.'

They went into 'The Bear' and Ramsay was proud that Cyril was wearing a 'Blue' scarf and knew most of the undergraduates in the pub. Perhaps Cyril represented the only possible compromise.

'Heard from Mrs Phillips,' Cyril said. 'Asked after you.'

'Oh, yes?'

'Pat is going up to Girton next term.'

'Who?' Ramsay asked. He knew quite well who Pat was.

'Patricia Phillips, don't you know?'

'Oh, you mean the "tennis-anyone" girl,' Ramsay said. Oxford had given him the phrase but it seemed spontaneous.

Cyril drank some beer and nodded.

'She's a very good games player, you know.'

'I can think of a few games I'd like to play with her,' Ramsay said. Cyril grinned. It was an extraordinary grin but it wasn't quite right. It looked like the Cheshire Cat's grin drawn by a cubist. Cyril had seen an ex-major who was telling a dirty story grin something like that and he decided to copy it but he hadn't got it quite right. He only looked idiotic. Ramsay remembered how perfectly Patricia had smiled in the English way.

The Queen arrived in Oxford on the next Thursday and Cyril was presented. He wore morning coat, cravat and topper and performed a long-remembered genuflection when the Queen shook hands with him. Ramsay displayed his invitation to Goldsmiths' Hall prominently on his mantelpiece, but he didn't go to London. He was not unimpressed by royalty and ceremonial and he would gladly have gone to meet the Queen of the Netherlands. The trouble was that this Queen was supposed to be *his* Queen and he felt he was a fraud who had no inherent right to be her subject. He added a sentence to his treatise:

> *The Negro finds it difficult to accept a personal sovereign because a modern sovereign represents a racial memory that the Negro has lost.*

The summer term contained certain facts – the sun again, the long twilights, the river, garden productions of Shakespeare, but Ramsay could not recover the enchantment he had lost on the first day. He drifted with Guy from place to place with good appetite as one takes one's pleasure in any university in any country. They hired a gramophone and borrowed classical records and with the curtains drawn, shutting out the sunlight, they argued themselves into believing they were in another world. Guy wrote what can only be called 'smoky' verse and Ramsay, who had no ear for music, tried to learn to read a score. But mostly they drifted about and got bad reports from their tutors at the end of term. Guy went off to Austria and Ramsay stayed in college getting drunk every night with those chaps who had just finished taking their finals or with those who came up later for 'vivas'. Then there was nobody left in college but himself. It was a centreless existence: he wasn't even lonely. He went into 'digs' and spent every day reading fiction in the Union Library until the Union, too, was closed. Then he went to Paris for a week.

He did all that one could do in Paris for a week in the middle of August, the buildings, the shows, the people to be looked at. It was an irritating week. Paris was interesting but nothing happened except that he met a girl from British Guiana he knew at Oxford who asked him if he had a copy of yesterday's *Times*, he was held up and 'frisked' by the police twice very late at night and some whores in Montmartre mistook him for an American and swore at him. When he returned to Oxford there was a letter from Guy Horne waiting for him.

'Dear boy,
I have an excellent idea for a birthday party in your honour next summer. When were you born by the way? We'll have three punts down the river. Punt 1 – Banks of flowers, a chorus of *gypsy* girls singing a Greek ode in French composed by myself. Punt 2 – You, surrounded by very very blonde girls and champagne bottles. Punt 3 – Myself and a be-bop band, playing *Tull's Delight*. Do you think that will get me a fellowship in a cry of dons at All Souls?

I got drunker and drunker and Vienna was lovelier and lovelier.

Seriously though, I have met two wonderful Nigerians at London University library where I go daily (being broke) to read some history. We have lunch together and I am beginning to grasp the colonial problem. What a mess!

I saw the Prince in Paris walking down the Champs-Elysées with *the* most gorgeous piece on that remarkable street.

Don't be depressed, Ramsay. Remember,
         "The Lillie of a Day
         Is fairer farre in May."
You must hold that lily gently in your medieval hand and if you see

that kind Lord on the High (but only on the High) *please* give it to him.

"He (you, not the kind Lord) was likely had he been put on, to have proved most royally."

Ever,

Guy.

PS – Come to London and see Helpmann's face and les girls!'

Ramsay was not depressed but restless. He did a month's half-hearted reading in the Radcliffe Camera. The year had brought one truth but it could not be transliterated into his treatise. It was the memory of a diminuendo from his week in Paris,

> doucement, bébé, doucement
> you black man, you blaack maaan,
> la bouche, bébé, la bouche!

The apotheosis of the negro. He wrote in his treatise:

The Negro is not a man but an inconsistent myth created by himself in the white man's image.

Evan Jones

The Lament of the Banana Man

Gal, I'm tellin' you, I'm tired fo' true,
Tired of Englan', tired o' you.
But I can' go back to Jamaica now . . .

I'm here in Englan', I'm drawin' pay,
I go to de underground every day —
Eight hours is all, half-hour fo' lunch,
M' uniform's free, an' m' ticket punch —
Punchin' tickets not hard to do,
When I'm tired o' punchin', I let dem through.

I get a paid holiday once a year.
Ol' age an' sickness can' touch me here.

I have a room o' m' own, an' a iron bed,
Dunlopillo under m' head,
A Morphy-Richards to warm de air,
A formica table, an easy chair.
I have summer clothes, an' winter clothes,
An' paper kerchiefs to blow m' nose.

My yoke is easy, my burden is light,
I know a place I can go to, any night.
Dis place Englan'! I'm not complainin',
If it col', it col', if it rainin', it rainin'.
I don' min' if it's mostly night,
Dere's always inside, or de sodium light.

I don' min' white people starin' at me
Dey don' want me here? Don't is deir country?
You won' catch me bawlin' any homesick tears
If I don' see Jamaica for a t'ousand years!

. . . Gal, I'm tellin' you, I'm tired fo' true,
Tired of Englan', tired o' you,
I can' go back to Jamaica now –
But I'd want to die there, anyhow.

Samuel Selvon

from The Lonely Londoners

When that first London summer hit Galahad he begin to feel so cold that he had to get a overcoat. Moses laugh like hell. 'You thought you get away from the weather, eh?' he say. 'You warm in the winter and cold in the summer, eh? Well is my turn to put on my light suit and cruise about.'

'I don't know why I hot in the winter and cold in the summer,' Galahad say, shivering.

But for all that, he getting on well in the city. He had a way, whenever he talking with the boys, he using the names of the places like they mean big romance, as if to say 'I was in Oxford Street' have more prestige than if he just say 'I was up the road'. And once he had a date with a frauline, and he make a big point of saying he was meeting she by Charing Cross, because just to say 'Charing Cross' have a lot of romance in it, he remember it had a song called 'Roseann of Charing Cross'. So this is how he getting on to Moses:

'I meeting that piece of skin tonight, you know.' And then, as if it is not very important, 'She waiting for me by Charing Cross Station.'

Jesus Christ, when he say 'Charing Cross', when he realize that is he, Sir Galahad, who going there, near that place that everybody in the world know about (it even have the name in the dictionary) he feel like a new man. It didn't matter about the woman he going to meet, just to say he was going there make him feel big and important, and even if he was just going to coast a lime, to stand up and watch the white people, still, it would have been something.

The same way with the big clock they have in Piccadilly Tube Station, what does tell the time of places all over the world. The time when he had a date with Daisy he tell her to meet him there.

'How you don't know where it is?' he say when she tell him she don't know where it is. 'Is a place that everybody know, everybody does have dates there, is a meeting place.'

Many nights he went there before he get to know how to move around the city, and see them fellars and girls waiting, looking at they wristwatch, watching the people coming up the escalator from the tube. You could tell that they waiting for somebody, the way how they getting on. Leaning up here, reading the *Evening News*, or smoking a cigarette, or walking round the circle looking at clothes in the glass case, and every time people come up the escalator, they watching to see, and if the person not there, they relaxing to wait till the next tube come. All these people there, standing up waiting for somebody. And then you would see a sharp piece of skin come up the escalator, in a sharp coat, and she give the ticket collector she ticket and look around, and same time the fellar who waiting throw away his cigarette and you could see a happy look in his face, and the girl come and hold his arm and laugh, and he look at his wristwatch. Then the two of them walk up the steps and gone to the Circus, gone somewhere, to the theatre, or the cinema, or just to walk around and watch the big life in the Circus.

Lord, that is life for you, that is it. To meet a craft there, and take she out some place.

'What you think, Moses?' he ask Moses.

'Ah, in you I see myself, how I was when I was new to London. All them places is like nothing to me now. Is like when you back home and you hear fellars talk about Times Square and Fifth Avenue, and Charing Cross and gay Paree. You say to yourself, "Lord, them places must be sharp." Then you get a chance and you see them for yourself, and is like nothing.'

'You remember that picture "Waterloo Bridge", with Robert Taylor? I went down by the bridge the other night, and stand up and watch the river.'

'Take it easy,' Moses say wearily.

But Galahad feel like a king living in London. The first time he take a craft out, he dress up good, for one of the first things he do after he get a work was to stock up with clothes like stupidness, as if to make up for all the hard times when he didn't have nice things to wear.

So this is Galahad dressing up for the date: he clean his shoes until they shine, then he put on a little more Cherry Blossom and give them a extra shine, until he could see his face in the leather. Next he put on a new pair of socks – nylon splice in the heel and the toe. He have to put on woollen underwear, though is summer. Then the shirt – a white Van Heusen. Which tie to wear? Galahad have so much tie that whenever he open the cupboard is only tie he seeing in front of him, and many times he just put out his hand and make a grab, and whichever one come he wear. But for this date he choose one of those woollen ties that the bottom cut off. Before he put on trousers and jacket he comb his hair. That is a big operation for Galahad, because he grow the hair real long and bushy, and it like a clump of grass on the head. First, he wet the hair with some water, then he push his finger in the hair-cream jar and scoop out some. He rub the cream on his hands, then he rub his hands on his head. The only mirror in the room is a small one that Galahad have tie on to the electric light cord, and the way he have it, it just a little bit higher than he is, so while he combing the grass he have to sort of look up and not forward. So this comb start going through the grass, stumbling across some big knot in Galahad hair, and water flying from the head as the comb make a pass, and Galahad concentrating on the physiognomy, his forehead wrinkled and he turning the head this way and that. Then afterwards he taking the brush and touching the hair like a tonsorial specialist, here and there, and when he finish, the hair comb well.

When Galahad put on trousers the seam could cut you, and the jacket fitting square on the shoulders. One thing with Galahad since he hit London, no foolishness about clothes: even Moses surprise at the change. Now if you bounce up Galahad one morning by the tube station when he coming from work, you won't believe is the same fellar you did see coasting in the park the evening before. He have on a old cap that was brown one time, but black now with grease and fingerprint, and a jacket that can't see worse days, and a corduroy trousers that would shame them ragandbone man. The shoes have big hole, like they laughing, and so Galahad fly out the tube station, his eyes red and bleary, and his body tired and bend up like a piece of wire, and he only stop to get a *Daily Express* by the station. For Galahad, like Moses, pick up a night work, because it have more money in it. He wasn't doing electrician, but with overtime he grossing about ten so why worry? So while other people going to work, Galahad coming from work. He does cross the road and go by the bakery and buy a hot bread to take home and eat. This time so, as he walking, he only studying sleep, and if a friend bawl out 'Aye, Galahad!' he pass him straight because his mind groggy and tired.

But when you dressing, you dressing. Galahad tailor is a fellar in the Charing Cross Road that Moses put him on to and the tailor surprise that Galahad know all the smartest and latest cut. He couldn't palm off no slack work on the old Galahad at all. And one thing, Galahad not stinting on money for clothes, because he get enough tone when he land up in tropical and watchekong. Don't matter if the test tell him twenty guineas, or thirty-five pounds, Galahad know what he want, and he tell the fellar is all right, you go ahead, cut that jacket so and so, and don't forget I want a twenty-three bottom on the trousers.

And the crowning touch is a long silver chain hanging from the fob, and coming back into the side pocket.

So, cool as a lord, the old Galahad walking out to the road, with plastic raincoat hanging on the arm, and the eyes not missing one sharp craft that pass, bowing his head in a polite 'Good evening' and not giving a blast if they answer or not. This is London, this is life oh lord, to walk like a king with money in your pocket, not a worry in the world.

Is one of those summer evenings, when it look like night would never come, a magnificent evening, a powerful evening, rent finish paying, rations in the cupboard, twenty pounds in the bank, and a nice piece of skin waiting under the big clock in Piccadilly Tube Station. The sky blue, sun shining, the girls ain't have on no coats to hide the legs.

'Mummy, look at that black man!' A little child, holding on to the mother hand, look up at Sir Galahad.

'You mustn't say that, dear!' The mother chide the child.

But Galahad skin like rubber at this stage, he bend down and pat the child cheek, and the child cower and shrink and begin to cry.

'What a sweet child!' Galahad say, putting on the old English accent, 'What's your name?'

But the child mother uneasy as they stand up there on the pavement with so many white people around: if they was alone she might have talked a little, and ask Galahad what part of the world he come from, but instead she pull the child along and she look at Galahad and give a sickly sort of smile, and the old Galahad, knowing how it is, smile back and walk on. —

If that episode did happen around the first time when he land up in London, oh Lord! He would have run to the boys, telling them he have big ballad. But at this stage Galahad like duck back when rain fall — everything running off. Though it used to have times when he lay down there on the bed in the basement room in the Water, and all the experiences like that come to him, and he say 'Lord, what it is we people do in this world that we have to suffer so? What it is we want that the white people and them find it so hard to give? A little work, a little food, a little place to sleep. We not asking for the sun, or the moon. We only want to get by, we don't even want to get on.' And

Galahad would take his hand from under the blanket, as he lay there studying how the night before he was in the lavatory and two white fellars come in and say how these black bastards have the lavatory dirty, and they didn't know that he was there, and when he come out they say hello mate have a cigarette. And Galahad watch the colour of his hand, and talk to it, saying, 'Colour, is you that causing all this, you know. Why the hell you can't be blue, or red or green, if you can't be white? You know is you that cause a lot of misery in the world. Is not me, you know, is you! I ain't do anything to infuriate the people and them, is you! Look at you, you so black and innocent, and this time so you causing misery all over the world!'

So Galahad talking to the colour Black, as if is a person, telling it that is not *he* who causing botheration in the place, but Black, who is a worthless thing for making trouble all about. 'Black, you see what you cause to happen yesterday? I went to look at that room that Ram tell me about in the Gate, and as soon as the landlady see you she say the room let already. She ain't even give me a chance to say good morning. Why the hell you can't change colour?'

Galahad get so interested in this theory about Black that he went and tell Moses. 'Is not we that the people don't like,' he tell Moses, 'is the colour Black.' But the day he went to Moses with this theory Moses was in an evil mood, because a new friend did just get in a thing with some white fellars by Praed Street, near Paddington Station. The friend was standing up there reading in the window about rooms to let and things to sell, and it had a notice saying Keep the Water White, and right there the friend start to get on ignorant (poor fellar, he was new in London) and want to get in big argument with the white people standing around.

So Moses tell Galahad, 'Take it easy, that is a sharp theory, why you don't write about it.'

Anyway all thought like that out of Galahad mind as he out on this summer evening, walking down the Bayswater Road on his way to the Circus. He go into the gardens, and begin to walk down to the Arch, seeing so much cat about the place, laying down on the grass, sitting and talking, all of them in pretty summer colours, the grass green, the sky blue, sun shining, flowers growing, the fountains spouting water, and Galahad Esquire strolling through all of this, three-four pounds in the pocket, sharp clothes on – lord oh lord – going to meet a first-class craft that waiting for him in the Circus. Once or twice, as he get a smile here and there, he made to forget Daisy and try to make some headway in the park.

By the Arch, he meet one of the boys.

'Where you going?' the test say.

'Have a date, man, going to pick up a little thing down the road.'

'Listen, listen here to the rarse this man talking, about how colonials shouldn't come to Brit'n, that the place overcrowding with spades.'

'I ain't have time, man, I late already.'

'Lend me ten shillings.'

'I can't make it now, come round tomorrow.'

'Oh God ease me up, man. A cup of char?'

Galahad give him a shilling and move away from the Arch, watching up at the clock on the Odeon although he have wristwatch. The clock saying half-past seven and he have to meet Daisy at eight. He start to walk a little faster, but was five past when he find himself in the Circus.

Always, from the first time he went there to see Eros and the lights, that circus have a magnet for him, that circus represent life, that circus is the beginning and the ending of the world. Every time he go there, he have the same feeling like when he see it the first night, drink Coca-Cola, any time is Guinness time, Bovril and the fireworks, a million flashing lights, gay laughter, the wide doors of theatres, the huge posters, ever-ready batteries, rich people going into tall hotels, people going to the theatre, people sitting and standing and walking and talking and laughing and buses and cars and Galahad Esquire, in all this, standing there in the big city, in London. Oh Lord.

He went down the steps into the station, and Daisy was expecting him to come by tube so she watching the escalators, and he walk up behind her and he put his hands over she eyes, and that evening people in the tube station must be bawl to see black man so familiar with white girl. But Galahad feeling too good to bother about the loud tones in them people eyes. Tonight is his night. This was something he uses to dream about in Trinidad. The time when he was leaving, Frank tell him: 'Boy, it have bags of white pussy in London, and you will eat till you tired.' And now, the first date, in the heart of London, dressed to kill, ready to escort the number around the town, anywhere she want to go, any place at all.

Daisy was dress up plenty, she look different than when she in the plant with a pair of jeans and a overalls on. All the grease and dirt wash off the hands, the hair comb well, the dress is a sort of cotton but it have all sorts of coloured designs on it and it look pretty, and she have on lipstick for so. She look real sharp, and when he was coming up he notice the trim legs, and the straight lines of the nylons, and the high-heel shoes.

Daisy move his hands and say, 'Oh, it's you. I thought you were coming by tube.' And she look a little embarrass, but Galahad didn't notice.

'What time it is now in Trinidad?' Galahad look at the big clock, watching for Trinidad; the island so damn small it only have a dot and the name. 'That is where I come from,' he tell Daisy, 'you see how far it is from England?'

'We'll be late,' Daisy say.

'Which part you want to go,' Galahad ask, 'anywhere at all. Tonight we on a big splurge.'

'They're showing *The Gladiator* at the Hippodrome, and I want to see it.'

'Pictures! Is pictures you want to go to tonight?'

'Well it's Sunday and all the theatres are closed.'

'Who acting in *The Gladiator*?'

'Victor Mature.'

'Well if that is what you want, all right. But I was thinking we could go some place and have a good time, being as is the only night I have off for the whole week, and you too.'

So they went to this theatre that showing *The Gladiator*, and Galahad feeling good with this piece of skin walking with him. But when he look at prices to enter, he couldn't help saying how it was a lot of money, not that he mind, but he know that that same picture would come down in the Water and show for two and six.

'This is the West End,' Daisy remind him.

'All right, even if is a pound we still going.'

After the picture they went to a restaurant and eat a big meal, and Galahad buy a bottle of French wine, telling the waiter to bring the best.

The summer night descend with stars, they walking hand in hand, and Galahad feeling hearts.

'It was a lovely evening —' Daisy begin.

'Come and go in the yard,' Galahad say.

'What?' Daisy say.

'The yard. Where I living.'

All this time he was stalling, because he feeling sort of shame to bring the girl in that old basement room, but if the date end in fiasco he know the boys would never finish giving him tone for spending all that money and not eating.

Daisy start to hesitate but he make haste and catch a number twelve, telling she that it all on the way home. When they hop off by the Water she was still getting on prim, but Galahad know was only grandcharge, and besides the old blood getting hot, so he walk Daisy brisk down the road, and she quiet as a mouse. They went down the basement steps and Galahad fumble for the key, and when he open the door a whiff of stale food and old clothes and dampness and dirt come out the door and he only waiting to hear what Daisy would say.

But she ain't saying nothing, and he walk through the passage and open the door and put the light on.

Daisy sit down on the bed and Galahad say: 'You want a cup of char?' And without waiting for any answer he full the pot in the tap and put it on the ring and turn the gas on. He feel so excited that he had to light a cigarette, and he keep saying 'Take it easy' to himself.

'Is this your room?' Daisy say, looking around and shifting about as if she restless.

'Yes,' Galahad say. 'You like it?'

'Yes,' Daisy say.

Galahad throw a copy of *Ebony* to her and she begin to turn the pages.

With all the excitement Galahad taking off the good clothes carefully and slowly, putting the jacket and trousers on the hanger right away, and folding up the shirt and putting it in the drawer.

When the water was boiling he went to the cupboard and take out a packet of tea, and he shake some down in the pot.

Daisy look at him as if he mad.

'Is that how you make tea?' she ask.

'Yes,' Galahad say. 'No foolishness about it. Tea is tea — you just drop some in the kettle. If you want it strong, you drop plenty. If you want it weak, you drop little bit. And so you make a lovely cuppa.'

He take the kettle off and rest it on a sheet of *Daily Express* on the ground. He bring two cups, a spoon, a bottle of milk and a packet of sugar.

'Fix up,' he say, handing Daisy a cup.

They sit down there sipping the tea and talking.

'You get that raise the foreman was promising you?' Galahad ask, for something to say.

'What did you say? You know it will take me some time to understand everything you say. The way you West Indians speak!'

'What wrong with it?' Galahad ask. 'Is English we speaking.'

And so he coasting a little oldtalk until the tea finish, and afterwards he start to make one set of love to Daisy.

'It was battle royal in that basement, man,' he tell Moses afterwards, and he went on to give a lot of detail, though all of that is nothing to a old veteran like Moses, is only to Galahad is new because is the first time with a white number. Moses smile a knowing smile, a tired smile, and 'Take it easy,' he tell Sir Galahad.

.　　.　　.　　.　　.　　.

Oh what a time it is when summer come to the city and all them girls throw away heavy winter coat and wearing light summer frocks so you could see the legs and shapes that was hiding away from the cold blasts and you could coast a lime in the park and negotiate ten shillings or a pound with the sports as the case may be or else they have a particular bench near the Hyde Park Corner that they call the Play Around Section where you could go and sit with one of them what a time summer is because you bound to meet the boys coasting lime in the park and you could go walking through the gardens and see all them pretty pieces of skin taking suntan and how the old geezers like the sun they would sit on the benches and smile everywhere you turn the English people smiling isn't it a lovely day as if the sun burn away all the tightness and strain that was in their faces for the winter and on a nice day every manjack and his brother going to the park with his girl and laying down on the green grass and making love in the winter you would never think that the grass would ever come green again but if you don't keep your eyes open it look like one day the trees naked and the next day they have clothes on sometimes walking up to the Bayswater Road from Queensway you could look on a winter day and see how grim the trees looking and a sort of fog in the distance though right near to you ain't no fog but that is only deceiving because if somebody down the other side look up by where you are it would look to them as if it have fog by where you are and this time so the sun in the sky like a forceripe orange and it giving no heat at all and the atmosphere like a sullen twilight hanging over the big city but it different too bad when is summer for then the sun shine for true and the sky blue and a warm wind blowing it look like when is winter a kind of grey nasty colour does come to the sky and it stay there and you forget what it like to see blue skies like back home where blue sky so common people don't even look up in the air and you feeling miserable and cold but when summer come is fire in the town big times fête like stupidness and you have to keep the blood cool for after all them cold and wet months you like you roaring to go though to tell truth winter don't make much difference to some of the boys they blazing left and right as usual all the year round to talk of all the episodes that Moses had with woman in London would take bags of ballad Moses move through all the nationalities in the world and then he start the circle again everybody know how after the war them rich English family sending to the continent to get domestic and over there all them girls think like the newspapers say about the Jamaicans that the streets of London paved with gold so they coming by the boatload and the boys making contact and having big times with the girls working during the day and coming round by the yard in the evening for a cuppa and to hit one or two but anyone of Moses encounter is big episode because coasting about the Water it ain't have no man with a sharper eye than he not even Cap could ask him for anything and one summer evening he was walking when he spot a number and he smile and she smile back and after a little preliminary about the weather Moses take her for a drink in the pub and after that he coast a walk with she in Kensington Gardens and they sit down on the grass and talk about how lovely the city is in the summer and Moses say how about coming to my yard she went but afterwards Moses nearly dead with fright because the woman start to moan and gasp and wriggle and twist up she body like a piece of wire when Moses ask she what happen she only moaning Moses start to get cold sweat because he know that if anything happen to the woman and the police find her in his yard that he wouldn't stand a chance the way how things against the boys from in front so he begin to rub the woman down and pat she and try to make she drink some water what happen to you Moses ask frighten like hell that the woman might conk off on his hands the woman only gasping and calling out for her mother and Moses sweating just then the bell ring and Moses went to the door and see Daniel Daniel he say boy a hell of a thing happening here man I just pick up a woman up the road and bring she in the yard and it look like if she dying what Daniel say as if he don't understand wait here Moses say and he run back in the room listen he tell the woman my friend come and you have to go put on your clothes by the time Moses went and call Daniel inside the woman was calm and cool as if nothing happen she look all right to me Daniel say eyeing the piece as if he ready to charge but Moses was too frighten to keep the woman around though she sit down on the bed and begin to talk calmly boy he tell Daniel you wouldn't believe me but the woman did look as if she going to dead only lying because I happen to come round while you have she here Daniel say but Moses so relieve that she looking all right that he didn't bother with Daniel he just tell her to come and go right away so he take her out to the Bayswater Road to catch a bus the heel of my shoe is coming off she say will you come with me to get it fixed sure Moses say but as soon as they hop on the bus and it begin to drive off Moses hop off again and leave she going to Marble Arch what a gambol does go on in the park on them summer nights oh sometimes the girls wishing it would get dark quickly and you have them parading all down the Bayswater Road from the Arch to the Gate and you could see them fellars going up and talking for a minute and if they agree they go in the park or somewhere else together and if not the fellar walk on but these fellars that cruising they could size up the situation in one glance as they pass by and know if they like this one or that one you does meet all sorts of fellars from all walks of life don't ever be surprised at who you meet up cruising and reclining in the park it might be your boss or it might be some big professional fellar because it ain't have no discrimination when it comes to that in the park in the summer see them girls in little groups here and there talking and how they could curse you never hear curse until one of them sports curse you if you approach one and she don't like your terms she tell you to — off right away and if you linger she tell you to double — off but business is brisk in the park in the summer one night one of them hustle from behind a tree pulling up her clothes and she bawl out Mary the police and if you see how them girls fade out and make races with the tight skirts holding the legs close together and the high heels going clopclop but that was no handicap when they take off it have some fellars who does go in the park only to cruise around and see what they could see you could always tell these tests they have on a coat with the collar turn up and they hand in they pocket and they breezing through the park hiding from tree to tree like if they playing hide and see one night Moses was liming near the park and a car pull up that had a fellar and a old-looking woman in it the fellar start to talk friendly and invite Moses home for a cup of coffee and Moses went just to see what would happen and what happen was the fellar play as if he fall asleep and give Moses a free hand because it have fellars who does get big thrills that way but Moses didn't do anything because he know what the position like and even though the fellar offer him three pounds he smile and was polite and tell him that he sorry good night introducing Galahad to the night life Moses explain to him about short time and long time and how to tackle the girls and he take Galahad one night and let him loose in the park Galahad say I going to try and he broach a group under the trees about a hundred yards from the corner by the Arch but from the time he begin to talk the girl tell him to — off Galahad stand up to argue but Moses pull him away those girls not catholic at all Galahad say Moses say it have some of them who don't like the boys and is all the fault of Cap because Cap don't like to pay let us cut through the park and go by Hyde Park Corner Galahad say when they reach there Moses pick up a sharp thing who was talking to two English fellars and he take her to the yard afterwards the girl tell him how she used to take heroin at one time and she show him the marks on her arm where she inject the kick Moses stay with the thing regular for a week then he get tired and tell Cap he have a girl if he interested and Cap give the usual answer so Moses tell him to come in the yard in the night that the girl would be there Cap went and Moses left the two of them in the room and went for a walk when he come back three hours later Cap was in the bathroom and the thing was standing up before the gas fire warming up the treasury your friend have any money she ask Moses yes Moses say he have bags of money he is the son of a Nigerian king and when he goes back home he will rule more than a million people the girl ask Moses if he want anything take it easy Moses say when Cap come back Moses tell him to drop the girl up the road and the girl went with Cap thinking that he have plenty money when Cap get to the corner he tell her to wait he going to change a five-pound note as he don't go around with small change and he left the girl standing up there and never went back meantime Moses sit down on the bed and the bed fall down when Cap come back he say Cap you are a hell of a man you break my bed Cap say sorry Moses say this is the third time you break my bed Cap say it was warm and nice in the bed Moses say what I will tell the landlord this thing happening so often and he had was to put a box and prop up the bed to sleep summer does really be hearts like if you start to live again you coast a lime by the Serpentine and go for a row on the river or you go bathing by the Lido though the water never warm no matter how hot the sun is you would be feeling hot out of the water but the minute you jump in you start to shiver and have to get out quick but it does be as if around that time of the year something strange happen to everybody they all smiling and as if they living for the first time so you get to wondering if it ain't have a certain part of the population what does lie low during the cold months and only take to the open when summer come for it have some faces in the Water that Moses never see until summer come or maybe they have enough money to go Montego Bay in winter and come back to the old Brit'n when they know the weather would be nice listen to this ballad what happen to Moses one summer night one splendid summer night with the sky brilliant with stars like in the tropics he was liming in Green Park when a English fellar come up to him and say you are just the man I am looking for who me Moses say yes the man say come with me Moses went wondering what the test want and the test take him to a blonde who was standing up under a tree and talk a little so Moses couldn't hear but Blondie shake her head then he take Moses to another one who was sitting on a bench and she say yes so the test come back to Moses and want to pay Moses to go with the woman Moses was so surprise that he say yes quickly and he went with the thing and the test hover in the background afterwards he ask Moses if he would come again and Moses say it look like a good preposition to me I don't mind and he carry on for a week the things that does happen in this London people wouldn't believe when you tell them they would cork their ears when you talk and say that isn't true but some ballad happen in the city that people would bawl if they hear right there in Hyde Park how them sports must bless the government for this happy hunting ground the things that happen there in the summer hard to believe one night two sports catch a fellar hiding behind some bushes with a flash camera in his hand they mash up the camera and beat the fellar where all these women coming from you never know but every year the ranks augmented with fresh blood from the country districts who come to see the big life in London and the bright lights also lately in view of the big set of West Indians that storming Brit'n it have a lot of dark women who in the racket too they have to make a living and you could see them here and there with the professionals walking on the Bayswater Road or liming in the park learning the tricks of the trade it have some white fellars who feel is a big thrill to hit a black number and the girls does make them pay big money but as far as spades hitting spades it ain't have nothing like that for a spade wouldn't hit a spade when it have so much other talent on parade don't think that you wouldn't meet real class in the park even in big society it have hustlers one night Moses meet a pansy by Marble Arch tube station and from the way the test look at him Moses know because you could always tell these tests unless you real green you have a lovely tie the pansy say yes Moses say you have a lovely hat yes Moses say you have a very nice coat yes Moses say everything I have is nice I like you the pansy say I like you too Moses say and all this time he want to dead with laugh I have a lovely model staying in my flat in Knightsbridge the pansy say she likes to go with men but I don't like that sort of thing myself would you like to come to my flat sure Moses say we will go tomorrow night as I have an important engagement tonight I will meet you right here by the station the test say but so many people are here Moses say I might miss you if you don't see me you can phone but what will we do when I come to your flat Moses say playing stupid and the

test tell him what and what they wouldn't do one night he and Galahad
was walking up Inverness Terrace when a car pass going slow and the
door open and a fellar fling one of the sports out the poor girl fall down
and roll to the pavement all the other sports in the area rally and run
up to she and pick she up and ask she what happen she say she went
with the fellar but he didn't want to pay and she give him two cuff in his
face and he pitch she out the car another night a big Jamaican fellar
take two home and had them running out of the house and he throw
their clothes for them from the window people wouldn't believe you
when you tell them the things that happen in the city but the cruder
you are the more the girls like you you can't put on any English accent
for them or play ladeda or tell them you studying medicine in Oxford
or try to be polite and civilize they don't want that sort of thing at all
they want you to live up to the films and stories they hear about black
people living primitive in the jungles of the world that is why you will
see so many of them African fellars in the city with their hair high up
on the head like they ain't had a trim for years and with scar on their
face and a ferocious expression going about with some real sharp
chicks the cruder you are the more they like you the whole blasted set
of them frustrated like if they don't know what it is all about what
happen to you people Moses ask a cat one night and she tell him how
the black boys so nice and could give them plenty of thrills people
wouldn't believe or else they would cork their ears and say they don't
want to know but the higher the society the higher the kicks they want
one night Moses meet a nice woman driving in a car in Piccadilly and
she pick him up and take him to a club in Knightsbridge where it had a
party bags of women and fellars all about drinking champagne and
whisky this girl who pick him up get high and start to dance the cancan
with some other girls when they fling their legs up in the air they going
around to the tables where the fellars sitting Moses sit down there
wondering how this sort of thing happening in a place where only the
high and the mighty is but with all of that they feel they can't get big
thrills unless they have a black man in the company and when Moses
leave afterwards they push five pounds in his hand and pat him on the
back and say that was a jolly good show it have a lot of people in
London who cork their ears and wouldn't listen but if they get the
chance they do the same thing themselves everybody look like they
frustrated in the big city the sex life gone wild you would meet women
who beg you to go with them one night a Jamaican with a woman in
Chelsea in a smart flat with all sorts of surrealistic painting on the walls
and contemporary furniture in the G-plan the poor fellar bewildered

and asking questions to improve himself because the set-up look like the World of Art but the number not interested in passing on any knowledge she only interested in one thing and in the heat of emotion she call the Jamaican a black bastard though she didn't mean it as an insult but as a compliment under the circumstances but the Jamaican fellar get vex and he stop and say why the hell you call me a black bastard and he thump the woman and went away all these things happen in the blazing summer under the trees in the park on the grass with the daffodils and tulips in full bloom and a sky of blue oh it does really be beautiful then to hear the birds whistling and see the green leaves come back on the trees and in the night the world turn upside down and everybody hustling that is life that is London oh lord Galahad say when the sweetness of summer get in him he say he would never leave the old Brit'n as long as he live and Moses sigh a long sigh like a man who live life and see nothing at all in it and who frighten as the years go by wondering what it is all about.

Louise M. Meriwether

A Happening in Barbados

The best way to pick up a Barbadian man, I hoped, was to walk alone down the beach with my tall, brown frame squeezed into a skin-tight bathing suit. Since my hotel was near the beach and Dorothy and Alison, my two travelling-companions, had gone shopping, I managed this quite well. I had not taken more than a few steps on the glittering, white sand before two black men were on either side of me vying for attention.

I chose the tall, slim-hipped one over the squat, muscle-bound man who was also grinning at me. But apparently they were friends, because Edwin had no sooner settled me under his umbrella then the squat one showed up with a beach chair and two other boys in tow.

Edwin made the introductions. His temporary rival was Gregory, and the other two were Alphonse and Dimitri.

Gregory was ugly. He had thick, rubbery lips, a scarcity of teeth, and a broad nose splattered like a pyramid across his face. He was all massive shoulders and bulging biceps. No doubt he had a certain animal magnetism, but personally I preferred a lean man like Edwin, who was well built but slender, his whole body fitting together like a symphony. Alphonse and Dimitri were clean-cut and pleasant looking.

They were all too young — twenty to twenty-five at the most — and Gregory seemed the oldest. I inwardly mourned their youth and settled down to make the most of my catch.

The crystal blue sky rivalled the royal blue of the Caribbean for beauty and our black bodies on the white sand added to the munificence of colours. We ran into the sea like squealing children when the sudden raindrops came, then shivered on the sand under a makeshift tent of umbrellas and damp towels waiting for the sun to reappear while nourishing ourselves with straight Barbados rum.

As with most of the West Indians I had already met on my whirlwind tour of Trinidad and Jamaica who welcomed American Negroes with open arms, my new friends loved their island home, but work was scarce and they yearned to go to America. They were hungry for news of how Negroes were faring in the States.

Edwin's arm rested casually on my knee in a proprietary manner and I smiled at him. His thin, serious face was smooth, too young for a razor, and when he smiled back he looked even younger. He told me he was a waiter at the Hilton, saving his money to make it to the States. I had already learned not to be snobbish with the island's help. Yesterday's waiter may be tomorrow's prime minister.

Dimitri, very black with an infectious grin, was also a waiter, and lanky Alphonse was a tile setter.

Gregory's occupation was apparently women, for that's all he talked about. He was able to launch this subject when a bony, white woman — more peeling red than white, really — looking like a gaunt cadaver in a loose-fitting bathing suit, came out of the sea and walked up to us. She smiled archly at Gregory.

'Are you going to take me to the Pigeon Club tonight, Sugar?'

'No, mon,' he said pleasantly, with a toothless grin. 'I'm taking a younger pigeon.'

The woman turned a deeper red, if that were possible, and, mumbling something incoherent, walked away.

'That one is always after me to take her some place,' Gregory said. 'She's rich and she pays the bills but, mon, I don't want an old hag nobody else wants. I like to take my women away from white men and watch them squirm.'

'Come down, mon,' Dimitri said, grinning. 'She look like she's starving for what you got to spare.'

We all laughed. The boys exchanged stories about their experiences with predatory white women who came to the islands looking for some black action. But, one and all, they declared they liked dark-skinned meat the best, and I felt like a black queen of the Nile when Gregory winked at me and said: 'The blacker the berry, mon, the sweeter the juice.'

They had all been pursued and had chased some white tail too, no doubt, but while the others took it all in good humour, it soon became apparent that Gregory's exploits were exercises in vengeance.

Gregory was saying: 'I told that bastard, "You in my country now, mon, and I'll kick your ass all the way back to Texas. The girl agreed to dance with me and she don't need your permission." That white man's face turned purple but he sat back down and I danced with his girl. Mon, they hate to see me rubbing bellies with their women, 'cause they know once she rub bellies with me she wanna rub something else too.'

He laughed and we all joined in. Serves the white men right, I thought. Let's see how they liked licking *that* end of the stick for a change.

'Mon, you gonna get killed yet,' Edwin said, moving closer to me on the towel we shared. 'You're crazy. You don't care whose woman you mess with. But it's not gonna be a white man who kills you but some bad Bajan.'

Gregory led in the laughter, then held us spell-bound for the next hour with intimate details of his affair with Glenda, a young white girl spending the summer with her father on their yacht. Whatever he had, Glenda wanted it desperately, or so Gregory told it.

Yeah, I thought to myself, like LSD, a black lover is the thing this year. I had seen the white girls in the Village and at off-Broadway theatres clutching their black men tightly while I, manless, looked on with bitterness. I often vowed I would find me an ofay in self defense, but I could never bring myself to condone the wholesale rape of my slave ancestors by letting a white man touch me.

We finished the rum and the three boys stood up to leave, making arrangements to get together later with us and my two girl friends and go clubbing.

Edwin and I were left alone. He stretched out his smoothly muscled leg and touched my toes with his. I smiled at him and let our thighs come together. Why did he have to be so damned young? Then our lips met, his warm and demanding, and I thought, what the hell, maybe I will.

I was thirty-nine – goodbye, sweet bird of youth – an ungay divorcee, up tight and drinking too much, trying to disown the years which had brought only loneliness and pain. I had clawed my way up from the slums of Harlem via night school and was now a law clerk on Wall Street. But the fight upward had taken its toll. My husband, who couldn't claw as well as I, got lost somewhere in that concrete jungle. The last I saw of him he was peering under every skirt around, searching for his lost manhood.

I had always felt contempt for women who found their kicks by robbing the cradle. Now here I was on a Barbadoes beach with an amorous child young enough to be my son. Two sayings flitted unbidden across my mind: 'Judge not that ye be not judged,' and 'The thing which I feared is come upon me.' I thought, ain't it the goddamned truth?

Edwin kissed me again, pressing the length of his body against mine.

'I've got to go,' I gasped. 'My friends have probably returned and are looking for me. About ten, tonight?'

He nodded. I smiled at him and ran all the way to my hotel.

At exactly ten o'clock the telephone in our room announced we had company downstairs.

'Hot damn,' Alison said, putting on her eyebrows in front of the mirror. 'We're not going to be stood up.'

'Island men,' I said loftily, 'are dependable, not like the bums you're used to in America.'

Alison, freckled and willowy, had been married three times and was looking for her fourth. Her motto was, if at first you don't succeed, find another mother. She was a real estate broker in Los Angeles and we had been childhood friends in Harlem.

'What I can't stand,' Dorothy said from the bathroom, 'are those creeps who come to *your* apartment, drink up *your* liquor, then dirty up *your* sheets. You don't even get a lousy dinner out of the deal.'

She came out of the bathroom in her slip. Petite and delicate with a pixie grin, at thirty-five Dorothy looked more like one of the high school girls she taught than their teacher. She had never been married. Years ago, while she was holding on to her virginity with a miser's grip, her fiancé had messed up and knocked up one of her friends. Since then, all of Dorothy's affairs had been with married men, displaying perhaps a subconscious vendetta against all wives.

By ten-twenty we were downstairs and I was introducing the girls to our four escorts who eyed us with unconcealed admiration. We were looking good in our Saks Fifth Avenue finery. They were looking good, too, in soft shirts and loose slacks, all except Gregory, whose bulging muscles confined in clothing made him seem more gargantuan.

We took a cab, and a few minutes later were squeezing behind a table in a small, smoky room called the Pigeon Club. A Trinidad steel band was blasting out the walls and the tiny dance area was jammed with wiggling bottoms and shuffling feet. The white tourists, trying to do the hip-shaking calypso, were having a ball and looking awkward.

I got up to dance with Edwin. He had a natural grace and was easy to follow. Our bodies found the rhythm and became one with it, while our eyes locked in silent, ancient combat, his pleading, mine teasing.

We returned to our seats and to tall glasses of rum and cola tonic. The party had begun.

I danced every dance with Edwin, his clasp becoming gradually tighter until my face was smothered in his shoulder, my arms locked around his neck. He was adorable. Very good for my ego. The other boys took turns dancing with my friends, but soon preferences were set

— Alison with Alphonse and Dorothy with Dimitri. With good humour Gregory ordered another round and didn't seem to mind being odd man out, but he wasn't alone for long.

During the floor show featuring the inevitable limbo dancers, a pretty white girl, about twenty-two, with straight, red hair hanging down to her shoulder, appeared at Gregory's elbow. From his wink at me and self-satisfied grin, I knew this was Glenda from the yacht.

'Hello,' she said to Gregory. 'Can I join you, or do you have a date?'

Well, I thought, that's the direct approach.

'What are you doing here?' Gregory asked.

'Looking for you.'

Gregory slid over on the bench next to the wall and Glenda sat down as he introduced her to the rest of us. Somehow her presence spoiled my mood. We had been happy being black and I resented this intrusion from the white world. But Glenda was happy. She had found the man she set out to find and a swinging party to boot. She beamed a dazzling smile around the table.

Alphonse led Alison on to the dance floor and Edwin and I followed. The steel band was playing a wild calypso and I could feel my hair rising with the heat as I joined in the wildness.

When we returned to the table, Glenda applauded us, then turned to Gregory. 'Why don't you teach me to dance like that?'

He answered with his toothless grin and a leer, implying he had better things to teach her.

White women were always snatching our men, I thought, and now they want to dance like us.

I turned my attention back to Edwin and met his full stare.

'I want you,' he said, his tone as solemn as if he were in church.

I teased him with a smile, refusing to commit myself. He had a lusty, healthy appetite, which was natural, I supposed, for a twenty-one-year-old lad. Lord, but why did he have to be *that* young? I stood up to go to the ladies' room.

'Wait for me,' Glenda cried, trailing behind me.

The single toilet stall was occupied and Glenda leaned against the wall waiting for it, while I flipped open my compact and powdered my grimy face.

'You married?' she asked.

'Divorced.'

'When I get married I want to stay hooked for ever.'

'That's the way I planned it too,' I said drily.

'What I mean,' she rushed on, 'is that I've gotta find a cat who wants to groove only with me.'

Oh Lord, I thought, don't try to sound like us too. Use your own sterile language.

'I really dug this guy I was engaged to,' Glenda continued, 'but he couldn't function without a harem. I could have stood that maybe, but when he didn't mind if I made it with some other guy too, I knew I didn't want that kind of life.'

I looked at her in the mirror as I applied my lipstick. She had been hurt, and badly. Shook right down to her naked soul. So she was dropping down a social notch, according to her scale of values, and trying to repair her damaged ego with a black brother.

'You gonna make it with Edwin?' she asked, as if we were college chums comparing dates.

'I'm not a one night stand.' My tone was frigid. That's another thing I can't stand about white people. Too familiar, just because we're coloured.

'I dig Gregory,' she said, pushing her hair out of her eyes. 'He's kind of rough, but who wouldn't be, the kind of life he's led.'

'And what kind of life is that?' I asked.

'Didn't you know? His mother was a whore in an exclusive brothel for white men only. That was before, when the British owned the island.'

'I take it you like rough men?' I asked.

'There's usually something gentle and lost underneath,' she replied.

A white woman came out of the toilet and Glenda went in. Jesus, I thought. Gregory, gentle? The woman walked to the basin, flung some water in the general direction of her hands, and left.

'Poor Daddy is having a fit,' Glenda volunteered from the john, 'but there's not much he can do about it. He's afraid I'll leave him again and he gets lonely without me, so he just tags along and tries to keep me out of trouble.'

'And pays the bills?'

She answered with a laugh. 'Why not? He's loaded.'

Why not, I thought with bitterness. You white women have always managed to have your cake and eat it too. The toilet flushed with a roar like Niagara Falls. I opened the door and went back to our table. Let Glenda find her way back alone.

Edwin pulled my chair out and brushed his lips across the nape of my neck as I sat down. He still had not danced with anyone else and his apparent desire was flattering. For a moment I considered it. That's what I really needed, wasn't it? To walk down the moonlit beach wrapped in his arms, making it to some pad to be made? It would be a delightful story to tell at bridge sessions. But I shook my head at him and this time my smile was more sad than teasing.

Glenda came back and crawled over Gregory's legs to the seat beside him. The bastard. He made no pretence of being a gentleman. Suddenly, I didn't know which of them I disliked the most. Gregory winked at me. I don't know where he got the impression I was his conspirator, but got up to dance with him.

'That Glenda,' he grinned, 'she's the one I was on the boat with last night. I banged her plenty, in the room right next to her father. We could hear him coughing to let us know he was awake, but he didn't come in.'

He laughed, like a naughty schoolboy, and I joined in. He was a nerveless bastard all right, and it served Glenda right that we were laughing at her. Who asked her to crash our party, anyway? That's when I got the idea to take Gregory away from her.

'You gonna bang her again tonight?' I asked, a new teasing quality in my voice. 'Or are you gonna find something better to do?' To help him get the message I rubbed bellies with him.

He couldn't believe this sudden turn of events. I could almost see him thinking. With one stroke he could slap Glenda down a peg and repay Edwin for beating out his time with me on the beach that morning.

'You wanna come with me?' he asked, making sure of his quarry.

'What you got to offer?' I peered at him through half-closed lids.

'Big Bamboo,' he sang, the title of a popular calypso. We both laughed.

I felt a heady excitement of impending danger as Gregory pulled me back to the table.

The men paid the bill and suddenly we were all standing outside the club in the bright moonlight. Gregory deliberately uncurled Glenda's arm from his and took a step towards me. Looking at Edwin and nodding in my direction he said: 'She's coming with me. Any objections?'

Edwin inhaled a mouthful of smoke. His face was inscrutable. 'You want to go with him?' he asked me quietly.

I avoided his eyes and nodded. 'Yes.'

He flipped the cigarette with contempt at my feet and lit another one. 'Help yourself to the garbage,' he said, and leaned back against the building, one leg braced behind him. The others suddenly stilled their chatter, sensing trouble.

I was holding Gregory's arm now and I felt his muscles tense. 'No,' I said, as he moved towards Edwin. 'You've got what you want. Forget it.'

Glenda was ungracious in defeat. 'What about me?' she screamed. She stared from one black face to another, her glance lingering on Edwin. But he wasn't about to come to her aid and take Gregory's leavings.

'You can go home in a cab,' Gregory said, pushing her ahead of him and pulling me behind him to a taxi waiting at the curb.

Glenda broke from his grasp. 'You bastard. Who in the hell do you think you are, King Solomon? You can't dump me like this.' She raised her hands as if to strike Gregory on the chest, but he caught them before they landed.

'Careful, white girl,' he said. His voice was low but ominous. She froze.

'But why,' she whimpered, all hurt child now. 'You liked me last night. I know you did. Why are you treating me like this?'

'I didn't bring you here,' his voice was pleasant again, 'so don't be trailing me all over town. When I want you I'll come to that damn boat and get you. Now get in that cab before I throw you in. I'll see you tomorrow night. Maybe.'

'You go to hell.' She eluded him and turned on me, asking with incredible innocence: 'What did I ever do to you?' Then she was running past us towards the beach, her sobs drifting back to haunt me like a forlorn melody.

What had she ever done to me? And what had I just done? In order to degrade her for the crime of being white I had sunk to the gutter. Suddenly Glenda was just another woman, vulnerable and lonely, like me.

We were sick, sick, sick. All fucked up. I had thought only Gregory was hung up in his love-hate, black-white syndrome, decades of suppressed hatred having sickened his soul. But I was tainted too. I had forgotten my own misery long enough to inflict it on another woman who was only trying to ease her loneliness by making it with a soul brother. Was I jealous because she was able to function as a woman where I couldn't, because she realized that a man is a man, colour be damned, while I was crucified on my anti-white man cross? What if she were going black trying to repent for some ancient Nordic sin? How else could she atone except with the gift of herself? And if some black brother wanted to help a chick off her lily-white pedestal, he was entitled to that freedom, and it was none of my damned business anyway.

'Let's go, baby,' Gregory said, tucking my arm under his.

The black bastard. I didn't even like the ugly ape. I backed away from him. 'Leave me alone,' I screamed. 'Goddammit, just leave me alone!'

For a moment we were all frozen into an absurd fresco – Alison, Dorothy, and the two boys looking at me in shocked disbelief, Edwin hiding behind a nonchalant smoke screen, Gregory off balance and confused, reaching out towards me.

I moved first, towards Edwin, but I had slammed that door behind me. He laughed, a mirthless sound in the stillness. He knew. I had forsaken him, but at least not for Gregory.

Then I was running down the beach looking for Glenda, hot tears of shame burning my face. How could I have been such a bitch? But the white beach, shimmering in the moonlight, was empty. And once again, I was alone.

Nicolás Guillén

Ballad of My Two Grandfathers

Shadows that only I can see
my two grandfathers go with me.

Lance with head of bone
drum of leather and of wood:
my black grandfather.

Ruff round his broad throat,
grey warrior's armour:
my white grandfather.

Naked foot, body of rock,
these from my black man;
pupils of Antarctic glass,
these from my white man.

Africa of dank forests
and heavy, muffled gongs —
I am dying
          (says my black grandfather)
Black water of crocodiles,
green morning of coco palms.
I am weary
          (says my white grandfather)
O sails of bitter wind
galleon burning gold.
I am dying
          (says my black grandfather)

O coasts of virgin throats
cheated with glass trinkets.
I am weary
          (says my white grandfather)

O pure sun of beaten gold,
caught in the hoop of the tropics
O pure moon so round and clear
over the sleep of monkeys.

How many ships! How many ships!
How many Negroes! How many Negroes!
What long refulgence of sugar-cane!
What lashes those of the slave-trader!
Blood? Blood! Tears? Tears!
Half-opened veins and eye-lids
and empty day-breaks
and sunsets on plantations
and a great voice, a strong voice
shattering the silence.
And O the ships, so many ships,
so many Negroes.

          Shadows that only I can see
          my two grandfathers go with me.

Don Federico shouts to me
and Taita Facundo is silent;
and both dream on through the night,
I bring them together.
                    Federico.
Facundo. They both embrace.
They both sigh. They both
raise their proud heads
under the high stars
both of the same stature
black anguish and white anguish
Both of the same stature.
And they shout. And dream. And weep. And sing.
And sing – and sing – and sing.

                    Translated from the Spanish by G. R. Coulthard

Nicolás Guillén

Ballad of the River Sprites

Chase away the spirits
Chase away the river-sprites.

The muddy waters of the river
are deep and full of dead;
tortoise shells
black children's heads
At night the river puts out its arms
and tears at the silence
with its claws, which are claws
of a frenzied crocodile.
Under the screaming of the stars
under the incendiary moon
the river barks among the stones
and with invisible fingers
shakes the arches of the bridges
and strangles travellers.

Chase away the spirits
Chase away the river-sprites.

Dwarves with enormous navels
live in its restless waters
their short legs are bent,
erect, their long ears.

Help, they are eating my child,
his flesh black and pure,
they are drinking his blood
they are sucking his veins
they are closing his eyes
his big eyes like pearls.

Run, the bogey-man will kill you,
my pickny, my pickny
may your neck-string protect you.

Chase away the spirits
Chase away the river-sprites.

But Chango willed it otherwise.
A hand came out of the water
and dragged him away ... It was a water-sprite
It opened his skull in two halves,
it put out his two big eyes,
it pulled out his white teeth
and made a knot with his legs
and made a knot with his arms.

My pickny, my little pickny,
My sorrow is dreaming
of the depths of your river
and of your little dry veins
and your little wet heart.

Chase away the spirits
Chase away the river-sprites.
Ah, my pickny, little pickny,
I told you it would happen.

Translated from the Spanish by G. R. Coulthard

Ezekiel Mphahlele

Mrs Plum

I

My madam's name was Mrs Plum. She loved dogs and Africans and said that everyone must follow the law even if it hurt. These were three big things in Madam's life.

I came to work for Mrs Plum in Greenside, not very far from the centre of Johannesburg, after leaving two white families. The first white people I worked for as a cook and laundry woman were a man and his wife in Parktown North. They drank too much and always forgot to pay me. After five months I said to myself No. I am going to leave these drunks. So that was it. That day I was as angry as a red-hot iron when it meets water. The second house I cooked and washed for had five children who were badly brought up. This was in Belgravia. Many times they called me You Black Girl and I kept quiet. Because their mother heard them and said nothing. Also I was only new from Phokeng my home, far away near Rustenburg, I wanted to learn and know the white people before I knew how far to go with the others I would work for afterwards. The thing that drove me mad and made me pack and go was a man who came to visit them often. They said he was cousin or something like that. He came to the kitchen many times and tried to make me laugh. He patted me on the buttocks. I told the master. The man did it again and I asked the madam that very day to give me my money and let me go.

These were the first nine months after I had left Phokeng to work in Johannesburg. There were many of us girls and young women from Phokeng, from Zeerust, from Shuping, from Kosten, and many other places who came to work in the cities. So the suburbs were full of blackness. Most of us had already passed Standard Six and so we learned more English where we worked. None of us likes to work for white farmers, because we know too much about them on the farms near our homes. They do not pay well and they are cruel people.

At Easter time so many of us went home for a long weekend to see

our people and to eat chicken and sour milk and *morogo* – wild spin-
ach. We also took home sugar and condensed milk and tea and coffee
and sweets and custard powder and tinned foods.

It was a home-girl of mine, Chimane, who called me to take a job in
Mrs Plum's house, just next door to where she worked. This is the third
year now. I have been quite happy with Mrs Plum and her daughter
Kate. By this I mean that my place as a servant in Greenside is not as
bad as that of many others. Chimane too does not complain much. We
are paid six pounds a month with free food and free servant's room. No
one can ever say that they are well paid, so we go on complaining
somehow. Whenever we meet on Thursday afternoons, which is time off
for all of us black women in the suburbs, we talk and talk and talk:
about our people at home and their letters; about their illnesses; about
bad crops; about a sister who wanted a school uniform and books and
school fees; about some of our madams and masters who are good, or
stingy with money or food, or stupid or full of nonsense, or who kill
themselves and each other, or who are dirty – and so many things I
cannot count them all.

Thursday afternoons we go to town to look at the shops, to attend a
women's club, to see our boy friends, to go to bioscope some of us. We
turn up smart, to show others the clothes we bought from the black
men who sell soft goods to servants in the suburbs. We take a number
of things and they come round every month for a bit of money until we
finish paying. Then we dress the way of many white madams and girls. I
think we look really smart. Sometimes we catch the eyes of a white
woman looking at us and we laugh and laugh until we nearly drop on the
ground because we feel good inside ourselves.

II

What did the girl next door call you? Mrs Plum asked me the first day I
came to her. Jane, I replied. Was there not an African name? I said yes,
Karabo. All right, Madam said. We'll call you Karabo, she said. She
spoke as if she knew a name is a big thing. I knew so many whites who
did not care what they called black people as long as it was all right for
their tongue. This pleased me, I mean Mrs Plum's use of *Karabo*; because the only time I heard the name was when I was home or when
my friends spoke to me. Then she showed me what to do: meals, meal
times, washing, and where all the things were that I was going to use.

My daughter will be here in the evening, Madam said. She is at
school. When the daughter came, she added, she would tell me some of

the things she wanted me to do for her every day.

Chimane, my friend next door, had told me about the daughter Kate, how wild she seemed to be, and about Mr Plum who had killed himself with a gun in a house down the street. They had left the house and come to this one.

Madam is a tall woman. Not slender, not fat. She moves slowly, and speaks slowly. Her face looks very wise, her forehead seems to tell me she has a strong liver: she is not afraid of anything. Her eyes are always swollen at the lower eyelids like a white person who has not slept for many many nights or like a large frog. Perhaps it is because she smokes too much, like wet wood that will not know whether to go up in flames or stop burning. She looks me straight in the eyes when she talks to me, and I know she does this with other people too. At first this made me fear her, now I am used to her. She is not a lazy woman, and she does many things outside, in the city and in the suburbs.

This was the first thing her daughter Kate told me when she came and we met. Don't mind mother, Kate told me. She said, She is sometimes mad with people for very small things. She will soon be all right and speak nicely to you again.

Kate, I like her very much, and she likes me too. She tells me many things a white woman does not tell a black servant. I mean things about what she likes and does not like, what her mother does or does not do, all these. At first I was unhappy and wanted to stop her, but now I do not mind.

Kate looks very much like her mother in the face. I think her shoulders will be just as round and strong-looking. She moves faster than Madam. I asked her why she was still at school when she was so big. She laughed. Then she tried to tell me that the school where she was was for big people, who had finished with lower school. She was learning big things about cooking and food. She can explain better, me I cannot. She came home on weekends.

Since I came to work for Mrs Plum Kate has been teaching me plenty of cooking. I first learned from her and Madam the word *recipes*. When Kate was at the big school, Madam taught me how to read cookery books. I went on very slowly at first, slower than an ox-wagon. Now I know more. When Kate came home, she found I had read the recipe she left me. So we just cooked straight-away. Kate thinks I am fit to cook in a hotel. Madam thinks so too. Never never! I thought. Cooking in a hotel is like feeding oxen. No one can say thank you to you. After a few months I could cook the Sunday lunch and later I could cook specials for Madam's or Kate's guests.

Madam did not only teach me cooking. She taught me how to look after guests. She praised me when I did very very well; not like the white people I had worked for before. I do not know what runs crooked in the heads of other people. Madam also had classes in the evenings for servants to teach them how to read and write. She and two other women in Greenside taught in a church hall.

As I say, Kate tells me plenty of things about Madam. She says to me she says, My mother goes to meetings many times. I ask her I say, What for? She says to me she says, For your people. I ask her I say, My people are in Phokeng far away. They have got mouths, I say. Why does she want to say something for them? Does she know what my mother and what my father want to say? They can speak when they want to. Kate raises her shoulders and drops them and says, How can I tell you Karabo? I don't say your people – your family only. I mean all the black people in this country. I say Oh! What do the black people want to say? Again she raises her shoulders and drops them, taking a deep breath.

I ask her I say, With whom is she in the meeting?

She says, With other people who think like her.

I ask her I say, Do you say there are people in the world who think the same things?

She nods her head.

I ask, What things?

So that a few of your people should one day be among those who rule this country, get more money for what they do for the white man, and – what did Kate say again? Yes, that Madam and those who think like her also wanted my people who have been to school to choose those who must speak for them in the – I think she said it looks like a *Kgotla* at home who rule the villages.

I say to Kate I say, Oh I see now. I say, Tell me Kate why is Madam always writing on the machine, all the time every day nearly?

She replies she says, Oh my mother is writing books.

I ask, You mean a book like those? – pointing at the books on the shelves.

Yes, Kate says.

And she told me how Madam wrote books and other things for newspapers and she wrote for the newspapers and magazines to say things for the black people who should be treated well, be paid more money, for the black people who can read and write many things to choose those who want to speak for them.

Kate also told me she said, My mother and other women who think like her put on black belts over their shoulders when they are sad and they want to show the white government they do not like the things being done by whites to blacks. My mother and the others go and stand where the people in government are going to enter or go out of a building.

I ask her I say, Does the government and the white people listen and stop their sins? She says No. But my mother is in another group of white people.

I ask, Do the people of the government give the women tea and cakes? Kate says, Karabo! How stupid; oh!

I say to her I say, Among my people if someone comes and stands in front of my house I tell him to come in and I give him food. You white people are wonderful. But they keep standing there and the government people do not give them anything.

She replies, You mean strange. How many times have I taught you not to say *wonderful* when you mean *strange!* Well, Kate says with a short heart and looking cross and she shouts, Well they do not stand there the whole day to ask for tea and cakes stupid. Oh dear!

Always when Madam finished to read her newspapers she gave them to me to read to help me speak and write better English. When I had read she asked me to tell her some of the things in it. In this way, I did better and better and my mind was opening and opening and I was learning and learning many things about the black people inside and outside the towns which I did not know in the least. When I found words that were too difficult or I did not understand some of the things I asked Madam. She always told me You see this, you see that, eh? with a heart that can carry on a long way. Yes, Madam writes many letters to the papers. She is always sore about the way the white police beat up black people; about the way black people who work for whites are made to sit at the Zoo Lake with their hearts hanging, because the white people say our people are making noise on Sunday afternoon when they want to rest in their houses and gardens; about many ugly things that happen when some white people meet black man on the pavement or street. So Madam writes to the papers to let others know, to ask the government to be kind to us.

In the first year Mrs Plum wanted me to eat at table with her. It was very hard, one because I was not used to eating at table with a fork and knife, two because I heard of no other kitchen worker who was handled like this. I was afraid. Afraid of everybody, of Madam's guests if they found me doing this. Madam said I must not be silly. I must show that African servants can also eat at table. Number three, I could not eat some of the things I loved very much: mealie-meal porridge with sour milk or *morogo*, stamped mealies mixed with butter beans, sour porridge for breakfast and other things. Also, except for morning porridge, our food is nice when you eat with the hand. So nice that it does not stop in the mouth or the throat to greet anyone before it passes smoothly down.

We often had lunch together with Chimane next door and our garden boy – Ha! I must remember never to say *boy* again when I talk about a man. This makes me think of a day during the first few weeks in Mrs Plum's house. I was talking about Dick her garden man and I said 'garden boy'. And she says to me she says, Stop talking about a 'boy', Karabo. Now listen here, she says, You Africans must learn to speak properly about each other. And she says white people won't talk kindly about you if you look down upon each other.

I say to her I say Madam, I learned the word from the white people I worked for, and all the kitchen maids say 'boy'.

She replies she says to me, Those are white people who know nothing, just low-class whites. I say to her I say I thought white people know everything.

She said, You'll learn, my girl, and you must start in this house, hear? She left me there thinking, my mind mixed up.

I learned. I grew up.

III

If any woman or girl does not know the Black Crow Club in Bree Street, she does not know anything. I think nearly everything takes place inside and outside that house. It is just where the dirty part of the City begins, with factories and the market. After the market is the place where Indians and Coloured people live. It is also at the Black Crow that the buses turn round and back to the black townships. Noise, noise, noise all the time. There are women who sell hot sweet potatoes and fruit and monkey nuts and boiled eggs in the winter, boiled mealies and the other things in the summer, all these on the pavements. The streets are always full of potato and fruit skins and monkey nut shells. There is always a strong smell of roast pork. I think it is because of Piel's cold storage down Bree Street.

Madam said she knew the black people who work in the Black Crow. She was happy that I was spending my afternoon on Thursday in such a club. You will learn sewing, knitting, she said, and other things that you like. Do you like to dance? I told her I said, Yes, I want to learn. She paid the two shillings fee for me each month.

We waited on the first floor, we the ones who were learning sewing; waiting for the teacher. We talked and laughed about madams and masters, and their children and their dogs and birds and whispered about our boy friends.

Sies! My Madam you do not know – *mojuta oa'nete* – a real miser . . .

Jo – jo – jo! you should see our new dog. A big thing like this. People! Big in a foolish way . . .

What! Me, I take a master's bitch by the leg, me, and throw it away so that it keeps howling, *tjwe – tjwe! ngo – wu ngo – wu!* I don't play about with them, me . . .

Shame, poor thing! God sees you, true . . . !

They wanted me to take their dog out for a walk every afternoon and I told them I said It is not my work in other houses the garden man does it. I just said to myself I said they can go to the chickens. Let them bite their elbow before I take out a dog, I am not so mad yet . . .

Hei! It is not like the child of my white people who keeps a big white rat and you know what? He puts it on his bed when he goes to school. And let the blankets just begin to smell of urine and all the nonsense and they tell me to wash them. *Hei,* people . . . !

Did you hear about Rebone, people? Her Madam put her out, because her master was always tapping her buttocks with his fingers. And yesterday the madam saw the master press Rebone against himself . . .

Jo – jo – jo! people . . . !

Dirty white man!

No, not dirty. The madam smells too old for him.

Hei! Go and wash your mouth with soap, this girl's mouth is dirty . . .

Jo, Rebone, daughter of the people! We must help her to find a job before she thinks of going back home.

The teacher came. A woman with strong legs, a strong face, and kind eyes. She had short hair and dressed in a simple but lovely floral frock. She stood well on her legs and hips. She had a black mark between the two top front teeth. She smiled as if we were her children. Our group began with games, and then Lilian Ngoyi took us for sewing. After this she gave a brief talk to all of us from the different classes.

I can never forget the things this woman said and how she put them to us. She told us that the time had passed for black girls and women in the suburbs to be satisfied with working, sending money to our people and going to see them once a year. We were to learn, she said, that the world would never be safe for black people until they were in the government with the power to make laws. The power should be given by the Africans who were more than the whites.

We asked her questions and she answered them with wisdom. I shall put some of them down in my own words as I remember them.

Shall we take the place of the white people in the government?

Some yes. But we shall be more than they as we are more in the country. But also the people of all colours will come together and there are good white men we can choose and there are Africans some white people will choose to be in the government.

There are good madams and masters and bad ones. Should we take the good ones for friends?

A master and a servant can never be friends. Never, so put that out of your head, will you! You are not even sure if the ones you say are good are not like that because they cannot breathe or live without the work of your hands. As long as you need their money, face them with respect. But you must know that many sad things are happening in our country and you, all of you, must always be learning, adding to what you already know, and obey us when we ask you to help us.

At other times Lilian Ngoyi told us she said, Remember your poor people at home and the way in which the whites are moving them from place to place like sheep and cattle. And at other times again she told us she said, Remember that a hand cannot wash itself, it needs another to do it.

I always thought of Madam when Lilian Ngoyi spoke. I asked myself, What would she say if she knew that I was listening to such words. Words like: A white man is looked after by his black nanny and his mother when he is a baby. When he grows up the white government looks after him, sends him to school, makes it impossible for him to suffer from the great hunger, keeps a job ready and open for him as soon as he wants to leave school. Now Lilian Ngoyi asked she said, How many white people can be born in a white hospital, grow up in white streets, be clothed in lovely cotton, lie on white cushions; how many whites can live all their lives in a fenced place away from people of other colours and then, as men and women learn quickly the correct ways of thinking, learn quickly to ask questions in their minds, big questions that will throw over all the nice things of a white man's life? How many? Very very few! For those whites who have not begun to ask, it is too late. For those who have begun and are joining us with both feet in our house, we can only say Welcome!

I was learning. I was growing. Every time I thought of Madam, she became more and more like a dark forest which one fears to enter, and

which one will never know. But there were several times when I thought,
This woman is easy to understand, she is like all other white women.

What else are they teaching you at the Black Crow, Karabo?

I tell her I say, nothing, Madam. I ask her I say Why does Madam
ask?

You are changing.

What does Madam mean?

Well, you are changing.

But we are always changing Madam.

And she left me standing in the kitchen. This was a few days after I
had told her that I did not want to read more than one white paper a
day. The only magazines I wanted to read, I said to her, were those
from overseas, if she had them. I told her that white papers had pictures of white people most of the time. They talked mostly about white
people and their gardens, dogs, weddings and parties. I asked her if she
could buy me a Sunday paper that spoke about my people. Madam
bought it for me. I did not think she would do it.

There were mornings when, after hanging the white people's washing
on the line Chimane and I stole a little time to stand at the fence and
talk. We always stood where we could be hidden by our rooms.

Hei, Karabo, you know what? That was Chimane.

No – what? Before you start, tell me, has Timi come back to you?

Ach, I do not care. He is still angry. But boys are fools they always
come back dragging themselves on their empty bellies. *Hei* you know
what?

Yes?

The Thursday past I saw Moruti KK. I laughed until I dropped on the
ground. He is standing in front of the Black Crow. I believe his big
stomach was crying from hunger. Now he has a small dog in his armpit,
and is standing before a woman selling boiled eggs and – *hei* home-girl!
– tripe and intestines are boiling in a pot – oh – the smell! you could
fill a hungry belly with it, the way it was good. I think Moruti KK is
waiting for the woman to buy a boiled egg. I do not know what the
woman was still doing. I am standing nearby. The dog keeps wriggling
and pushing out its nose, looking at the boiling tripe. Moruti keeps
patting it with his free hand, not so? Again the dog wants to spill out of
Moruti's hand and it gives a few sounds through the nose. *Hei* man,
home-girl! One two three the dog spills out to catch some of the good
meat! It misses falling into the hot gravy in which the tripe is swimming I do not know how. Moruti KK tries to chase it. It has tumbled on
to the woman's eggs and potatoes and all are in the dust. She stands up

and goes after KK. She is shouting to him to pay, not so? Where am I at that time? I am nearly dead with laughter the tears are coming down so far.

I was myself holding tight on the fence so as not to fall through laughing. I held my stomach to keep back a pain in the side.

I ask her I say, Did Moruti KK come back to pay for the wasted food?

Yes, he paid.

The dog?

He caught it. That is a good African dog. A dog must look for its own food when it is not time for meals. Not these stupid spoiled angels the whites keep giving tea and biscuits.

Hmm.

Dick our garden man joined us, as he often did. When the story was repeated to him the man nearly rolled on the ground laughing.

He asks who is Reverend KK?

I say he is the owner of the Black Crow.

Oh!

We reminded each other, Chimane and I, of the round minister. He would come into the club, look at us with a smooth smile on his smooth round face. He would look at each one of us, with that smile on all the time, as if he had forgotten that it was there. Perhaps he had, because as he looked at us, almost stripping us naked with his watery shining eyes – funny – he could have been a farmer looking at his ripe corn, thinking many things.

KK often spoke without shame about what he called ripe girls – *matjitjana* – with good firm breasts. He said such girls were pure without any nonsense in their heads and bodies. Everybody talked a great deal about him and what they thought he must be doing in his office whenever he called in so-and-so.

The Reverend KK did not belong to any church. He baptized, married, and buried people for a fee, who had no church to do such things for them. They said he had been driven out of the Presbyterian Church. He had formed his own, but it did not go far. Then he later came and opened the Black Crow. He knew just how far to go with Lilian Ngoyi. She said although she used his club to teach us things that would help us in life, she could not go on if he was doing any wicked things with the girls in his office. Moruti KK feared her, and kept his place.

IV

When I began to tell my story I thought I was going to tell mostly about Mrs Plum's two dogs. But I have been talking about people. I think Dick is right when he says What is a dog! And there are so many dogs cats and parrots in Greenside and other places that Mrs Plum's dogs do not look special. But there was something special in the dog business in Madam's house. The way in which she loved them, maybe.

Monty is a tiny animal with long hair and small black eyes and a face nearly like that of an old woman. The other, Malan, is a bit bigger, with brown and white colours. It has small hair and looks naked by the side of the friend. They sleep in two separate baskets which stay in Madam's bedroom. They are to be washed often and brushed and sprayed and they sleep on pink linen. Monty has a pink ribbon which stays on his neck most of the time. They both carry a cover on their backs. They make me fed up when I see them in their baskets, looking fat, and as if they knew all that was going on everywhere.

It was Dick's work to look after Monty and Malan, to feed them, and to do everything for them. He did this together with garden work and cleaning of the house. He came at the beginning of this year. He just came, as if from nowhere, and Madam gave him the job as she had chased away two before him, she told me. In both those cases, she said that they could not look after Monty and Malan.

Dick had a long heart, even although he told me and Chimane that European dogs were stupid, spoiled. He said One day those white people will put ear rings and toe rings and bangles on their dogs. That would be the day he would leave Mrs Plum. For, he said, he was sure that she would want him to polish the rings and bangles with Brasso.

Although he had a long heart, Madam was still not sure of him. She often went to the dogs after a meal or after a cleaning and said to them Did Dick give you food sweethearts? Or, Did Dick wash you sweethearts? Let me see. And I could see that Dick was blowing up like a balloon with anger. These things called white people! he said to me. Talking to dogs!

I say to him I say, People talk to oxen at home do I not say so?

Yes, he says, but at home do you not know that a man speaks to an ox because he wants to make it pull the plough or the wagon or to stop or to stand still for a person to inspan it. No one simply goes to an ox looking at him with eyes far apart and speaks to it. Let me ask you, do you ever see a person where we come from take a cow and press it to his stomach or his cheek? Tell me!

And I say to Dick I say, We were talking about an ox, not a cow.

He laughed with his broad mouth until tears came out of his eyes. At a certain point I laughed aloud too.

One day when you have time, Dick says to me, he says, you should look into Madam's bedroom when she has put a notice outside her door.

Dick, what are you saying? I ask.

I do not talk, me. I know deep inside me.

Dick was about our age, I and Chimane. So we always said *moshiman'o* when we spoke about his tricks. Because he was not too big to be a boy to us. He also said to us *Hei, lona banyana kelona* — Hey you girls, you! His large mouth always seemed to be making ready to laugh. I think Madam did not like this. Many times she would say What is there to make you laugh here? Or in the garden she would say This is a flower and when it wants water that is not funny! Or again, if you did more work and stopped trying to water my plants with your smile you would be more useful. Even when Dick did not mean to smile. What Madam did not get tired of saying was, If I left you to look after my dogs without anyone to look after you at the same time you would drown the poor things.

Dick smiled at Mrs Plum. Dick hurt Mrs Plum's dogs? Then cows can fly. He was really — really afraid of white people, Dick. I think he tried very hard not to feel afraid. For he was always showing me and Chimane in private how Mrs Plum walked, and spoke. He took two bowls and pressed them to his chest, speaking softly to them as Madam speaks to Monty and Malan. Or he sat at Madam's table and acted the way she sits when writing. Now and again he looked back over his shoulder, pulled his face long like a horse's making as if he were looking over his glasses while telling me something to do. Then he would sit on one of the armchairs, cross his legs and act the way Madam drank her tea; he held the cup he was thinking about between his thumb and the pointing finger, only letting their nails meet. And he laughed after every act. He did these things, of course, when Madam was not home. And where was I at such times? Almost flat on my stomach, laughing.

But oh how Dick trembled when Mrs Plum scolded him! He did his house-cleaning very well. Whatever mistake he made, it was mostly with the dogs; their linen, their food. One white man came into the house one afternoon to tell Madam that Dick had been very careless when taking the dogs out for a walk. His own dog was waiting on Madam's stoop. He repeated that he had been driving down our street; and Dick had let loose Monty and Malan to cross the street. The white man made plenty of noise about this and I think wanted to let Madam know how useful he had been. He kept on saying Just one inch, *just* one inch. It was lucky I put on my brakes quick enough ... But your boy kept on smiling – Why? Strange. My boy would only do it twice and only twice and then ... ! His pass. The man moved his hand like one writing, to mean that he would sign his servant's pass for him to go and never come back. When he left, the man said Come on Rusty, the boy is waiting to clean you. Dogs with names, men without, I thought.

Madam climbed on top of Dick for this, as we say.

Once one of the dogs, I don't know which – Malan or Monty – took my stocking – brand new, you hear – and tore it with its teeth and paws. When I told Madam about it, my anger as high as my throat, she gave me money to buy another pair. It happened again. This time she said she was not going to give me money because I must also keep my stockings where the two gentlemen would not reach them. Mrs Plum did not want us ever to say *Voetsek* when we wanted the dogs to go away. Me I said this when they came sniffing at my legs or fingers. I hate it.

In my third year in Mrs Plum's house, many things happened, most of them all bad for her. There was trouble with Kate; Chimane had big trouble; my heart was twisted by two loves; and Monty and Malan became real dogs for a few days.

Madam had a number of suppers and parties. She invited Africans to some of them. Kate told me the reasons for some of the parties. Like her mother's books when finished, a visitor from across the seas and so on. I did not like the black people who came here to drink and eat. They spoke such difficult English like people who were full of all the books in the world. They looked at me as if I were right down there whom they thought little of – me a black person like them.

One day I heard Kate speak to her mother. She says I don't know why you ask so many Africans to the house. A few will do at a time. She said something about the government which I could not hear well. Madam replies she says to her You know some of them do not meet white people often, so far away in their dark houses. And she says to Kate that they do not come because they want her as a friend but they just want a drink for nothing.

I simply felt that I could not be the servant of white people and of blacks at the same time. At my home or in my room I could serve them without a feeling of shame. And now, if they were only coming to drink!

But one of the black men and his sister always came to the kitchen to talk to me. I must have looked unfriendly the first time, for Kate talked to me about it afterwards as she was in the kitchen when they came. I know that at that time I was not easy at all. I was ashamed and I felt that a white person's house was not the place for me to look happy in front of other black people while the white man looked on.

Another time it was easier. The man was alone. I shall never forget that night, as long as I live. He spoke kind words and I felt my heart grow big inside me. It caused me to tremble. There were several other visits. I knew that I loved him, I could never know what he really thought of me, I mean as a woman and he as a man. But I loved him, and I still think of him with a sore heart. Slowly I came to know the pain of it. Because he was a doctor and so full of knowledge and English I could not reach him. So I knew he could not stoop down to see me as someone who wanted him to love me.

Kate turned very wild. Mrs Plum was very much worried. Suddenly it looked as if she were a new person, with new ways and new everything. I do not know what was wrong or right. She began to play the big gramophone aloud, as if the music were for the whole of Greenside. The music was wild and she twisted her waist all the time, with her mouth half-open. She did the same things in her room. She left the big school and every Saturday night now she went out. When I looked at her face, there was something deep and wild there on it, and when I thought she looked young she looked old, and when I thought she looked old she was young. We were both twenty-two years of age. I think that I could see the reason why her mother was so worried, why she was suffering.

Worse was to come.

They were now openly screaming at each other. They began in the sitting room and went upstairs together, speaking fast hot biting words, some of which I did not grasp. One day Madam comes to me and says You know Kate loves an African, you know the doctor who comes to supper here often. She says he loves her too and they will leave the country and marry outside. Tell me, Karabo, what do your people think of this kind of thing between a white woman and a black man? It *cannot* be right is it?

I reply and I say to her We have never seen it happen before where I come from.

That's right, Karabo, it is just madness.

Madam left. She looked like a hunted person.

These white women, I say to myself I say these white women, why do not they love their own men and leave us to love ours!

From that minute I knew that I would never want to speak to Kate. She appeared to me as a thief, as a fox that falls upon a flock of sheep at night. I hated her. To make it worse, he would never be allowed to come to the house again.

Whenever she was home there was silence between us. I no longer wanted to know anything about what she was doing, where or how.

I lay awake for hours on my bed. Lying like that, I seemed to feel parts of my body beat and throb inside me, the way I have seen big machines doing, pounding and pounding and pushing and pulling and pouring some water into one hold which came out at another end. I stretched myself so many times so as to feel tired and sleepy.

When I did sleep, my dreams were full of painful things.

One evening I made up my mind, after putting it off many times. I told my boy-friend that I did not want him any longer. He looked hurt, and that hurt me too. He left.

The thought of the African doctor was still with me and it pained me to know that I should never see him again; unless I met him in the street on a Thursday afternoon. But he had a car. Even if I did meet him by luck, how could I make him see that I loved him? Ach, I do not believe he would even stop to think what kind of woman I am. Part of that winter was a time of longing and burning for me. I say part because there are always things to keep servants busy whose white people go to the sea for the winter.

To tell the truth, winter was the time for servants; not nannies, because they went with their madams so as to look after the children. Those like me stayed behind to look after the house and dogs. In winter so many families went away that the dogs remained the masters and madams. You could see them walk like white people in the streets. Silent but with plenty of power. And when you saw them you knew that they were full of more nonsense and fancies in the house.

There was so little work to do.

One week word was whispered round that a home-boy of ours was going to hold a party in his room on Saturday. I think we all took it for a joke. How could the man be so bold and stupid? The police were always driving about at night looking for black people; and if the whites next door heard the party noise – *oho*! But still, we were full of joy and wanted to go. As for Dick, he opened his big mouth and nearly fainted when he heard of it and that I was really going.

During the day on the big Saturday Kate came.

She seemed a little less wild. But I was not ready to talk to her. I was surprised to hear myself answer her when she said to me Mother says you do not like a marriage between a white girl and a black man, Karabo.

Then she was silent.

She says But I want to help him, Karabo.

I ask her I say You want to help him to do what?

To go higher and higher, to the top.

I knew I wanted to say so much that was boiling in my chest. I could not say it. I thought of Lilian Ngoyi at the Black Crow, what she said to us. But I was mixed up in my head and in my blood.

You still agree with my mother?

All I could say was I said to your mother I had never seen a black man and a white woman marrying, you hear me? What I think about it is my business.

I remembered that I wanted to iron my party dress and so I left her. My mind was full of the party again and I was glad because Kate and the doctor would not worry my peace that day. And the next day the sun would shine for all of us, Kate or no Kate, doctor or no doctor.

The house where our home-boy worked was hidden from the main road by a number of trees. But although we asked a number of questions and counted many fingers of bad luck until we had no more hands for fingers, we put on our best pay-while-you-wear dresses and suits and clothes bought from boys who had stolen them, and went to our home-boy's party. We whispered all the way while we climbed up to the house. Someone who knew told us that the white people next door were away for the winter. Oh, so that is the thing! we said.

We poured into the garden through the back and stood in front of his room laughing quietly. He came from the big house behind us, and were we not struck dumb when he told us to go into the white people's house! Was he mad? We walked in with slow footsteps that seemed to be sniffing at the floor, not sure of anything. Soon we were standing and sitting all over on the nice warm cushions and the heaters were on. Our home-boy turned the lights low. I counted fifteen people inside. We saw how we loved one another's evening dress. The boys were smart too.

Our home-boy's girl-friend Naomi was busy in the kitchen preparing food. He took out glasses and cold drinks – fruit juice, tomato juice, ginger beers, and so many other kinds of soft drink. It was just too nice. The tarts, the biscuits, the snacks, the cakes, *woo*, that was a party, I tell you. I think I ate more ginger cake than I had ever done in my life. Naomi had baked some of the things. Our home-boy came to me and said I do not want the police to come here and have reason to arrest us, so I am not serving hot drinks, not even beer. There is no law that we cannot have parties, is there? So we can feel free. Our use of this house is the master's business. If I had asked him he would have thought me mad.

I say to him I say, You have a strong liver to do such a thing.

He laughed.

He played pennywhistle music on gramophone records – Miriam Makeba, Dorothy Masuka, and other African singers and players. We danced and the party became more and more noisy and more happy. *Hai*, those girls Miriam and Dorothy, they can sing, I tell you! We ate more and laughed more and told more stories. In the middle of the party, our home-boy called us to listen to what he was going to say. Then he told us how he and a friend of his in Orlando collected money to bet on a horse for the July Handicap in Durban. They did this each year but lost. Now they had won two hundred pounds. We all clapped hands and cheered. Two hundred pounds *woo*!

You should go and sit at home and just eat time, I say to him. He laughs and says You have no understanding not one little bit.

To all of us he says Now my brothers and sisters enjoy yourselves. At home I should slaughter a goat for us to feast and thank our ancestors. But this is town life and we must thank them with tea and cake and all those sweet things. I know some people think I must be so bold that I could be midwife to a lion that is giving birth, but enjoy yourselves and have no fear.

Madam came back looking strong and fresh.

The very week she arrived the police had begun again to search servants' rooms. They were looking for what they called loafers and men without passes who they said were living with friends in the suburbs against the law. Our dog's-meat boys became scarce because of the police. A boy who had a girl-friend in the kitchens, as we say, always told his friends that he was coming for dog's meat when he meant he was visiting his girl. This was because we gave our boy-friends part of the meat the white people bought for the dogs and us.

One night a white and a black policeman entered Mrs Plum's yard. They said they had come to search. She says no, they cannot. They say Yes, they must do it. She answers No. They forced their way to the back, to Dick's room and mine. Mrs Plum took the hose that was running in the front garden and quickly went round to the back. I cut across the floor to see what she was going to say to the men. They were talking to Dick, using dirty words. Mrs Plum did not wait, she just pointed the hose at the two policemen. This seemed to surprise them. They turned round and she pointed it into their faces. Without their seeing me I went to the tap at the corner of the house and opened it more. I could see Dick, like me, was trying to keep down his laughter. They shouted and tried to wave the water away, but she kept the hose pointing at them, now moving it up and down. They turned and ran through the back gate, swearing the while.

That fixes them, Mrs Plum said.

The next day the morning paper reported it.

They arrived in the afternoon – the two policemen – with another. They pointed out Mrs Plum and she was led to the police station. They took her away to answer for stopping the police while they were doing their work.

She came back and said she had paid bail.

At the magistrate's court, Madam was told that she had done a bad thing. She would have to pay a fine or else go to prison for fourteen days. She said she would go to jail to show that she felt she was not in the wrong.

Kate came and tried to tell her that she was doing something silly going to jail for a small thing like that. She tells Madam she says This is not even a thing to take to the high court. Pay the money. What is £5?

Madam went to jail.

She looked very sad when she came out. I thought of what Lilian Ngoyi often said to us: You must be ready to go to jail for the things you believe are true and for which you are taken by the police. What did Mrs Plum really believe about me, Chimane, Dick, and all the other black people? I asked myself. I did not know. But from all those things she was writing for the papers and all those meetings she was going to where white people talked about black people and the way they are treated by the government, from what those white women with black bands over their shoulders were doing standing where a white government man was going to pass, I said to myself I said This woman, *hai*, I do not know she seems to think very much of us black people. But why was she so sad?

Kate came back home to stay after this. She still played the big gramophone loud-loud-loud and twisted her body at her waist until I thought it was going to break. Then I saw a young white man come often to see her. I watched them through the opening near the hinges of the door between the kitchen and the sitting room where they sat. I saw them kiss each other for a long time. I saw him lift up Kate's dress and her white-white legs begin to tremble, and – oh I am afraid to say more, my heart was beating hard. She called him Jim. I thought it was funny because white people in the shops call black men Jim.

Kate had begun to play with Jim when I met a boy who loved me and I

loved. He was much stronger than the one I sent away and I loved him
more, much more. The face of the doctor came to my mind often, but
it did not hurt me so any more. I stopped looking at Kate and her Jim
through openings. We spoke to each other, Kate and I, almost as freely
as before but not quite. She and her mother were friends again.

Hallo, Karabo, I heard Chimane call me one morning as I was starch-
ing my apron. I answered. I went to the line to hang it. I saw she was
standing at the fence, so I knew she had something to tell me. I went to
her.

Hallo!

Hallo, Chimane!

O kae?

Ke teng. Wena?

At that moment a woman came out through the back door of the
house where Chimane was working.

I have not seen that one before, I say, pointing with my head.

Chimane looked back. Oh, that one. *Hei,* daughter-of-the-people,
Hei, you have not seen miracles. You know this is Madam's mother-in-
law as you see her there. Did I never tell you about her?

No, never.

White people, nonsense. You know what? That poor woman is
here now for two days. She has to cook for herself and I cook for the
family.

On the same stove?

Yes, She comes after me when I have finished.

She has her own food to cook?

Yes, Karabo. White people have no heart no sense.

What will eat them up if they share their food?

Ask me, just ask me. God! She clapped her hands to show that only
God knew, and it was His business, not ours.

Chimane asks me she says, Have you heard from home?

I tell her I say, Oh daughter-of-the-people, more and more deaths.
Something is finishing the people at home. My mother has written. She
says they are all right, my father too and my sisters, except for the
people who have died. Malebo, the one who lived alone in the house I
showed you last year, a white house, he is gone. Then teacher Sedimo.
He was very thin and looked sick all the time. He taught my sisters not
me. His mother-in-law you remember I told you died last year – no, the
year before. Mother says also there is a woman she does not think I
remember because I last saw her when I was a small girl she passed away
in Zeerust she was my mother's greatest friend when they were girls.

She would have gone to her burial if it was not because she has swollen feet.

How are the feet?

She says they are still giving her trouble. I ask Chimane, How are your people at Nokaneng? They have not written?

She shook her head.

I could see from her eyes that her mind was on another thing and not her people at that moment.

Wait for me Chimane eh, forgive me, I have scones in the oven, eh! I will just take them out and come back, eh!

When I came back to her Chimane was wiping her eyes. They were wet.

Karabo, you know what?

E—e. I shook my head.

I am heavy with child.

Hau!

There was a moment of silence.

Who is it, Chimane?

Timi. He came back only to give me this.

But he loves you. What does he say have you told him?

I told him yesterday. We met in town.

I remembered I had not seen her at the Black Crow.

Are you sure, Chimane? You have missed a month?

She nodded her head.

Timi himself — he did not use the thing?

I only saw after he finished, that he had not.

Why? What does he say?

He tells me he says I should not worry I can be his wife.

Timi is a good boy, Chimane. How many of these boys with town ways who know too much will even say Yes it is my child?

Hai, Karabo, you are telling me other things now. Do you not see that I have not worked long enough for my people? If I marry now who will look after them when I am the only child?

Hm. I hear your words. It is true. I tried to think of something soothing to say.

Then I say You can talk it over with Timi. You can go home and when the child is born you look after it for three months and when you are married you come to town to work and can put your money together to help the old people while they are looking after the child.

What shall we be eating all the time I am at home? It is not like those days gone past when we had land and our mother could go to the fields until the child was ready to arrive.

The light goes out in my mind and I cannot think of the right answer. How many times have I feared the same thing! Luck and the mercy of the gods that is all I live by. That is all we live by – all of us.

Listen, Karabo. I must be going to make tea for Madam. It will soon strike half-past ten.

I went back to the house. As Madam was not in yet, I threw myself on the divan in the sitting-room. Malan came sniffing at my legs. I put my foot under its fat belly and shoved it up and away from me so that it cried *tjunk – tjunk – tjunk* as it went out. I say to it I say Go and tell your brother what I have done to you and tell him to try it and see what I will do. Tell your grandmother when she comes home too.

When I lifted my eyes he was standing in the kitchen door, Dick. He says to me he says *Hau!* now you have also begun to speak to dogs!

I did not reply. I just looked at him, his mouth ever stretched out like the mouth of a bag, and I passed to my room.

I sat on my bed and looked at my face in the mirror. Since the morning I had been feeling as if a black cloud were hanging over me, pressing on my head and shoulders. I do not know how long I sat there. Then I smelled Madam. What was it? Where was she? After a few moments I knew what it was. My perfume and scent. I used the same cosmetics as Mrs Plum's. I should have been used to it by now. But this morning – why did I smell Mrs Plum like this? Then, without knowing why, I asked myself I said, Why have I been using the same cosmetics as Madam? I wanted to throw them all out. I stopped. And then I took all the things and threw them into the dustbin. I was going to buy other kinds on Thursday; finished!

I could not sit down. I went out and into the white people's house. I walked through and the smell of the house made me sick and seemed to fill up my throat. I went to the bathroom without knowing why. It was full of the smell of Madam. Dick was cleaning the bath. I stood at the door and looked at him cleaning the dirt out of the bath, dirt from Madam's body. *Sies!* I said aloud. To myself I said, Why cannot people wash the dirt of their own bodies out of the bath? Before Dick knew I was near I went out. Ach, I said again to myself, why should I think about it now when I have been doing their washing for so long and cleaned the bath many times when Dick was ill. I had held worse things from her body times without number . . .

I went out and stood mid-way between the house and my room, looking into the next yard. The three-legged grey cat next door came to the fence and our eyes met. I do not know how long we stood like that looking at each other. I was thinking, Why don't you go and look at your grandmother like that? when it turned away and mewed hopping on the three legs. Just like someone who feels pity for you.

In my room I looked into the mirror on the chest of drawers. I thought Is this Karabo this?

Thursday came, and the afternoon off. At the Black Crow I did not see Chimane. I wondered about her. In the evening I found a note under my door. It told me if Chimane was not back that evening I should know that she was at 660 3rd Avenue, Alexandra Township. I was not to tell the white people.

I asked Dick if he could not go to Alexandra with me after I had washed the dishes. At first he was unwilling. But I said to him I said, Chimane will not believe that you refused to come with me when she sees me alone. He agreed.

On the bus Dick told me much about his younger sister whom he was helping with money to stay at school until she finished; so that she could become a nurse and a midwife. He was very fond of her, as far as I could find out. He said he prayed always that he should not lose his job, as he had done many times before, after staying a few weeks only at each job; because of this he had to borrow monies from people to pay his sister's school fees, to buy her clothes and books. He spoke of her as if she were his sweetheart. She was clever at school, pretty (she was this in the photo Dick had shown me before). She was in Orlando Township. She looked after his old people, although she was only thirteen years of age. He said to me he said Today I still owe many people because I keep losing my job. You must try to stay with Mrs Plum, I said.

I cannot say that I had all my mind on what Dick was telling me. I was thinking of Chimane: what could she be doing? Why that note?

We found her in bed. In that terrible township where night and day are full of knives and bicycle chains and guns and the barking of hungry dogs and of people in trouble. I held my heart in my hands. She was in pain and her face, even in the candlelight, was grey. She turned her eyes at me. A fat woman was sitting in a chair. One arm rested on the other and held her chin in its palm. She had hardly opened the door for us after we had shouted our names when she was on her bench again as if there were nothing else to do.

She snorted, as if to let us know that she was going to speak. She said There is your friend. There she is my own-own niece who comes from the womb of my own sister, my sister who was made to spit out my mother's breasts to give way for me. Why does she go and do such an evil thing. *Ao!* you young girls of today you do not know children die so fast these days that you have to thank God for sowing a seed in your womb to grow into a child. If she had let the child be born I should have looked after it or my sister would have been so happy to hold a grand-child on her lap, but what does it help? She has allowed a worm to cut the roots, I don't know.

Then I saw that Chimane's aunt was crying. Not once did she mention her niece by her name, so sore her heart must have been. Chimane only moaned.

Her aunt continued to talk, as if she was never going to stop for breath, until her voice seemed to move behind me, not one of the things I was thinking: trying to remember signs, however small, that could tell me more about this moment in a dim little room in a cruel township without street lights, near Chimane. Then I remembered the three-legged cat, its grey-green eyes, its *miau*. What was this shadow that seemed to walk about us but was not coming right in front of us?

I thanked the gods when Chimane came to work at the end of the week. She still looked weak, but that shadow was no longer there. I wondered Chimane had never told me about her aunt before. Even now I did not ask her.

I told her I told her white people that she was ill and had been fetched to Nokaneng by a brother. They would never try to find out. They seldom did, these people. Give them any lie, and it will do. For they seldom believe you whatever you say. And how can a black person work for white people and be afraid to tell them lies. They are always asking the questions, you are always the one to give the answers.

Chimane told me all about it. She had gone to a woman who did these things. Her way was to hold a sharp needle, cover the point with the finger, and guide it into the womb. She then fumbled in the womb until she found the egg and then pierced it. She gave you something to ease the bleeding. But the pain, spirits of our forefathers!

Mrs Plum and Kate were talking about dogs one evening at dinner. Every time I brought something to table I tried to catch their words. Kate seemed to find it funny, because she laughed aloud. There was a word I could not hear well which began with *sem*—: whatever it was, it was to be for dogs. This I understood by putting a few words together. Mrs Plum said it was something that was common in the big cities of America, like New York. It was also something Mrs Plum wanted and Kate laughed at the thought. Then later I was to hear that Monty and Malan could be sure of a nice burial.

Chimane's voice came up to me in my room the next morning, across the fence. When I come out she tells me she says *Hei* child-of-my-father, here is something to tickle your ears. You know what? What? I say. She says, These white people can do things that make the gods angry. More godless people I have not seen. The madam of our house says the people of Greenside want to buy ground where they can bury their dogs. I heard them talk about it in the sitting-room when I was giving them coffee last night. *Hei*, people, let our forefathers come and save us!

Yes, I say, I also heard the madam of our house talk about it with her daughter. I just heard it in pieces. By my mother one day these dogs will sit at table and use knife and fork. These things are to be treated like people now, like children who are never going to grow up.

Chimane sighed and she says *Hela batho*, why do they not give me some of that money they will spend on the ground and on gravestones to buy stockings! I have nothing to put on, by my mother.

Over her shoulder I saw the cat with three legs. I pointed with my head. When Chimane looked back and saw it she said *Hm*, even *they* live like kings. The mother-in-law found it on a chair and the madam said the woman should not drive it away. And there was no other chair, so the woman went to her room.

Hela!

I was going to leave when I remembered what I wanted to tell Chimane. It was that five of us had collected £1 each to lend her so that she could pay the woman of Alexandra for having done that thing for her. Then, when Chimane's time came to receive money which we collected each month and which we took in turns, she would pay us back. We were ten women and each gave £2 at a time. So one waited ten months to receive £20. Chimane thanked us for helping her.

I went to wake up Mrs Plum as she had asked me. She was sleeping late this morning. I was going to knock at the door when I heard strange noises in the bedroom. What is the matter with Mrs Plum? I asked myself. Should I call her, in case she is ill? No, the noises were not those of a sick person. They were happy noises but like those a person makes in a dream, the voice full of sleep. I bent a little to peep through the keyhole. What is this? I kept asking myself. Mrs Plum! Malan! What is she doing this one! Her arm was round Malan's belly and pressing its back against her stomach at the navel, Mrs Plum's body in a nightdress moving in jerks like someone in fits ... her leg rising and falling ... Malan silent like a thing to be owned without any choice it can make to belong to another.

The gods save me! I heard myself saying, the words sounding like wind rushing out of my mouth. So this is what Dick said I would find out for myself!

No one could say where it all started; who talked about it first; whether the police wanted to make a reason for taking people without passes and people living with servants and working in town or not working at all. But the story rushed through Johannesburg that servants were going to poison the white people's dogs. Because they were too much work for us: that was the reason. We heard that letters were sent to the newspapers by white people asking the police to watch over the dogs to stop any wicked things. Some said that we the servants were not really bad, we were being made to think of doing these things by evil people in town and in the locations. Others said the police should watch out lest we poison madams and masters because black people did not know right from wrong when they were angry. We were still children at heart, others said. Mrs Plum said that she had also written to the papers.

Then it was the police came down on the suburbs like locusts on a cornfield. There were lines and lines of men who were arrested hour by hour in the day. They liked this very much, the police. Everybody they took, everybody who was working was asked, Where's the poison eh? Where did you hide it? Who told you to poison the dogs eh? If you tell us we'll leave you to go free, you hear? and so many other things.

Dick kept saying It is wrong this thing they want to do to kill poor dogs. What have these things of God done to be killed for? Is it the dogs that make us carry passes? Is it dogs that make the laws that give us pain? People are just mad they do not know what they want, stupid! But when white policeman spoke to him, Dick trembled and lost his tongue and the things he thought. He just shook his head. A few moments after they had gone through his pockets he still held his arms stretched out, like the man of straw who frightens away birds in a field. Only when I hissed and gave him a sign did he drop his arms. He rushed to a corner of the garden to go on with his work.

Mrs Plum had put Monty and Malan in the sitting-room, next to her. She looked very much worried. She called me. She asked me she said Karabo, you think Dick is a boy we can trust? I did not know how to answer. I did not know whom she was talking about when she said *we*. Then I said I do not know, Madam. You know! she said. I looked at her. I said I do not know what Madam thinks. She said she did not think anything, that was why she asked. I nearly laughed because she was telling a lie this time and not I.

At another time I should have been angry if she lied to me, perhaps. She and I often told each other lies, as Kate and I also did. Like when she came back from jail, after that day when she turned a hosepipe on two policemen. She said life had been good in jail. And yet I could see she was ashamed to have been there. Not like our black people who are always being put in jail and only look at it as the white man's evil game. Lilian Ngoyi often told us this, and Mrs Plum showed me how true those words are. I am sure that we have kept to each other by lying to each other.

There was something in Mrs Plum's face as she was speaking which made me fear her and pity her at the same time. I had seen her when she had come from prison; I had seen her when she was shouting at Kate and the girl left the house; now there was this thing about dog poisoning. But never had I seen her face like this before. The eyes, the nostrils, the lips, the teeth seemed to be full of hate, tried, fixed on doing something bad; and yet there was something on that face that told me she wanted me on her side.

Dick is all right madam, I found myself saying. She took Malan and Monty in her arms and pressed them to herself, running her hands over their heads. They looked so safe, like a child in a mother's arm.

Mrs Plum said All right you may go. She said Do not tell anybody what I have asked about Dick eh?

When I told Dick about it, he seemed worried.

It is nothing, I told him.

I had been thinking before that I did not stand with those who wanted to poison the dogs, Dick said. But the police have come out, I do not care what happens to the dumb things, now.

I asked him I said Would you poison them if you were told by someone to do it?

No. But I do not care, he replied.

The police came again and again. They were having a good holiday, everyone could see that. A day later Mrs Plum told Dick to go because she would not need his work any more.

Dick was almost crying when he left. Is madam so unsure of me? he asked. I never thought a white person could fear me! And he left.

Chimane shouted from the other yard. She said, *Hei ngoana'rona*, the boers are fire-hot eh?

Mrs Plum said she would hire a man after the trouble was over.

A letter came from my parents in Phokeng. In it they told me my uncle had passed away. He was my mother's brother. The letter also told me of other deaths. They said I would not remember some, I was sure to know the others. There were also names of sick people.

I went to Mrs Plum to ask her if I could go home. She asks she says When did he die? I answer I say It is three days, madam. She says So that they have buried him? I reply Yes Madam. Why do you want to go home then? Because my uncle loved me very much madam. But what are you going to do there? To take my tears and words of grief to his grave and to my old aunt, madam. No you cannot go, Karabo. You are working for me you know? Yes, madam. I, and not your people pay you. I must go madam, that is how we do it among my people, madam. She paused. She walked into the kitchen and came out again. If you want to go, Karabo, you must lose the money for the days you will be away. Lose my pay, madam? Yes Karabo.

The next day I went to Mrs Plum and told her I was leaving for Phokeng and was not coming back to her. Could she give me a letter to say that I worked for her. She did, with her lips shut tight. I could feel that something between us was burning like raw chillies. The letter simply said that I had worked for Mrs Plum for three years. Nothing more. The memory of Dick being sent away was still an open sore in my heart.

The night before the day I left, Chimane came to see me in my room. She had her own story to tell me. Timi, her boy-friend, had left her — for good. Why? Because I killed his baby. Had he not agreed that you should do it? No. Did he show he was worried when you told him you were heavy? He was worried, like me as you saw me, Karabo. Now he says if I kill one I shall eat all his children up when we are married. You think he means what he says? Yes, Karabo. He says his parents would have been very happy to know that the woman he was going to marry can make his seed grow.

Chimane was crying, softly.

I tried to speak to her, to tell her that if Timi left her just like that, he had not wanted to marry her in the first place. But I could not, no, I could not. All I could say was Do not cry, my sister, do not cry. I gave her my handkerchief.

Kate came back the morning I was leaving, from somewhere very far I cannot remember where. Her mother took no notice of what Kate said asking her to keep me, and I was not interested either.

One hour later I was on the Railway bus to Phokeng. During the early part of the journey I did not feel anything about the Greenside house I had worked in. I was not really myself, my thoughts dancing between

Mrs Plum, my uncle, my parents, and Phokeng, my home. I slept and woke up many times during the bus ride. Right through the ride I seemed to see, sometimes in sleep, sometimes between sleep and waking, a red car passing our bus, then running behind us. Each time I looked out it was not there.

Dreams came and passed. He tells me he says You have killed my seed I wanted my mother to know you are a woman in whom my seed can grow ... Before you make the police take you to jail make sure that it is for something big you should go to jail for, otherwise you will come out with a heart and mind that will bleed inside you and poison you ...

The bus stopped for a short while, which made me wake up.

The Black Crow, the club women ... *Hei*, listen! I lie to the madam of our house and I say I had a telegram from my mother telling me she is very sick. I show her a telegram my sister sent me as if mother were writing. So I went home for a nice weekend ...

The laughter of the women woke me up, just in time for me to stop a line of saliva coming out over my lower lip. The bus was making plenty of dust now as it was running over part of the road they were digging up. I was sure the red car was just behind us, but it was not there when I woke.

Any one of you here who wants to be baptized or has a relative without a church who needs to be can come and see me in the office ... A round man with a fat tummy and sharp hungry eyes, a smile that goes a long, long way ...

The bus was going uphill, heavily and noisily.

I kick a white man's dog, me, or throw it there if it has not been told the black people's law ... This is Mister Monty and this is Mister Malan. Now get up you lazy boys and meet Mister Kate. Hold out your hands and say hallo to him ... Karabo, bring two glasses there ... Wait a bit — What will you chew boys while Mister Kate and I have a drink? Nothing? Sure?

We were now going nicely on a straight tarred road and the trees rushed back. Mister Kate. What nonsense, I thought.

Look Karabo, madam's dogs are dead. What? Poison. I killed them. She drove me out of a job did she not? For nothing. Now I want her to feel she drove me out for something. I came back when you were in your room and took the things and poisoned them ... And you know what? She has buried them in clean pink sheets in the garden. *Ao*, clean clean good sheets. I am going to dig them out and take one sheet do you want the other one? Yes, give me the other one I will send it to my mother ... *Hei*, Karabo, see here they come. Monty and Malan. The bloody fools they do not want to stay in their hole. Go back you silly fools. Oh you do not want to move eh? Come here, now I am going to throw you in the big pool. No, Dick! No Dick! no, no! Dick! They cannot speak do not kill things that cannot speak. Madam can speak for them she always does. No! Dick ... !

I woke up with a jump after I had screamed Dick's name, almost hitting the window. My forehead was full of sweat. The red car also shot out of my sleep and was gone. I remembered a friend of ours who told us how she and the garden man had saved two white sheets in which their white master had buried their two dogs. They went to throw the dogs in a dam.

When I told my parents my story Father says to me he says, So long as you are in good health my child, it is good. The worker dies, work does not. There is always work. I know when I was a boy a strong sound body and a good mind were the biggest things in life. Work was always there, and the lazy man could never say there was no work. But today people see work as something bigger than everything else, bigger than health, because of money.

I reply I say, Those days are gone Papa. I must go back to the city after resting a little to look for work. I must look after you. Today people are too poor to be able to help you.

I knew when I left Greenside that I was going to return to Johannesburg to work. Money was little, but life was full and it was better than sitting in Phokeng and watching the sun rise and set. So I told Chimane to keep her eyes and ears open for a job.

I had been at Phokeng for one week when a red car arrived. Somebody was sitting in front with the driver, a white woman. At once I knew it to be that of Mrs Plum. The man sitting beside her was showing her the way, for he pointed towards our house in front of which I was sitting. My heart missed a few beats. Both came out of the car. The white woman said Thank you to the man after he had spoken a few words to me.

I did not know what to do and how to look at her as she spoke to me. So I looked at the piece of cloth I was sewing pictures on. There was a tired but soft smile on her face. Then I remembered that she might want to sit. I went inside to fetch a low bench for her. When I remembered it afterwards, the thought came to me that there are things I never think white people can want to do at our homes when they visit for the first time: like sitting, drinking water or entering the house. This is how I thought when the white priest came to see us. One year at

Easter Kate drove me home as she was going to the north. In the same way I was at a loss what to do for a few minutes.

Then Mrs Plum says, I have come to ask you to come back to me, Karabo. Would you like to?

I say I do not know, I must think about it first.

She says, Can you think about it today? I can sleep at the town hotel and come back tomorrow morning, and if you want to you can return with me.

I wanted her to say she was sorry to have sent me away, I did not know how to make her say it because I know white people find it too much for them to say Sorry to a black person. As she was not saying it, I thought of two things to make it hard for her to get me back and maybe even lose me in the end.

I say, You must ask my father first, I do not know, should I call him?

Mrs Plum says, Yes.

I fetched both Father and Mother. They greeted her while I brought benches. Then I told them what she wanted.

Father asks Mother and Mother asks Father. Father asks me. I say if they agree, I will think about it and tell her the next day.

Father says, It goes by what you feel my child.

I tell Mrs Plum I say, if you want me to think about it I must know if you will want to put my wages up from £6 because it is too little.

She asks me, How much will you want?

Up by £4.

She looked down for a few moments.

And then I want two weeks at Easter and not just the weekend. I thought if she really wanted me she would want to pay for it. This would also show how sorry she was to lose me.

Mrs Plum says, I can give you one week. You see you already have something like a rest when I am in Durban in the winter.

I tell her I say I shall think about it.

She left.

The next day she found me packed and ready to return with her. She was very much pleased and looked kinder than I had ever known her. And me, I felt sure of myself, more than I had ever done.

Mrs Plum says to me, You will not find Monty and Malan.

Oh?

Yes, they were stolen the day after you left. The police have not found them yet. I think they are dead myself.

I thought of Dick ... my dream. Could he? And she ... did this woman come to ask me to return because she had lost two animals she loved?

Mrs Plum says to me she says, You know, I like your people, Karabo, the Africans.

And Dick and Me? I wondered.

Paule Marshall

Brazil

Three trumpets, two saxophones, a single trombone; a piano, drums and a bass fiddle. Together in the dimness of the night club they shaped an edifice of sound glittering with notes and swaying to the buffeting of the drums the way a tall building sways imperceptibly to the wind when, suddenly, one of the trumpets sent the edifice toppling with a high, whinnying chord that seemed to reach beyond sound into silence. It was a signal and the other instruments quickly followed, the drums exploding into the erotic beat of a samba, the bass becoming a loud pulse beneath the shrieking horns – and in the midst of the hysteria, a voice announced, first in Portuguese and then in English, 'Ladies and gentlemen, the Casa Samba presents *O Grande Caliban e a Pequena Miranda* – The Great Caliban and the Tiny Miranda!'

The music ended in a taut, expectant silence and in the darkness a spotlight poured a solid cone of light on to the stage with such force smoke seemed to rise from its wide edge and drift out across the audience. Miranda stood within the cone of light, alone but for the shadowy forms of the musicians behind her, as rigid and stiff-faced as a statue. She was a startlingly tall, long-limbed woman with white skin that appeared luminous in the spotlight and blonde hair piled like whipped cream above a face that was just beginning to slacken with age and was all the more handsome and arresting because of this. Her brief costume of sequins and tulle gave off what seemed an iridescent dust each time she breathed, and a smile was affixed like a stamp to her mouth, disguising an expression that was, at once, calculating and grasping – but innocently so, like a child who has no sense of ownership and claims everything to be his. Blue eye shadow sprinkled with gold dust and a pair of dramatic, blue-tinged eyelashes hid her sullen, bored stare.

She filled the night club with a powerful animal presence, with a decisive, passionless air that was somehow Germanic. And she was part German, one of those Brazilians from Rio Grande do Sul who are mixed German, Portuguese, native Indian and sometimes African. With her the German had triumphed. She was a Brunhild without her helmet and girdle of mail, without her spear.

There was a rap on the drums and Miranda clutched one of her buttocks as if she had been struck there; another rap, louder this time, and she clutched the other, feigning shock and outrage.

'Hey, lemme in, stupid!' a rough male voice called in Portuguese behind her, and she whirled like a door that had been kicked open as a dark, diminutive figure burst around her thigh, wearing a scarlet shirt with billowing sleeves and a huge *C* embroidered on the breast like the device of a royal house, a pair of oversized fighter's trunks of the same scarlet which fell past his knees and a prize fighter's high-laced shoes.

He was an old man. His hair beneath the matted wig he wore had been grey for years now and his eyes under their crumpled lids were almost opaque with rheum and innocent with age. Yet, as he turned to Miranda with a motion of kicking the door shut, his movements were deft and fluid – his body was still young, it seemed – and as he turned to the audience his face, despite the wrinkles which like fine incisions had drawn his features into an indistinct knot, was still mobile, eloquent, subtle, each muscle beneath the black skin under his absolute control.

Applause greeted him and he assumed the stance of a prize fighter, his body dropping to a wary, menacing crouch, his head ducking and weaving and his tiny fists cocked as he did a dazzling swift dance on his toes ... Suddenly he unleashed a flurry of savage jabs, first in the direction of Miranda, who quailed, then at the audience. He pommelled the air and when the knock-out blow finally came, it was an uppercut so brilliantly timed, so visually lethal, that those in the audience who had never seen him before jerked their heads out of the way of that fist. 'Joe Louis, the champion,' he cried, and held up a triumphant right hand.

He always opened his act this way and the caricature had made him famous and become his trademark. But he had burlesqued at other times in his long career, and just as effectively, a rustic gazing up at Rio's high buildings of tinted glass and steel for the first time (this was his favourite since, fifty years ago, he had himself come to Rio from a small jewel-mining town in Minas Gerais), an American who had just missed his plane (and it had never mattered that his skin was black or that he spoke Portuguese, the illusion had held), a matron from the Brazilian upper class whose costume had begun unravelling during the carnival ball at Copacabana Palace ... and others.

He had been Everyman, so much so that it had become difficult over his thirty-five years in show business to separate out of the welter of faces he could assume his face, to tell where O Grande Caliban ended and he, Heitor Baptista Guimares, began. He had begun to think about this dimly ever since the night he had decided to retire – and to be vaguely disturbed.

Their act was mostly slapstick, with Caliban using the cowed Miranda as a butt for his bullying and abuse. And it was this incongruous and contradictory relationship – Caliban's strength, his bossiness despite his age and shrivelled body and Miranda's weakness, which belied her imposing height and massive limbs – that was the heart of their act. It shaped everything they did. When they sang, as they were doing now, his voice was an ominous bass rumble beneath her timid soprano. They broke into a dance routine and Miranda took little mincing steps while Caliban spurred his body in a series of impressive leaps and spins, and forced his legs wide in a split.

It looked effortless, but he felt his outraged muscles rebel as he repeated the split, his joints stiffen angrily. He smiled to disguise both his pain and the disgust he felt for his ageing body. He was suddenly overwhelmed by rage and, as usual when his anger became unbearable and he felt helpless, he blamed Miranda. She caught his angry scowl and paused for an instant that was no longer than the natural pause between her dance steps, bewildered, thinking that she had done something wrong and then understanding (she knew him far better now that they openly hated each other), and her own anger streaked across her eyes even as her smile remained intact.

Half-way through their act Miranda left the stage and, alone with the spotlight narrowed to just his face, Caliban spun off a ream of old off-colour jokes and imitations. Everything he did was flawlessly timed and full of the subtlety and slyness he had perfected over the years, but he was no longer funny. The audience laughed, but for reasons other than his jokes: the Brazilians out of affection and loyalty, and the tourists, mostly Americans from a Moore-McCormack ship in the harbour, out of a sense of their own well-being and in relief – relief because in the beginning when Caliban's dark face had appeared around Miranda's white thigh they had tensed, momentarily outraged and alarmed until, with smiles that kept slipping out of place, they had reminded each other that this was Brazil after all, where white was never wholly white, no matter how pure it looked. They had begun laughing then in loud, self-conscious gusts, turning to each other for cues and reassurance, whispering, 'I don't know why I'm laughing. I don't understand a word of Spanish. Or is this the place where they speak Portuguese?'

Miranda returned for a brief, noisy finale and at the very end she reversed the roles by scooping Caliban up with one hand and marching triumphantly off stage with him kicking, his small arms flailing, high above her head.

'*Senhor* and *Senhoras, O Grande Caliban e a Pequena Miranda!*'

Usually, they took two curtain calls, the first with Miranda still holding the protesting Caliban aloft and the other with Caliban on the ground and in command again, chasing the frightened Miranda across the stage. But, tonight, as soon as they were behind the wing, he ordered her to set him down and when she did, he turned and walked towards his dressing-room without a word, his legs stiff with irritability and his set shoulders warning her off.

'Hey, are you crazy, where are you going? The curtain call . . .'

'You take it,' he said, without turning. 'You think it's your show, so you take it.'

She stared after him, helpless and enraged, her eyes a vaporous grey which somehow suggested that her mind was the same grey swirl, and her hair shining like floss in the dimness and dust backstage. Then she bounded after him, an animal about to attack. 'Now what did I do wrong?' she shouted against the dwindling sound of the applause.

He turned abruptly and she stopped. 'Everything,' he said quietly. 'You did everything wrong. You were lousy.'

'So were you.'

'Yes, but only because of you.'

'Bastard, whenever something's worrying you or you feel sick, you take it out on me. I swear you're like a woman changing life. Nobody told you to try doing the split out there tonight, straining yourself. You're too old. You should retire. You're finished.'

'Shut up.'

'Why don't you take out your worries on the little mamita you have home, your holiest of virgins . . . ?' He walked rapidly away and she cried after him, gesturing furiously, her voice at a scathing pitch, 'Yes, go home to mamita, your child bride. And has the holiest of virgins given birth to your little Jesus yet?'

'Pig,' he said, and opened the door to his dressing-room.

'Children of old men come out crooked.' She began to cry, the false eyelashes staining her cheeks blue.

'Barren bitch.'

'Runt! Despoiler of little girls.'

He slammed the door on her, jarring the mirror on his dressing table so that his reflection wavered out of shape within its sombre, mottled depth. He remained near the door, waiting for the mirror to settle and his own anger to subside, aware, as always, of a critical silence in the room. It was a pleasant silence, welcoming him when his performance was good, but mocking and cold – as it was now – when he failed. And he was aware of something else in the room, a subtle disturbance he had sensed there ever since the night, two months ago, when he had decided to retire. He had thought, at first, that the disturbance was due to something out of place within the familiar disorder or to some new object which had been placed there without his knowing it. But after searching and finding nothing, he had come to believe that what he felt was really a disturbance within himself, some worry he could not define which had become dislodged and escaped along with his breath and taken a vague, elusive form outside of him. Each night it awaited him in the cubicle of a dressing-room and watched him while he took off his make-up and dressed, mute yet somehow plaintive, like the memory of someone he had known at another time, but whose face he could no longer remember.

Taking off the scarlet shirt, he tossed it among the other costumes littering the room and, sitting at the dressing table, began taking off the make-up, pausing each time the bulb over the mirror flickered out as the music, playing now for the patrons' dancing, jarred the walls. As his face emerged it was clear that it had once been appealing – the way a child's face is – with an abrupt little nose flattened at the tip, a wry mouth and softly moulded contours which held dark shadows within their hollows – a face done in miniature over which the black skin had been drawn tight and eyes which held like a banked fire the intensity of the Latin.

He avoided looking at his face now that he was old. Without the make-up it reminded him of a piece of old fruit so shrivelled and spotted with decay that there was no certainty as to what it had been originally. Above all, once he removed the make-up, his face was without expression, bland, as though only on stage made up as Caliban in the scarlet shirt and baggy trunks was he at all certain of who he was. Caliban might have become his reality.

So that now, while his hands did the work of his eyes, he gazed absently at his body, imposing on his slack shoulders and on the sunken chest which barely stirred with his breathing the dimmed memory of his body at the height of his fame (he could not remember what it had looked like before becoming Caliban). He had held himself like a military man then, very erect, his small shoulders squared, all of him stretching it seemed towards the height which had been denied him – and this martial stance, so incongruous somehow, had won him the almost hysterical admiration of the crowds. Yet, in the midst of this admiration, he had always felt vaguely like a small animal who had been fitted out in an absurd costume and trained to amuse, some Lilliputian in a kingdom of giants who had to play the jester in order to survive. The world had been scaled without him in mind – and his rage and contempt for it and for those who belonged was always just behind his smile, in the vain, superior lift of his head, in his every gesture.

He pulled on a robe of the same red satin, with a large C embroidered on the breast, hiding himself. He flung aside the towel he was using and the light flickered and then flickered again as the door opened and the porter, Henriques, who also served as Caliban's valet, entered with the cup of *café Sinho* he always brought him after the last show.

Caliban watched the reflection take shape behind his in the mirror: the bloated form dressed in a discarded evening jacket with a cummerbund spanning his vast middle, the face a white globule until the beaked nose which absorbed it appeared, and then the fringe of black hair which Henriques kept waved and pomaded. Caliban felt comforted and younger suddenly, so that as Henriques placed the coffee beside him he motioned him to a chair and, turning, said, his voice loud and casual but strained:

'Henriques, we are in business, old man. Or better out of business. The signs are finished. I saw them today. And they are good. Very bold. They used my red and it hits the eye like one of Caliban's uppercuts' – his fist cut through the air and, although Henriques laughed and nodded, no smile stirred within his old eyes.

'And, thank God, they got the C in Caliban right. I was worried about that because they got it all wrong on the posters they made for my tour last year. But it pleased me the way they did the C this time. Very large and sweeping. Up at the top it says, "O Grande Caliban retiring", in big print to catch the eye, with the C coming at you like a fist, then below that "Brazil's greatest and most beloved comedian leaving the stage after thirty-five years", and at the bottom, "See him perform for the last times this month at the Casa Samba." That's all. And enough, I think. It is more dramatic that way . . .'

'And when will they be put on display, Senhor Caliban?' Henriques asked with elaborate courtesy.

'The day after tomorrow. The posters will go up all over the city, but the big signs only down-town and in Copacabana. There'll be announcements in all the papers of course – a full-page ad which will run for a week, and on radio and television.'

'I have a confession, senhor,' Henriques said, his voice edging in beside Caliban's, which had grown louder, filling the room. 'I personally did not believe it. You know, senhor, how you sometimes talk about retiring but ... well, you know. But now with the signs and the announcements ...'

'The talk has ended, Henriques. Two more weeks. The signs are ready, old man!' He shouted as though informing someone beyond the room and held up two fingers the colour and shape of dried figs. 'Two weeks from tonight Caliban does his last boxing match. That night will mark my anniversary. Thirty-five years ago that same night I won the amateur contest at the Teatro Municipal. Do you remember the old Teatro Municipal? There's a clinic there now for the children of the poor. The night I won, the producer, Julio Baretos, right away booked me in his regular show and christened me O Grande Caliban. After that ...' His gesture summed up the success which had followed that night.

'And what is your real name, Senhor Caliban?' Henriques said.

Caliban paused, surprised for the moment, and then quickly said, 'Guimares. Heitor Guimares. Heitor Baptista Guimares.' He gave an embarrassed laugh. 'I haven't used it for so long I had to stop and think.'

'Perhaps you will begin using it now that you are retiring.'

'Of course,' he said, and sat back, his smile and gesture dying, his eyes becoming troubled again under their crumpled lids. He quickly drank the *café Sinho* and, as his glance met Henriques' over the cup, he gave a shapeless smile. 'Of course,' he repeated loudly, even as his gaze wandered over the costumes hung like the bright skins of imaginary animals on the walls, over the trunks containing his juggling and magician equipment. His eyes lingered on each object, possessing it. He tied the scarlet robe more securely around him.

'You are wise to retire,' Henriques said quietly. 'After all, you are not that old yet and you have a new life ahead what with a young wife and a child soon.'

'Of course,' Caliban murmured, and for a moment could not remember what his wife looked like.

'How many your age have that? Look at me. I haven't been able to have a woman for years now. And children? All my children have forgotten me. And you have money, Senhor Caliban, while we who are old and without must keep dragging around a dead carcass, breathing death over everybody, working till our end . . .' Henriques stirred heavily in the chair, looking, with the costumes draped behind him and the cummerbund girding his middle, like some old, sated regent.

'Yes,' he said, and followed Caliban's stare into space. 'You are retiring at the right time, senhor, and with dignity. Putting up the signs all over the city shows style. You are saying goodbye to Rio in the proper way, which is only right, since it was here that you became famous. Rio made you, after all.'

'Of course.'

'Now once a year during carnival you will perform before the President at Copacabana Palace Hotel and all of Rio will weep remembering your greatness . . .'

Caliban restrained him with a gesture and in the silence his dark skin seemed to grow ashen as if inside some abstract terror had cramped his heart. 'What to do, Henriques,' he said, and shrugged. 'I am an old man. Did you see me tonight? The last show especially? I could hardly move. I forgot lines so that the jokes didn't make sense. I was all right in the beginning, but once I gave the knock-out punch I was through. That punch took all my strength. I feel it here,' he touched his right shoulder, his chest. 'Oh, I know I could go on working at the Casa Samba for a while longer, I am an institution here, but I don't love it any more. I don't feel the crowd. And then that pig Miranda has gotten so lousy.'

'Did you have her name put on the signs?'

'To hell with her. No,' he shouted, swept suddenly by the same anger he had felt on stage. He jumped up and began dressing under Henriques' somnolent eye, wondering at the intensity of his anger, knowing remotely that it reached beyond Miranda to something greater.

'But haven't you told her?'

'I told her. I even told her about the signs. But like you she didn't believe me. She just laughed. The pig,' he cried suddenly, and the light flickered. 'Did you hear her cursing me just now, and cursing my wife and my unborn child. She has become crazy this past year. All because I married.' Suddenly, facing the door, he shouted, 'It's my business that I married, pig, not yours. And if I chose to marry a child of twenty-five, it is my business still.'

He waited, quivering, as though expecting Miranda to burst into the room. Then, turning again to Henriques, he said, 'You would not believe it, Henriques, but I still give her everything she wants even though I married. Last month she saw one of those fancy circular beds in a magazine from Hollywood and I had one custom made for her. A while back, she took out all the light fixtures and put in chandeliers, even in the kitchen, so that her place looks like the grand ballroom of the Copacabana Palace Hotel. I bought the chandeliers for her, of course, as I have bought nearly everything she has – while she has been saving her money all these years. And even though I married I still go and spend part of the evening with her before we come to the club ... So she complains I will have nothing to do with her any more. But after all, Henriques, I am an old man and I have a young wife. Besides it was always a little grotesque with her...'

'They say it's never good to keep a woman around once you're finished with her.'

'I should have kicked her out, yes – and long ago. She was never any good for me or for the act. From the very beginning she tried to take over both of us. And I only included her in the act for effect. She wasn't supposed to do anything more than stand there like a mannequin. But she kept insisting – she would wake me at night begging me to let her do more. And so ...' He motioned hopelessly and sat down.

'I should have never taken up with her.' Then he said softly, 'But she was a weakness with me in the beginning.' He gave Henriques an oblique, almost apologetic glance. 'And what I said just now was not true. She was good for me in the beginning – and we were good together. We were the same, you see. Me, as I am —' and with a gesture he offered Henriques his shrunken body —'and she, so tall, and she was skinny then. They were laughing at her the first time I saw her in a show at the Miramar almost fifteen years ago now. She couldn't dance. She couldn't sing. She hadn't bleached her hair yet and she looked lousy ... I understood what it was for her being so tall —' His voice dropped, becoming entangled with the memory. 'And she was good for the act in the beginning. She had imagination and the comic touch. She was the one who thought up the prize-fighter routine, which is still the most famous. But then something went wrong with her, Henriques, and she began doing everything wrong. I've been carrying her for years now. Perhaps I would have had another five, ten years left, if not for her. She has become a bane. She has used me till I'm dry, the pig!'

'But what of her now?'

Caliban, dressed in an expensive mohair suit with a white handkerchief embroidered with a red *C* in the breast pocket, patent-leather shoes with built-up heels and diamond cuff links glinting in turn with the many rings he wore, turned sharply towards the door as if to rush from the room and the question. 'What of her? That's not my worry. The day those signs go up is the day I finish with her, the parasite. Let her spend some of the money she sits on. She has talked for years about doing her own act. Now she'll have a chance to do it.'

'But does she have the talent for that?'

'No, and she knows it. Do you think she would have stayed with me all this time if she had, Henriques? Not Miranda.'

'Well, she will find someone to keep her. She is like Rio. There will always be somebody to admire her.' Henriques heaved up from the chair, and, as his unwieldy bulk filled the small room, the dusk whirred up like frightened birds and settled further away. He began picking up Caliban's clothes.

'Yes,' Caliban said thoughtfully, 'she will find somebody to use, the bitch. For a while anyway.' He hurried to the door, eager to escape the room which had suddenly become crowded with the image of Miranda and hot from his anger. As he opened it, he sensed the vague, illusory form of his fear rush past him like a draught and lead him through the clutter backstage, out the back door and across the denuded yard to the entrance, where the neon lights pulsed the name CASA SAMBA into the night and a large sign at the door announced the nightly appearance of O Grande Caliban.

The club was closing; the last of the crowd clustered under the awning while the doorman called up the taxis. Beyond the radius of neon lights the night itself was a vast awning under which the city slept, exhausted from its nightly revelry, its few remaining lights like dull reflections of the stars. Its mountains, like so many dark breasts thrusting into the sky, gave height and prominence and solidity to the night.

The Casa Samba had been built on the sloping street leading to the *Pão de Açúcar* and as Caliban walked towards his car he was aware, as if for the first time, of the mountain's high, solid cone, black against the lesser blackness of the sky, benevolent, rising protectively over the sleeping city. He could make out the cable line of the aerial railway looped in a slender thread between *Pão de Açúcar* and its satellite, Mount Urca. What had been for years just another detail in the familiar frieze that was Rio was suddenly separate and distinct, restored ... He paused beside his car, hoping (but unaware of the hope) that a part of himself which he had long since ceased to see might emerge into consciousness as the mountain had emerged, thinking (and he was aware of this) that there might be a wind the day after tomorrow when the signs announcing his retirement went up, a wind strong enough to tear them down before they could be read and whip them out to sea. He was half smiling, his worn eyelids closing with pleasure at the thought, when a taxi with a group of Americans from the night club stopped and one of them called to him in English, 'Say, do you speak English?'

He turned, annoyed. The man's voice, the harsh, unmelodic, almost guttural English he spoke, his pale face floating in the darkness seemed to snatch his pleasure, to declare that there would be no wind the day after tomorrow and the signs would remain. As the taxi's headlights singled him out, he felt as if he had been caught on stage without the armour of his scarlet shirt and loose trunks – suddenly defenceless, shorter than his five feet, insignificant. He quickly assumed his martial pose.

'I speak some little English,' he said stiffly.

'Well, then maybe you can explain to our driver here —' and the driver protested in Portuguese to Caliban that he had understood them and could speak English – 'that we want to go some place else, not back to the hotel, but to another night club. Are there any that stay open all night? Do you understand what I'm saying? Some place where we can dance.'

Without answering, Caliban turned and told the driver where to take them. Then he said in English, 'He will take you to a place.'

'Thanks. Say, aren't you the comedian from the club? What's your name again?'

He wanted to fling the full title – O Grande Caliban – in the man's face and walk away, but he could not even say Caliban. For some reason he felt suddenly divested of that title and its distinction, no longer entitled to use it.

The man was whispering to the others in the car. 'What was his name again? You know, the old guy telling the jokes. With the blonde.'

'The name is Heitor Guimares,' Caliban said suddenly.

'No, I mean your stage name.'

'Hey, wait, I remember,' someone in the car called. 'It was from Shakespeare. Caliban ...'

'Heitor Baptista Guimares,' he cried, his voice loud and severe, addressed not only to them but to the mountain and the night. Turning, he walked to his car.

He did not drive away but remained perched like a small, ruffled bird on the cushions he used to raise the driver's seat, his rings winking angrily in the dimness as he watched the tail-lights of the taxi define the slope as it sped down, trying to order his breathing, which had suddenly become a conscious and complex act. The tail lights vanished and with them the momentary annoyance he had felt with the tourists. He was alone then, with only the vague form of his anxiety (and he had never felt such loneliness) and the unfamiliar name echoing in his mind.

'Heitor Guimares', he said slowly. 'Heitor Guimares'. But although he repeated it until his tongue was heavy, it had no reality. It was the name of a stranger who had lived at another time.

By the time Caliban reached the modern house of glass walls and stone he had built in a suburb near Corcovado, the mountain of Christ, a thin, opalescent dawn had nudged aside the darkness, and, as he walked hesitantly across the patio, through the living-room, down the hall to the bedrooms, the sound of his raised heels on the tiles was like the failing pulse of the dying night.

He paused at the opened door of the master bedroom. He could not hear his wife's breathing but he could see it in the small, steady flame of the candle before the Madonna in the niche near the bed. In the faint light he made out her stomach, like a low hill on the wide plain of the bed, and the dark outline of her face framed by the pillows. He did not have to see that face to know its mildness and repose. The first time he had met her on the tour last year which had taken him through the small town in Minas Gerais where he had been born (she was the grand-daughter of a distant cousin of his and it had been easy to arrange the marriage), he had almost, instinctively, crossed himself. She had looked like a Madonna painted black. He had wanted to confess to her as to a priest, seeing her that first time. He would have confessed now if he could have named his fear – whispering to her while she slept. And she would have, blindly in her sleep, curved her body to receive him, nesting him within the warm hollow of her back as if he were the child she bore. He hesitated though, feeling, oddly, that he was no longer entitled to use the name Caliban.

He closed the door and went to the small room at the end of the hall which he used as a den and stretched out on the cot there without undressing. As always when he was troubled, he slept quickly and his dream was that he was caught in a mine shaft without a lantern to light his way.

As quickly, light rushed at him from one end of the shaft and he awoke to the afternoon sun which had invaded the room. Like a reveller the sunlight did a sprightly dance on the framed photographs on the walls (they were all of Caliban, one with the President of Brazil during the carnival of 1946 and another with Carmen Miranda the year before she died), on the mementoes and awards on top of the desk; it leaped across the floor and landed in the arms of his wife as she opened the door.

She did not enter the room but stood, like a petitioner, in the doorway, holding a cup of coffee as though it was an offering. She had already been to Mass, yet a thin haze from her long sleep filmed her eyes; her body, Caliban knew, would still be warm and pliant from the bed. He felt neither pleasure nor passion at the thought, though – and as if she understood this and blamed herself, she bowed her head.

'Caliban . . .' she said finally, and hesitated. Then: 'You have slept in all your clothes and in your rings.'

'It's nothing,' he said, and sat up, waving her off as she started forward to help him. 'I was tired last night, that's all.'

His body felt strange: sore as though he had been beaten while he slept, constricted by the clothes which seemed to have shrunk overnight. The taste of the name he had spoken aloud in the car was still in his mouth. 'Let me have the coffee,' he said.

The coffee was the colour and texture of his sleep and he drank it quickly, wishing that it was a potion which would bring on that sleep again. 'Is there a wind today?'

'Only at the top of the road, near the church.' And she quickly added, 'But I wore a coat.'

His thought had been of the signs, not of her, and, ashamed suddenly, he said in the paternal, indulgent tone he used with her, 'Tell me, Clara, how would you like to live somewhere else for a while? Somewhere in Minas again perhaps . . .'

She could not disguise her reluctance. 'Back to Minas? But what of your work?'

'You let me worry about that, little Clara.'

'And this house?'

'Sell it and build a bigger one there.'

'Yes, of course. But then Rio is nice too. I mean there is carnival here and . . .'

'We will come down for carnival each year.'

'Of course. Then there is the child. It would be nice if it were born in Rio. Perhaps after the child we could return to Minas . . .'

'No, I don't want a child of mine to be born in Rio and be called a *Carioca*.'

'Yes, Caliban.'

'Say Heitor,' he said sharply, startling her.

'Heitor?' She frowned.

'Don't you know my real name?'

'Of course.'

'Well, then, you can begin using it.'

She would have asked why (he could see the question stir within the haze), but she was not bold enough.

For the first time her timidity annoyed him and he leaped up, his movement so abrupt that she drew back. 'Tell me,' he said, appealing to her suddenly, 'did your mother ever speak about me? Or your grandmother? Did they ever talk about me as a young man? About Heitor?'

'Of course.'

'What did they say I was like?'

She was silent for so long he repeated the question, his voice high and urgent. 'What did they say?'

'I know they used to talk about how big a success you were . . .' she said hesitantly.

'As a young man, I said. Before I came to Rio. I was different then . . .'

'I know they used to talk, but I can't remember all that they said. I only know that when you were famous they always looked for your name in the papers.'

He sat down on the edge of the cot, showing his disgust with her by a limp wave and feeling unreasonably that she had failed him. It was as if he had married her hoping that she would bring, like a dowry, the stories and memories of him as a young man, as Heitor, only to discover that he had been cheated.

'Heitor Guimares . . . Senhora Guimares,' she was murmuring, touching herself and smiling abstractly.

'What are you laughing about? You don't like the name?'

'No, it's just that until I get used to it I will keep looking for someone else when I say it because I'm so used to you being Caliban.'

It was not clear whether he hurled the cup at her or at the floor, but it missed her and, as it broke on the tiles, the sunlight scuttled from the room and the spilled coffee spread in a dark stain between them. 'And who will you be looking for?' His shout was strident with the same abstract rage of the night before. 'Who? Tell me. Some boy your age perhaps? Some tall, handsome boy, eh, some *Carioca* who will dance with you in the streets during carnival and jounce you on my bed behind my back? Is he the one you will be looking for?'

She said nothing. She had uttered a muted cry when the cup broke, but now, as he leaped up again, she calmly placed her hands over her swollen stomach, protecting it from the violence of his movement and, as he shouted, her fat child's fingers spread wider, deflecting the sound.

'Tell me!' he charged her. 'Who is this person you will be looking for when you call my name?'

She remained as silent and resigned as the Virgin in their bedroom, her head bent in submission, her hands guarding the stomach.

Her silence was a defence he could not shake and as he stood there, menacing her with his shouts, he felt his anger rebound from the thick, invisible wall of silence which shielded her and flailed him. He was the victim of his own rage, and bruised, beaten, he rushed from the room, from her, his heels clattering like small hoofs on the tile.

'Caliban!' He heard her cry over the sound of the motor as he started the car, and then a snatch of words as he drove off: 'You have not changed your clothes.'

He realized this when he was some distance from the house and had calmed a little. And the feel of the stale, sodden clothes recalled the time when he had first come to Rio and had had to wear secondhand clothes that were invariably too large for him and shiny from long wear and smelling always of the former owners. That had been the time, of course, when he had been only Heitor Guimares and people calling him by that name had not looked for anyone else, nor had he felt strange saying it. He tried to restore those years in his mind, but the memories were without form or coherence. They filtered down at random, blown like dust through his mind, and as he reached out to snatch them – desperate suddenly to recapture that time and that self – they eluded his fingers.

One memory paused though: he saw a street, the Rua Gloria, and the restaurant where he had worked until he had won the contest at the Teatro Municipal. The pattern of the tile floor over which he had swung the mop three times a day, the tables – slabs of cheap white marble upon which he had placed the food – were suddenly clear. He had left a part of himself there. Suddenly he brought his foot down on the accelerator, standing up and gripping the steering wheel to give himself leverage, and the big car bounded forward, bearing him to the city and the Rua Gloria.

As the car swept down the mountain roads, the sea appeared, vast and benign, mirroring the sky's paleness and breaking the sun's image into fragments, then the bays – sure, graceful curves, forming an arabesque design with the hills between – and finally the city itself – white, opulent, languorous under the sun's caress, taking its afternoon rest now in preparation for the night.

The Rua Gloria was in the old section of Rio and Caliban found it easily, recognizing the house on the corner with its Moorish-style balcony and chequer-pane windows. The house was a ruin but somehow it promised that he would find the restaurant at the other end of the street. Parking the car, he started down, eager suddenly. Instinctively,

as if the years had not passed, his legs made the slight adjustment to
the sloping street and his feet sought out the old holes in the pavement; half-way down he passed the boys' school and his head turned
automatically, expecting the boys in the yard to wave and shout, 'Ohlá,
Senhor Heitor, when are you going to stop growing?'

There were boys in the yard now, playing soccer in the eddying dust,
and they looked no different from those he had known. But they did not
wave, and, although they shouted and rushed out the gate when he
passed, it was only because he was a stranger. They pointed to his
mohair suit, his shoes with the raised heels, his rings dancing in the
sunlight, whispering among themselves. And then one of them cried, 'O
Grande Caliban,' and, with that abruptness which Caliban had perfected, dropped to a fighter's crouch. The others took up his cry and
the name O Grande Caliban rose in a piercing chorale.

They trailed him, trumpeting the name, a scuffling retinue in their
school uniforms. Caliban stiffened each time they tossed his name into
the air like a football, but he welcomed them. They were a solid wall
between him and the apprehensiveness which trailed him. Because of
them he was certain that he would find the restaurant intact, like the
setting of a play which had not been dismantled.

And it was there, but unrecognizable save for the glazed tiles in the
entrance way which were all broken now and the stone doorsill in which
the old groove had been worn deeper. Where the awning had been, a
huge sign said BEBE COCA-COLA and below that, on the modern glass
front, was the new name of the restaurant: O RESTAURANTE GRANDE
CALIBAN.

The boys crowded behind him, pressing him inside, and he saw that
the tile floor whose every imperfection he could have traced in the dark
had been covered in bright linoleum; chrome chairs and tables had
replaced the marble tables and wire-back chairs, while booths covered
in simulated leather lined one wall. The air smelled of stale coffee and
as Caliban, jarred by the sight of faded newspaper photographs of
himself crowding the walls and a garish oil painting of him in the scarlet
shirt hanging over the bar, placed his hand on a table to steady himself, a fly there stirred its wings but did not move.

The only occupant was a man – the waiter or owner perhaps – half-
asleep at the bar, his stout haunches overlapping the stool. He stirred into wakefulness now with the same blind, stubborn movement as
the fly. He was a *sarará* with an abundance of sandy hair curling out of
the sweat-shirt he wore, fair skin pitted from smallpox and small, agate-
coloured eyes set within morose features. He turned, querulous with

sleep, and missing Caliban, who was, after all, no taller than most of the boys, he shouted, 'Get out of here, you little bandits, before you let in the flies.'

'We come with Caliban,' they hurled at him, 'O Grande Caliban.'

The man stared suspiciously and peered, his head lowered as though he was about to charge, through the fog of sleep. As he spotted Caliban his agate-coloured eyes glittered like one of Caliban's rings, and an awed smile groped its way around his mouth. 'Senhor Caliban ... ?' he whispered, and slipped from the stool into a bow so fluid and perfect it looked rehearsed.

'Senhor Caliban, it is a great honour ...' With a proud wave he presented Caliban with the large portrait over the bar, the photographs, the chrome chairs and the linoleum. 'Please ...' He motioned him to a booth, then to a table.

Caliban would have turned and left if the boys had not been behind him, barring his way. He wanted to escape, for the restaurant had profaned his past with chrome and simulated leather, and the portrait, the faded photographs, his name on the window had effaced the Heitor Guimares who had wielded the mop over the tiles.

'Who put up those pictures?' he asked sharply.

The man's smile faltered and he said, puzzled, 'I found them here when I bought the place, Senhor Caliban, all except the portrait. I did that. I am something of a painter — an artist like yourself, Senhor Caliban. I did it in your honour ...' He gave the supple bow again.

'Who owned the place before you?'

'A man named DaCruz. He had many debts so I got it cheap ...'

'Did he put them up?'

'No, I think it was his great-uncle, old Nacimento, the one, Senhor Caliban, who must have owned the restaurant when you worked here. Perhaps you've forgotten him?'

'Yes, I had forgotten,' Caliban said, and paused, trying to summon Nacimento's face from the blurred assortment of faces in his mind. 'Is he still alive?'

'He was the last time I heard, Senhor Caliban, but he is very sick because of course he is so old. And he has nothing now, I hear, and lives in the *favelas*.'

'Which one?'

'The one above Copacabana ... Senhor Caliban, a *café Sinho* perhaps?'

But Caliban had already turned and with an abrupt wave scattered the boys out of his way.

'A *café Sinho*, at least!' The man shouted from the doorway over the heads of the boys, but Caliban, his small back slanted forward, was already rushing up the street, his patent-leather shoes flashing in the sunlight.

Later, as Caliban climbed the first slope leading to the *favela*, his shoes became covered with red dust and clay. He could see just above him the beginning of the slums – a vast, squalid rookery for the poor of Rio clinging to the hill above Copacabana, a nest of shacks built with the refuse of the city: the discarded crates and boxes, bits of galvanized iron and tin, old worm-eaten boards and shingles – and all of this piled in confused, listing tiers along the hillside, the wood bleached grey by the sun. The *favela* was another city above Rio which boldly tapped its electricity from below – so that at night the hills were strewn with lights – and repulsed the government's efforts to remove it. It was an affront – for that squalor rising above Rio implied that Rio herself was only a pretence; it was a threat – for it seemed that at any moment the *favela* would collapse and hurtle down, burying the city below.

Caliban had long ago ceased to see the *favelas*. He would glance up at the hills occasionally to watch them shift miraculously as the shadows moving across them shifted, but his eye passed quickly over the ugliness there: it was too much a reminder of what he had known. Now the *favela* claimed his eye. It seemed to rush down at him, bringing with it a sure and violent death – and he remembered the stories of strangers who had ventured into the *favelas* and had either disappeared or been found garrotted the next day at the foot of the hill.

In pursuing the old man, it was as if, suddenly, he was pursuing his own death. And because he was exhausted, the thought of that death was almost pleasurable. He imagined the thronged cathedral, the crowds standing a thousand deep outside, the city hung in crêpe; he heard the priest intoning his name – and at the thought that perhaps no one would recognize the name Heitor Guimares, he stumbled and nearly fell.

The children of the *favela* appeared, slipping quietly down amid the scrub which lined the path, some of them balancing gallon tins of water on their heads or smaller children on their hips. They seemed born of the dust which covered them, like small, tough plants sprung from the worn soil, and their flat, incurious eyes seemed to mirror the defeated lives they had yet to live.

They watched him climb without comment, recognizing that he was a stranger from the city below who brought with him the trappings of that world: the flashing rings and stylish clothes. Their empty stares seemed to push him up the hill towards some final discovery.

Caliban could not look at them, and said, his eyes averted, '*Ohlá*, can any of you tell me where to find Nacimento, the old man?'

Their answer was a stolid silence and he called down the line, addressing each one in turn: 'Do you know him? Which is his house? Do you know who I'm talking about?' Finally he cried, his voice strained thin by the dust and his exertion, 'Do you know him; he is an old friend!'

'His house is the one there,' a boy said finally, pointing. 'The one beside the tree without a head.'

Caliban saw the tree, a dead palm without its head-dress of fronds, starting out of the ground like a derisive finger, and then the house beside it, a makeshift of old boards and tin and dried fronds. It looked untenanted: Nacimento might have died and left the house as a monument. Caliban turned to the children, the fear dropping like a weight inside him.

'He's there,' the boy said. 'He doesn't like the sun.'

And suddenly Caliban remembered Nacimento sending him to roll down the restaurant awning against the sun each afternoon. The warped door he pushed open now seemed to declare the age of the man inside and, as he entered the room, shutting out the glare behind him, it was as if the night was in hiding there, waiting for the sun to set before it rushed out and, charging down the hill, lay siege to the city.

'Nacimento . . .' he called softly. He could not see the old man but he heard his breathing – a thin *râle* like the fluting of an instrument Nacimento played to ease his loneliness. Presently Caliban made out a table because of a white cup there, then a cot whose legs had been painted white and finally the dark form of the old man.

He was seated before the boarded-up window, facing it as though it was open, and he was watching the sun arching down the sky or the children waiting around the dead palm for Caliban to emerge.

'Nacimento,' Caliban said, and knew that the old man was blind. 'Senhor Nacimento.'

'Is there someone?' the old man asked uncertainly, as though he could no longer distinguish between those voices which probably filled his fantasies sitting there alone and those that were real. He did not turn from the window.

'Yes, it is Heitor Guimares.'

'Who is the person?' The old man said formally, turning now.

'Heitor.'

'Heitor?'

'Yes, from the restaurant years ago. You remember. He . . . I used to be the waiter . . .'

'Heitor . . .' the old man said slowly, as though searching for the face to which the name belonged.

Hopeful, Caliban drew closer. He could see Nacimento's eyes now, two yellow smears in the dimness which reflected nothing and the face wincing, it seemed, in unrelieved pain.

'Yes, Heitor,' Caliban said coaxingly. 'You used to call me Little Heitor from Minas. You remember . . .'

'I know no Heitor,' the old man said sorrowfully, and then, starting apprehensively, he cried, 'Is the door closed? The sun ruins everything.'

Caliban's voice rose, tremulous and insistent. 'But of course you remember. After all, every day you used to tell me the same thing – to close the door, to roll down the awning against the sun. It was I – Heitor Guimares – who would sometimes tell a few jokes at night to keep the customers drinking. But then, you must remember because it was you, after all, who made me enter the amateur contest at the Teatro Municipal. You even went with me that night and gave me a shirt to wear with ruffles down the front like a movie star. The Teatro Municipal!' he shouted as the old man shook his head confusedly. 'We wept on each other's shoulder when they told me I had won and put me in the regular show with the name of Caliban . . .'

'O Grande Caliban,' the old man said severely.

'Yes, but I was Heitor Guimares when I worked for you, not Caliban.'

'O Grande Caliban. He was the best they ever had at the Teatro Municipal. I told him he would win and he was the best . . .'

'But I was Heitor then!'

'I know no Heitor,' Nacimento cried piteously, and turned to the boarded-up window, reaching up as though he would open it and call for help. 'I know no Heitor . . .'

Caliban believed him. It was no use. The old man, he understood, going suddenly limp, had retained only a few things: his fear of the sun, the name O Grande Caliban, a moment of success in a crowded theatre in which he had shared. That was all. The rest had been stripped away in preparation for his death which, in a way, had already begun. Caliban smelled its stench in the room suddenly and wanted to flee as he had fled the restaurant earlier. Groping towards the door, he jarred against the table and the cup there fell and broke. The old man whimpered at the sound and Caliban remembered his wife's muted outcry that morning over the other cup he had broken. The day seemed to be closing in on him, squeezing his life from him, and his panic was like a stitch in his side as he rushed out, forgetting to close the door behind him.

The night might have escaped through the open door and followed him down the hill, for as he sat in his car, crumpled with exhaustion, knowing that his search had been futile and he could do nothing now but go to Miranda as he did each evening at this time, he saw the first of the dusk surge across the hill in a dark, purposeful wave, drowning out the *favela*, and then charge down the slopes, deepening into night as it came.

The city, in quick defence, turned on her lights, and as Caliban drove out of the tunnel on to the road which followed the wide arc of Copacabana Bay he saw the lights go on in the apartment buildings and hotels piled like white angular cliffs against the black hills. Seen from a distance those lighted windows resembled very large, fine diamonds, an iridescent amber now in the last of the sunlight, which would turn to a fiery yellow once the darkness settled. Rio – still warm from the sun, murmurous with the cadence of the sea, bejewelled with lights – was readying herself for the nightly carousal, waiting for the wind to summon her lovers.

Caliban had been one of her lovers, but as he drove through her midst, he felt her indifference to his confusion, to his sense of a loss which remained nameless; moreover, he suspected that she had even been indifferent to his success. 'After all Rio has made you,' Henriques had said, but he had not added that she would quickly choose another jester to her court once he was gone. Caliban hated the city suddenly – and as that hate became unbearable he shifted its weight on to Miranda. He accused her. Hadn't Henriques said that she and Rio were the same? He brought his foot down on the accelerator and the car leaped forward like a startled horse, leaving black streaks on the road.

Oddly enough, Miranda's apartment, in a new building at the end of Copacabana, reflected the city. The great squares of black and white tile in the foyer suggested not only the stark white buildings reared against the dark hills and the sidewalks of Copacabana – a painstaking mosaic of small black and white stones, but the faces of the *Cariocas* themselves – endless combinations of black and white. The green rug in the living-room could have been a swatch cut from one of the hills, while the other furnishings there – elaborate period pieces of an ivory finish, marble tables cluttered with figurines, sofas of pale silk and down, white drapes and gilt-edged mirrors – repeated the opulence, self-indulgence, the lavish whiteness of the city. And the chandeliers with their fiery crystal spears, which rustled like frosted leaves as Caliban slammed the door, caught the brilliance of Rio at night.

For the first time Caliban was aware of how the room expressed the city, and of himself, reflected in one of the mirrors, in relation to it. He was like a house pet, a tiny dog, who lent the room an amusing touch but had no real place there. The pale walls and ivory furniture, the abundance of white throughout stripped him of importance, denied him all significance. He felt like whimpering as the old man, Nacimento, had whimpered when the cup broke – and he must have unknowingly, for Miranda suddenly called from the adjoining bedroom, 'What in the hell are you muttering to yourself about out there?'

He turned and through the half-opened door saw her enthroned amid a tumble of pink satin cushions on the circular bed he had bought her, while her maid massaged her feet in a basin of scented water – the girl's black hands wavering out of shape under the water. Miranda had already dressed her hair for the night club – the stiff froth of blonde curls piled high above her white brow – and applied her make-up (she had spent the afternoon at it, Caliban knew), but her body beneath the sheer pink dressing-gown was still bare, the tops of the breasts a darker pink than the gown. Knowing how slack those breasts had become, Caliban felt repelled, weary and then angry again; he understood suddenly that her refusal ever to leave him and marry, to have children and use those ample breasts, was, simply, her desire to remain the child herself – wilful, dependent, indulged – and that she had used him to this end, just as she would use someone else now that she had exhausted him.

As always when he was truly angry, he became calm, and in that calm he could always feel his nerves, the muscles of his abrupt little arms and legs, his heart, quietly marshalling their force for the inevitable outburst. He came and stood in the doorway, very still, the only exterior signs of his anger a tightness around his mouth, a slight tension to his wide nose and a chill light within his even gaze.

Without looking up from polishing her nails, Miranda said querulously, 'You come in late slamming my doors and then you stand outside talking to yourself. Where have you been all day anyway? People have been calling here looking for you after they called your house and that stupid child you married said she didn't know where you had gone.'

She glanced up, still sullen and truculent from their quarrel the night before – and stiffened. Her maid felt her foot go taut and turned, puzzled.

'Go home, Luiz,' he said quietly.

Miranda screamed, the sound jarring the bottle of nail polish from her hand and it spilled, staining the pink covers red. 'No, Luiz . . .' She reached towards the girl. 'Wait, Luiz . . .'

'Go home, Luiz,' he repeated.

The girl stood up then as though jerked to her feet and, holding the basin of water, looked from him to Miranda for a single distraught moment and then broke for the door, the water sloshing on the rug. As she passed him, Caliban said gently, 'Good night, Luiz,' and closed the door behind her.

'*Luiz!*'

Caliban came and sat across the bed from her and deliberately placed his trouser leg with the red dust and clay from the *favela* against the pink coverlet.

Miranda stared at the leg, her grey eyes dull with hysteria and disbelief, at the nail polish streaked like fresh blood on the bedclothes and her hands, at the trail of water the maid had left on the rug and then across to the closed door. Her skin blanched with terror and her scream convulsed the air again, higher this time, so that the chandelier over her bed swayed anxiously. And still screaming, cursing incoherently, she frantically began drawing up the sheet around her.

'Tell me,' Caliban said evenly, 'do you know a Heitor Guimares?'

She did not hear him at first and he waited until her scream broke off and then repeated in the same quiet tone, 'I asked you if you know somebody named Heitor Guimares?'

'Who?' The word was uttered at the same high pitch as her scream. 'Heitor Guimares.'

'Heitor who . . . ? Guimares. No. Who is that? I don't know anybody by that name. Guimares . . . ?' Wary, suspicious, she said after a pause, 'Why do you ask?' and then emboldened by his silence, shouted, 'What is this? Why do you come asking me about someone I don't know. Who's this Heitor Guimares anyway? Why do you come in here looking as if you slept in the sewers and muttering to yourself, scaring me, scaring my maid, slamming my doors and ruining my bed with your dirt. Oh, God, what's wrong now? It's going to be hell tonight. You'll do everything wrong in the show and blame me. You're old!' she screamed, and started up in the bed. 'And losing your mind. You should retire. Go back to Minas, peasant . . . And that little bitch, she's fired. I won't pay her a cent for ruining the rug. Everything ruined . . .' she said tragically, and paused, looking tearfully down at the spilled nail polish on her hands, quiet for the moment, and then her head snapped up. 'Who is this Heitor Guimares now? I lie here alone all day, all night, alone, always alone, and then you come in here accusing me of someone I don't know. Bastard! Suppose I did know someone by that name. It would be my business. You don't own me. I'm not your scared little mamita. Heitor Guimares! Who is he? Somebody has been feeding you lies.'

'I am Heitor Guimares.'

She stared at him, the rest of what she had to say lying dead on her lips and the wildness still in her eyes. Then her bewilderment collapsed into a laugh that was as shrill, in relief, as her scream had been. The sheet she was holding around her dropped and her arm shot out, stiff with scorn. 'You? No, senhor, you are Caliban. O Grande Caliban!' And leaping from the bed, her great breasts swinging, she dropped to his familiar fighter's crouch, her fists cocked menacingly and her smile confirming what the others – his wife that morning, the boys on the Rua Gloria chanting behind him, the man in the restaurant that had been made into a shrine, and, finally, the old man, Nacimento – had all insisted was true, and what he, and certainly Miranda, had really known all along: simply, that Caliban had become his only reality and anything else he might have been was lost. The image Miranda had created for him was all he had now and once that was taken – as it would be tomorrow when the signs announcing his retirement went up – he would be left without a self.

Miranda did not see him pick up the small boudoir chair, for her head was lowered over her fists and she was doing the little shuffling fighter's dance he had made famous. But as the chair cut the air above her, her head snapped up, her hand started up and she watched its flight with the mocking smile her shock and stupefaction had fixed on her face. She tried to move but could not. It was too late anyway; the chair smashed into the low-hanging chandelier and brought it down in a roar of shattered crystal on to the bed – and in the light from the small lamps along the walls the bed seemed to explode in a thick, mushrooming cloud of pink dust.

Caliban's destruction of the apartment was swift and complete. It was as if the illusion of strength he had created on stage for so long had been finally given to him. While Miranda stood transfixed, a dazed horror spreading like a patina over her face (and she was never to lose that expression), he hauled down drapes and curtains, overturned furniture, scattered drawers and their frivolous contents across the floor, broke the figurines against the white walls, smashed the mirrors and his reflection there – and then, with a jagged piece of glass, slashed open the silk sofas and chairs so that the down drifted up over the wreckage like small kites. Finally, wielding a heavy curtain rod as if it were a lance, he climbed on to a marble table and swung repeatedly at the large chandelier in the living-room, sending the glass pendants winging over the room. With each blow he felt the confusion and despair congested within him fall away, leaving an emptiness which, he knew, would remain with him until he died. He wanted to sleep suddenly, beside his wife, in the room with the Madonna.

A glass spear struck Miranda, who had staggered, weeping and impotent, to the door, and she shrieked. Her outcry was the sound of the trumpet the night before, a high, whinnying note that reached beyond all sound into a kind of silence. The scream broke her paralysis and she rushed at him with a powerful animal grace, the gown flaring open around her bare body, and reaching up caught the rod.

He let it go, but from his high place he leaned down and struck her with his small fist on her head, and the hair cascaded down like a curtain over her stunned face.

He was at the elevator, the automatic door sliding open in front of him, when he heard her frightened, tearful voice calling him down the hall. 'Caliban! Caliban! Where are you going? The show! Are you crazy – what about the show tonight? Oh, Mary, full of grace, look what the bastard's done. The place! He's killed me inside. Oh, God, where is he going? Crazy bastard, come back here. What did I do? Was it me, Caliban? Caliban, *meu negrinho*, was it me   ?'

Peter Blackman

In Memory of Claudia Jones

She said
I walk with the humble
Yet not in humility
We scale the winds
My feet shall be
No swifter than their feet
My limbs shall share
No strength that is not theirs
When we move we move mountains

I live that men may walk together
Work together love together
Live possess this earth together
Till this be done
I may not rest
Till murder sleep
I may not rest
While children weep
A hungry shame unwept
I may not rest
Till this be done
No task too bitter
Nor any way too sore
Myself small purchase of sure victory

Speak to me of death
When I am dead
Then only
Now
I cannot understand
Nor bid death's pride daunt mine

Here room is not spread for tears
Here amid the dust the heart sings
Out of the darkness a voice cries
Light answers light
Leaping from peak to peak.

Aimé Césaire

For the Third World

Oh my island, half asleep and so restless
on the sea.
And suddenly from the points of danger
history makes the sign I had been waiting for.
I see nations sprouting,
red and green and I greet you.
Banners, throats filled with ancient air.
Mali, Guinea, Ghana.

And I see you, men
not at all clumsy under this new sun.

Listen,
from my distant island
from my brooding island,
I call out to you — Ho.
And your voices answer me
and what they say means:
the day is bright. And it is true
even through storms and night
the day is bright for you.

From here I see Kivu descend towards
Tanganyika by the silver stairway of Ruzuzi
(a big girl at each step
bathing the night with the rustling of her hair).

From here I see, knotted together
Benoue, Logone, Tchad:
bound together Senegal and Niger
from here, I hear the Nyaragongo
roaring.

Hatred.
Empty noise, leavings of the hyena,
under a stiff wind, we were all covered
with bruises.
I have seen the slavers' jaws growing smaller.

I see Africa, multiple and one
vertical in the thunderstorm's change of fortune
with its swellings and nodules,
slightly apart, but within reach
of the century, like a heart in reserve.

And again I say, Oh mother
   and I raise up my strength
   bowing down my face.
   Oh my land.

Let me crumble it gently between thumb and forefinger
Let me rub my chest with it, my arms,
my left arm
and let me caress my right arm with it.

Ho, my earth is good,
   Your voice also is good
   it has the appeasing power of a sunset.

Land forge granary. Land showing the way.
It is here a truth is found, light
eclipsing the cruel old artificial gold.

See,
   Africa is no longer
   in the diamond of misery
   a black heart breaking.

Our Africa is a hand out of a gauntlet,
it is a straight hand, palm outwards
fingers tightly pressed together.

It is a swollen hand
a wounded open hand
held out,
   brown, yellow, white

to all the hands, the wounded hands
of the world.

Translated from the French by G. R. Coulthard

Biographical Notes

Blackman, Peter. Poet. Born Barbados, West Indies. First came to Britain, 1933. Visited Africa, 1937. *My Song is for All Men* set to music by Alan Bush.

Brathwaite, Edward. Poet. Born Barbados, West Indies, 1930. Works include: *Masks, Islands, Rights of Passage.*

Césaire, Aimé. Poet. Born Martinique, 1913. Educated Ecole Normale, Paris. Has served for many years as Mayor of Fort de France and as Deputy to the French National Assembly. Works include: *Les Armes Miraculeuses, Henri Christophe.*

Dawes, Neville. Novelist. Born Jamaica, West Indies. Has lived in England and in Ghana. Now works at Institute of Jamaica.

Ellison, Ralph. Novelist. Born Oklahoma, USA, 1914. Works include: *Invisible Man,* and *Shadow and Act* (criticism).

Guillén, Nicolás. Born Cuba, 1902. Most renowned of Cuba's modern poets. Works include: *Tengo* and *El Gran 300.*

Hernton, Calvin C. Poet and critic. Born USA. Works include: *Sex and Racism in America, The Coming of Chronos to the House of Nightsong.*

Jones, Evan. Poet. Born Jamaica, West Indies. Has lived and taught in USA. Now resident in London.

Kane, C. H. Novelist. Born Senegal, 1928. Read law, philosophy at University of Paris. *Ambiguous Adventure* won Grand Prix Littéraire de l'Afrique Noir (1962).

Lamming, George. Novelist. Born Barbados, West Indies, 1927. Novels include: *In the Castle of My Skin, Natives of My Person.*

Marshall, Paule. Novelist. Born in Brooklyn, New York, of West Indian parents. Novels include: *Brown Girl, Brown Stones* and *The Chosen Place, The Timeless People.*

Meriwether, Louise M. Novelist. Born in Harlem, USA. Author of the novel: *Daddy Was a Numbers Runner.*

Mphahlele, Ezekiel. Novelist. Born Pretoria, South Africa, 1919. Now lectures at University of Denver, Colorado, USA. Works include: *Down Second Avenue, The African Image, The Wanderers.*

Ngugi Wa Thiong'o (Ngugi, James). Novelist. Born Kenya, 1938. Educated Makerere University and University of Leeds. Works include: *A Grain of Wheat, The River Between.*

Ousmane, Sembene. Novelist. Born Senegal, 1923. Became docker and trade union leader in Marseilles. Works include: *Le Docker Noir, L'Harmattan.*

Oyono, Ferdinand. Novelist. Born Cameroon, 1929. Novels include: *House Boy*.

p'Bitek, Okot. Born Uganda, 1931. Has taught at University College, Nairobi, Kenya.

Selvon, Samuel. Novelist. Born Trinidad, West Indies, 1923. Has lived in England since 1950. Novels include: *A Brighter Sun, Ways of Sunlight, Turn Again, Tiger*.

Senghor, Léopold Sédar. Poet. Born Senegal, 1906. Educated Lycée Louis le Grand and Sorbonne. Now President of Senegal. Works include: *Chants d'Ombres, Nocturnes*.

Soyinka, Wole. Poet, novelist and playwright. Born Western Nigeria, 1935. Lectures at University of Ife. Plays include: *A Dance of the Forests, The Road*.

Walcott, Derek. Poet and playwright. Born St Lucia, West Indies, 1930. Works include: *The Castaways, The Gulf, Dream on Monkey Mountain* (plays).

Young, A. L. Poet. Born Mississippi, USA, 1939. Author of the novel, *Snakes*.

PICADOR

Outstanding international fiction

NATIVES OF MY PERSON *by* George Lamming   60p

This exceptionally powerful novel can be read on two levels. The story
of a 17th-century voyage of colonization, it vividly depicts the horrors
of the slave trade, the claustrophobic intensity of life on board ship
and also the private passions, intrigues and rivalries in the lives of the
captain and crew of the *Reconnaissance*. But the voyage is also sym-
bolic; the true theme is freedom in its fullest sense: the struggle against
guilt and fear in the relationship between men and women, and the
struggle of nations to achieve real independence. Private and public
values are inextricable; there are many natives within each person.

'Glittering ... evocative ... undoubtedly George Lamming's finest
novel ... it is a profoundly revolutionary and original work'
                              NEW YORK TIMES BOOK REVIEW

'The protagonists symbolize aspects of the human possibility of which
we can never learn enough ... thrilling ... most exceptionally infused
with poetic vision' SUNDAY TIMES

'Lamming is one of the best we have' ANTHONY BURGESS